FROM AN ANTIQUE LAND

Ancient and Modern in the Middle East

JULIAN HUXLEY

With over 50 photographs

by the author

CEDRIC CHIVERS LTD
Portway
BATH

First published 1954
by
Max Parrish & Co. Ltd.
This edition published
by
Cedric Chivers Ltd.
as a
New Portway Special Reprint
by arrangement with the copyright holder
at the request of
The London and Home Counties Branch
of
The Library Association
1972

SBN 85594 660 1

Printed in Great Britain by
Redwood Press Limited, Trowbridge & London
Bound by Cedric Chivers Ltd, Bath

CONTENTS

CONTENTS

ILLUSTRATIONS

Plates in four-colour photogravure are shown in italics

ILLUSTRATIONS

ILLUSTRATIONS

The cover design is from a photograph of
the Arch of Ctesiphon by the Author

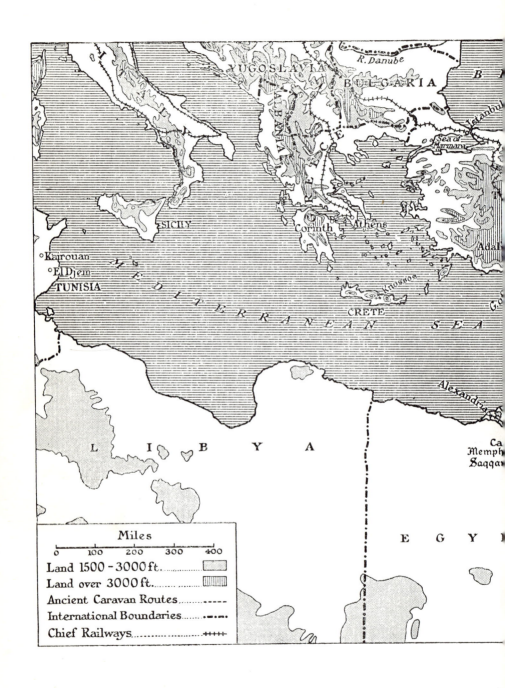

Land 1500 - 3000 ft.

Land over 3000 ft.

Ancient Caravan Routes

International Boundaries

Chief Railways

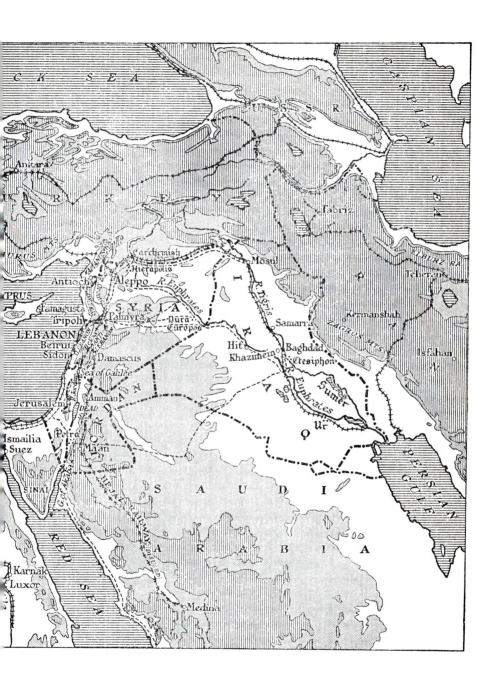

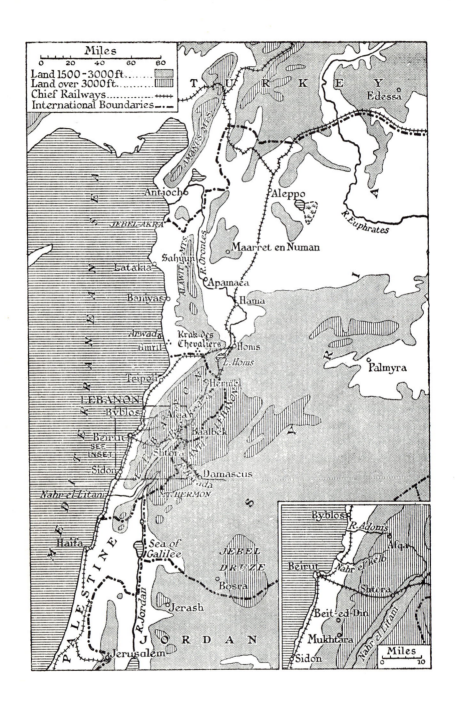

Miles
0   20   40   60   80

Land 1500-3000ft........
Land over 3000ft........
Chief Railways............
International Boundaries...-.-.-

T U R K E Y

Edessa

AMANUS MTS.

Antioch

JEBEL-AKRA

Aleppo

R. Euphrates

R. Orontes

Maarret en Numan

Sahyun

ALAWITE MTS.

Latakia

Apamaea

Baniyas

Hama

Arwad
Amrit

Krak des
Chevaliers

Homs

L. Homs

Palmyra

Tripoli

Hermel

LEBANON

Byblos

Afqa

ANTI-LEBANON

Beirut

Baalbek

SEE
INSET

Shtora

Sidon

Damascus

Barada

Nahr el Litani

MT. HERMON

Haifa

PALESTINE

Sea of
Galilee

JEBEL
DRUZE

Bosra

R. Jordan

Jerash

J O R D A N

Jerusalem

MEDITERRANEAN SEA

S Y R I A

Byblos

R. Adonis

Beirut

Afqa

Nahr el Kelb

Shtora

Beit ed Din

Mukhtara

Nahr el Litani

Sidon

Miles
0   10

I

INTRODUCTION

In 1948, I had the good fortune of having to visit a number of countries in the Middle East, both before and after the General Conference of Unesco, which was being held that year in Beirut. I say good fortune, and it was good fortune. But it was also hard work. Travelling on Unesco affairs is a high-speed business: there are so many international meetings to attend, so many countries to visit, and there is all the work at headquarters piling up against the hour of one's return. I have been looking at my diary, and am appalled at the amount of ground I covered. My first official journey, paving the way for the Unesco Conference, comprised nine countries, and took me to Rome; Constantinople, Ankara; Beirut, Byblos, Tripoli, Baalbek; Damascus, Amman, Petra, Jerash; Baghdad, Ctesiphon; Teheran, Isfahan; Cairo; Tunisia. My second, for the Conference itself, took me again to Constantinople, for a meeting of the Executive Board; to Beirut and the Lebanon; to Damascus and Palmyra. After the Conference was over, and I was a free man again, my wife and I were invited with the Executive Board to Cairo, whence we were able to visit Ismailia and Luxor; and then we explored various parts of the Lebanon and the Syrian Coast – the Alawit Mountains, Aleppo, Hama, Homs; Athens, Delphi, Knossos; Paestum and Naples; and so home.

Everywhere I went the kindness of the authorities insisted on supplementing my official contacts and visits to educational and scientific institutions by showing me something of the cultural and historical background of their country.

It was a wonderful experience, though the rain of new impressions was sometimes bewildering. But whenever possible, I kept notes at the time, and I took a great many photographs. When I returned to England, I resolved to take advantage of my good fortune by writing about my journeys. In order to do this, I began to read all kinds of books which would help to bring order into my impressions and to extend my knowledge of the regions I had visited. That knowledge is still, I fear, extremely scrappy; but at least it is centred on personal experience, a direct extension of my impressions on the spot.

I have not attempted to give chapter and verse for all my statements, nor to provide lists of books for further reading: that would be too pretentious. But I have referred to a certain number of books which I found particularly helpful. Here I would like to mention a few general works which I repeatedly found myself consulting: Ralph Turner's monumental *The Great Cultural Traditions*, of which the first two volumes have so far appeared; Arnold Toynbee's *A Study of History*; Breasted's *Ancient Times*; Jacques Pirenne's *Les Grands Courants de L'Histoire Universelle*; Frazer's *Golden Bough* (the one-volume edition); Philip Hitti's *History of Syria*; Ronald Latham's *In Quest of Civilization*; and I must not forget the indispensable *Encyclopaedia Britannica*.

This new impression (1961) is not in any sense a revision. However, some minor alterations and additions have been made in view of recent changes in the region.

★

Years ago, I was told the story of John Burns finding his patriotic feelings get the better of him (and his aspirates) when the American and the Canadian whom he was entertaining on the Terrace at Westminster persisted in belittling the Thames in favour of the huge rivers of their respective countries. 'Gentlemen,' he said, or is said to have said, 'the Saint Lawrence is cold muddy water; the Mississippi is warm muddy water: but this 'ere Thames is liquid 'istory.'

With a twist of the metaphor, one might say that the Middle East is solid history. At any rate, it is history in greater mass and variety than anywhere else; history of the maximum possible extent, since the region actually gave birth to history. There alone civilization began. Everywhere else, as for instance in our own islands, civilization diffused in from somewhere else. Only in the Middle East did the original transformation take place; only there are to be found the first spontaneous developments of that novel form of human organization we call civilized society.

Before he knows what is happening, the traveller in the Middle East finds himself travelling in time as well as space, between epoch and epoch as well as between country and country. Whether he likes it or not, he is being forced to explore history as well as a region. His journeys into the past, a thousand years here, four thousand there, may be even more exciting than his physical displacements, and almost as fatiguing. The Middle East is a region: but it is also and even more an historical process. To write about the Middle East is to write something about history.

The word *History* is one of those general semantic omnibuses which convey a number of different meanings to a number of different destinations. It may simply be used as a term for the objective sequence of events in time. Within this limitation, it can be used for any and every such sequence, as 'the history of life' or 'the history of the solar system'; or it can be restricted to the sequence of human events; or still further restricted to the historian's sense, of recorded history. Now that history and pre-history have established a complete continuity, this last distinction has become troublesome and sometimes misleading. On the other hand, in spite of the physical continuity of human evolution with biological evolution, there is a real discontinuity between the two in regard to their methods and their course. Accordingly, when using the word in its objective sense, I shall speak of 'history' *tout court*, or of 'human history', to mean the sequence of events since man first originated, and shall use 'recorded history' when I mean the history of historians.

But, strictly speaking, *history* should not be used in a purely objective sense, any more than *colour*, for instance, should be used to denote the objective physical radiations on which it depends. Scientific laws would perhaps be a better comparison, for they are not automatically presented to our minds by outer events, as are colours, but come into being as the result of intellectual effort. They do not exist objectively in nature. In nature, events happen; and scientific laws are one of the ways in which we formulate our understanding of how they happen.

History is in similar case. Only by a convenient form of shorthand – convenient, but sometimes misleading – can it be used to denote the objective sequence of human events. It is properly only our knowledge of that sequence, our formulation of how they happened. The accumulation of brute facts is a prerequisite for history as it is for science; but the raw historical data are not history, any more than the raw scientific data are science. The same old facts, when combined with others and harmonized in a new point of view, may produce something quite new in science, as the facts of geology and biology have ceased to support the idea of special creation, and became part of the new scientific concept of evolution, or the facts concerning falling bodies became part of an Einsteinian instead of a Newtonian universe. So too history is constantly developing into something novel: new kinds of history are constantly being born. This is partly due to the collection of new historical data, new facts about past events; but partly – since human history includes the present, and since it is subjective as well as objective – to the discovery by each succeeding present of new ways of looking at life, new questions to ask of the facts, new formulations by which they may be ordered.

History, in other words, is not merely a set of facts: it is also the building up of the facts into a comprehensible whole, a coherent picture of the world of human development.

The picture of the world presented by history depends very largely upon the assumptions, conscious or unconscious, made by each epoch, its intellectual climate, the principles which govern its thinking, and in particular by the theory or philosophy of history which happens to prevail. It depends, in fact, on the stage of history's own development, much as the picture of the world we each of us possess depends on the development of our individual minds. The infant passes from one set of assumptions to another: even today he normally begins with the unconscious assumption that events are controlled by magic, then passing to the animistic assumption that objects have mental properties akin to our own. Later in development, he may in our industrial societies grow into the conscious assumptions of materialist applied science, while in preceding centuries he would probably have adopted the theistic assumption, of divine control. History is itself a process; and as a process, it involves the development of a series of assumptions.

In societies without recorded history, there is often the assumption of an ancestral stability, which of course helps to ensure stability and to impede change. In early civilizations, there may be the assumption of blind fate overruling the active principles of human life; this was an important element in early Greek mytho-theology, and remained to colour Greek classical history.

There may be the assumption of a divine ruler influencing history according to his personal will, or, as in eighteenth-century thought, less directly, through the impersonal order of things he has established. In any case monotheism logically involves the assumption of the unity of all history.

In the East, there is often the assumption that history is without significance, an interminable process without direction, or an infinity of cyclical repetition. Elsewhere there has often been a millenary assumption – that history will be fulfilled or transcended by some particular happening at some particular time. This had a powerful effect on events in the decades before the year A.D. 1000; and exists in a rather special form in Marxist history. Marxism, however, includes a second assumption – that the course of history is inevitable: it assumes that the inevitability of capitalism's collapse and of revolution must and will eventually lead to the millenary state of the classless society.

On a different level, so to speak, is the assumption – generally tacit and often unconscious – that history exists for the better commemoration or even the glorification of the historian's own community. It may manifest itself in the selection practised among the multiplicity of facts; but often (as in many British and United States school histories of the American Revolution) it selects among conflicting moral interpretations. This assumption can be transformed into a principle by recalling that the writing of history is not something existing in vacuo, but has, like science, a social function; in other words, that history is written and taught *for* someone.

All human beings, unlike any animals, live in and through a culture, a tradition, and history is in one of its aspects an organ for conserving and transmitting patterns of cultural tradition, for making them more explicit and more effective. When I say conserving I do not of course mean that history should always be conservative in our political sense, nor do I imply that tradition is necessarily opposed to change. We may conserve a seed in order to let it develop, and a tradition may be a tradition of change just as well as one of static rigidity.

So long as human society is organized in the form of nations, histories will be needed which make the national tradition come alive and help the nation in its task of dealing with the raw material of events. This does not say that other histories will not be needed also, histories related to a more extended area and a more enduring sweep of time. The evolutionary assumption points to this extended goal for history – the goal of recording events and human actions, mistakes as well as achievements, so as to provide both instruction and useful lessons, both warning and inspiration, to the human species as a whole.

On the other hand, the commemorative assumption can swell up and become justificatory propaganda, deliberately distorting history in the interests of an existing system. George Orwell in *1984* showed us in all its horror the logical conclusion of this unjustifiable justification of the authority which happens to be in power. But in less extreme form it has been common enough. In the U.S.S.R. today the historian's attitude to his subject is well illustrated by Pokrovsky's dictum, that 'history is politics projected into the past', which presumably justifies such distortions as the virtual erasure of Trotsky's name from the history of the Revolution, the general attack on 'objectivism', and the astonishing claims recently made for Russian priority in all sorts of discoveries and inventions.

There are thus at least three distinct elements involved in present-day Soviet assumptions about history. That this should be so reminds us of the multiple causation so often at work in human affairs, for whose unravelling we need what Stuart Chase calls a multivalent logic. The complacent nineteenth century constructed its history on the assumption of automatic progress; and now the disillusioned existentialism of today is insinuating its assumption of the non-significance of history or of anything except the individual and his actions.

However, much more important to our present-day history than the existentialist assumption are the assumptions of relativism. In its extreme form, relativism maintains that the actual course of human history is always merely relative to the conditions of time and place, so that there are no universal or general principles to be discovered behind history's course; and also that the historical picture produced by each period is merely relative to the ideas and assumptions of that period, so that there is no way of arriving at a generally valid world history. The writing of history is always selective: the relativists assume that this selection of questions to be asked, or values to be considered, is bound always to be a purely relative one, even if, once it has been made, the later steps of the process – at any rate, in the hands of a good historian – are, as Max Weber said, determined by the facts, and therefore in principle objective and universal.

The trends towards relativism have been accentuated by the trends away from unity. The trend away from unity is manifested for one thing in the fragmentation of the world into separate nation-states, each demanding its own separate history as an organ of its own continuance. For another it is linked with the fragmentation of the so-called universal religions into rival sects, and the decline of belief in the possibility of religious universality and a theistic Absolute. And finally it is linked with the fragmentation of history itself into a number of specialisms. It is possible to see history in relation to economics, or to ideas, or to social and political organization, or to technical development; it is becoming increasingly difficult to discover any general or universal approach in which the different points of view can be reconciled.

It is true that an historian like Toynbee claims to have arrived empirically at a universal generalization: for him, all history is a matter of challenge and response. But apart from the awkward fact that the response is sometimes zero, or that the challenge may produce a collapse instead of a healthy reaction, the principle is so general that it has little of the concrete functions that principles play in the natural sciences. In setting out to explain everything, it really explains nothing. Like the principles of dialectical materialism, it enables one to experience the satisfaction of 'explaining' events *post hoc*, but does not provide a firm or detailed framework of intellectual comprehension, as does a scientific principle like the conservation of energy or a scientific theory like the gene theory of heredity.

The result is that, as Professor Aron has remarked, 'the absence and the need of a philosophy of history are both equally characteristic of our time'. However, as an outsider who has found himself straying into the historians' preserves from the domain of biology, I wonder whether a proper application of the idea of evolution may not provide the key.

It certainly will not do so if we try to transfer the ideas and regularities of biological evolution directly to human history. But once we have established not only the fact of continuity between biological and human evolution, but the fact of the discontinuity of their methods and the qualitative difference in their results, the situation begins to clarify itself. The key is provided by the idea of evolution, but the lock must be sought for among the properties of humanity: and if so, the philosophy we are in search of will be one of evolutionary humanism.

An evolutionary humanism could now, I am sure, prove a fruitful and well-grounded assumption for history. Some of the earlier historical assumptions have been mere figments of the human imagination: the assumption of infinitely recurring cycles, for instance, or of a millenary goal and end.

Others, like the economic determinism of Marxist dialectics, base themselves only on part of the facts, and then take the part for the whole. But evolutionary humanism is as comprehensive as can well be, now that science has revealed the whole of phenomenal reality as a continuously evolving process. Yet it is not so vague as to be useless, since it concentrates on humanism, in the sense of the properties and potentialities of man: and of these too a comprehensive and objective view is beginning to appear, as the result of history, psychology and the other human sciences.

On this assumption, the general aim of history is to record the progress made by the various segments of our species in realizing human potentialities. It should give a picture of the different methods by which this has been effected, and of the setbacks to the process as well as the successes. The process has an economic and material basis but cannot be fully described or comprehended in economic and material terms alone: mental and spiritual forces enter into it, and mental and spiritual fulfilment provides the most important standard for its evaluation.

How are cultural patterns transmitted and developed? How do new discoveries and new modes of realization become incorporated in cultural traditions, how are they modified by the political framework of the societies in which they operate? What have been the obstacles to advance, what the new difficulties resulting from each successful step? What are the blind alleys to avoid, and what regressions have occurred? How is social organization related to individual fulfilment on the one hand and to progressive social change on the other? These are among the questions which an evolutionary humanist approach prompts the historian to put to the facts of history.

One of the unique properties of the human species is that it can function as a microcosm, both by way of creating some sort of representation of the macrocosm, and by way of purpose, in becoming in some sort a conscious representative of the macrocosm in its further evolution. The microcosm is a very late product of evolution: it could not be anything more than a few distorted and scattered reflections until the mind of man arrived on the scene. Even in man, these microcosmic functions were rudimentary at first; but they have developed rapidly, and history can be an important microcosmic organ of our species.

However, I am straying from my subject. My aim in the following pages has been a modest one – merely to present the impressions made upon me personally by my rapid voyage in the Middle East. But I hope that my readers will see them against the framework of evolutionary humanism that has been in the background of my mind throughout.

I spent a good deal of time and energy in taking photographs, and I have to thank my publishers for their generosity in reproducing so many of these in their original colour, as well as many others in black and white. Colour is essential for capturing much of the Middle Eastern scene. I am also grateful to them for seeing this book through the press in my long absence.

I would also like to thank the authorities in all the countries I visited for their help in arranging for me to see so much in so short a time. I thank them for Palmyra, Petra, Isfahan, Byblos, Santa Sophia, Kairouan, Luxor, Saqqara, Ctesiphon and dozens of other unforgettable memories. And I thank the many acquaintances I made on my journey for their friendliness and hospitality.

Three members of the Unesco Secretariat, Claude Berkeley of Great Britain, Manolo Jimenez of Mexico and Emil Raadi of Persia, participated in my first tour of the region. I should like to tender them my personal thanks for all they did to make it a success. I enjoyed their company as much as I profited by their official labours. Without the invaluable help of my personal secretary, Mrs Paulette Mathews, through the strenuous weeks of the General Conference, I should have had no time or energy left for further exploration of the Lebanese scene. Finally, I want to thank my wife. Her perceptive mind doubled my capacity for absorbing new impressions at the time, and her vivid memory has been invaluable for their later recording.

2

THE LAND

In APRIL I MOTORED FROM
Beirut to Damascus. We had climbed in great sweeps up the western face of
the Lebanon to the pass, and were beginning to descend when round a corner
we slid into the view of the 'other side'. The horizon was occupied by the long
rampart of the Anti-Lebanon. Beyond and above this in the south-east there
rose the snows of Hermon, and between it and us there lay a huge trough, extending out of sight both to north and south (pl. 3, opposite p. 40). This was
the Bekaa, once one of the granaries of Rome, with Baalbek as its capital.

The map showed it as the source of two rivers – the famous Orontes, and
the Litani. Both escape from it in a geographically improbable fashion,
through deep gorges in the coastward rampart, whose crest, at both points
of penetration, is over a thousand feet above the level of the rivers' sources.
The fine relief map in the American University at Beirut later illuminated
what had happened; the rivers had been captured, as the geographers call it,
by streams of the coastal slope which had cut back and back until they had
tapped the waters of the interior trough. This is diagrammatically clear with
the Litani, whose waters must originally have travelled on southwards towards the Jordan. With the Orontes, matters are a little more complicated,
but essentially similar: a comparatively small stream, by cutting back
through the great Amanus range behind Antioch, has tapped a new collecting
ground and become a big river.

At the moment I was overpowered by the physical spectacle. A giant
trough traversing an entire country, with mountain ranges for sides, is both

impressive and very strange. I asked for the car to stop for a longer look. And as I was looking I suddenly realized what the Bekaa was. It was the other end of the Great Rift Valley of East Africa, two thousand five hundred miles to the south, which I had seen twenty years before.

Here is one of the strangest large-scale features to be seen on the earth's surface. We are confronted by a system of cracks extending from the gorge-like basins of Lakes Nyasa and Tanganyika in the south (where the system has two main forks) to the single trough which runs up against the Taurus mountains in the north. Normally, the rift is bordered by parallel cracks on either side, giving rise to a trough – how much by the dropping of the centre, how much by the squeezing up of the two sides, the geologists are not yet quite certain. It seems obvious that when the bottom of the trough is far below sea-level, as in the lower Jordan Valley and for a stretch south of the Dead Sea, or in the basin of Lake Tanganyika, it must have been squeezed down. But usually, it seems, there has been compression, with an upthrust of the sides.

Later in the year, when I climbed to the edge of the rift-scarp west of Petra, the extent to which the great trough had dropped was forcibly brought home. From the crest, the eye had a distant panorama of arid mountains rising up on the western horizon. From this the eye dropped down and down over steep buttresses to where the floor of the rift lay hundreds of feet below sea-level. The contrast between the height on which I stood and the depth of the valley floor below me was even more striking than in the Bekaa. The rift never failed to impress me, by the image which it conjured up of crustal cracking on a planetary scale.

Actually, as I discovered later from Dr W. B. Fisher's recently published book on the geography of the region,* I was wrong in imagining that the Bekaa is precisely comparable to the Great Rift of East Africa. It is in part a 'false rift', with a continuous downthrow fault along its west side only: its steep eastern rim is made by the abrupt upfold of the Anti-Lebanon. However, the western fault is all part of the great rift system of crustal cracks. At this northern end, the rifting forces have become a little weakened, and have spread out, as it were, in a tangle of minor cracks and faults. One

* *The Middle East*, London, Methuen, 1950. See also Arthur Holmes's *Principles of Physical Geology*, and L. Picard, Bull. Geol. Dept., Hebrew University, Jerusalem, 1943. Dubertret and Weulersse's *Manuel de Géographie: Syrie, Liban et Proche Orient* (Beirut) should also be mentioned as a useful general work on the region.

of these cuts sideways across the main north-south line of the system just north of Tripoli: the downthrow thus produced abruptly truncates the northern end of the Lebanon range (producing striking scenery rather like that of North Wales), and provides a corridor for human movement between the coast and the far interior – the easiest to be found in the whole region from Egypt to Turkey.

In most of the system, there has been double parallel cracking, with the production of true rift-troughs. These of course bear no relation to the erosion valleys of the normal drainage-system, and for that reason become the home of great lakes which, like Tanganyika, start by having no outlet, or, like the Dead Sea, may never find one. They are also inevitably lines of weakness, and at one place that weakness has been played upon, it seems, to put a marine separation between two once continuous areas. The entire Red Sea and the Straits of Bab-el-Mandeb, with its forked prolongations to Suez and Akaba, have probably come into being through the entire bulk of Africa having drifted a trifle westwards along part of the rift crack, the whole movement being pivoted round the Sinai Peninsula. This would explain the facts, first, that the two sides of the Red Sea are scarps like those on either side of a typical rift-trough; secondly that where the ponderous leverage of the drifting continent exerted its greatest force, the break – from Aden eastwards – is at right angles to the original line of weakness; and thirdly, that the inter-continental gap grows slightly wider from its pivot in the north-west to the Straits of Bab-el-Mandeb in the south-east. This tendency for blocks of the solid earth's crust, floating viscously in the slightly less solid underlying material, to move westwards, is all that is left today of Wegener's theory of continental drift.

According to most geologists, the rifting which led to this particular weakness and subsequent split and drift in the Red Sea area was a geologically late event, dating, at earliest, from the middle Tertiary. Before that, Arabia must have been continuous with Africa as well as with the Eurasiatic continent. This would account for the strong African element in the fauna of the Arabian-Syrian region – the hyenas, the ostriches, the antelopes, the crocodiles,* which survived in the Dog River close to Beirut into the later nineteenth century, and the hyenas which surprisingly still occur in the Lebanon today. The region reveals its African affinities in another way. Like the great

---

* N. B. Marshall (*Nature*, 1950, **166**, 763) states that the connection between the Red Sea and the Indian Ocean dates back only some 9 to 10 million years.

mass of Africa south of the Sahara, since geologically very remote times it has neither been submerged with formation of new strata, nor has it been subjected to the throes of mountain-building by crustal folding. The reason is that the entire area is built upon a sort of basement of very ancient crystalline rocks, so rigid that it has managed to resist the pressures which give rise to folding. As a result, in most of the region there are no ranges of great fold-mountains with their up-and-down folds that the geologists call anticlines and synclines, and their occasional great overthrusts or *nappes*, as in the Alps.

The region to the north of this rigid continental block was for quite a long period (long even by geological standards) occupied by a marine basin, the basin of what geologists call the Tethys Sea. In this basin, formed by downwarping of the earth's crust, layer upon layer of sediment was consolidated into stratified rocks. But these are not nearly so resistant to deformation as the crystalline basement, and when the accumulating pressures and tensions in the earth's crust threw it once more into a crisis of mountain-building, they yielded to the forces; through a system of great folds, they gave rise to the ranges that run through the Middle East from southern Palestine to the Taurus and from the Taurus to the Zagros and the Elburz. These seem all to be portions of the great fold-system of the Old World, induced by the mid-Tertiary orogenic squeeze, that runs from the Atlas and the Alps to the Himalayas and New Guinea.

These geological deductions are not so remote from human affairs as might seem at first sight. As one steams down the Red Sea, the sight of the bare, arid mountains to the east is a reminder of the height and extent of the great Arabian plateau beyond. This would not be one of the world's most impenetrable deserts if it were not so high and flat; and it is so high and flat because it rests on a great block of this rigid continental mass of crystalline rocks. In the Middle East, the rift itself has influenced human life by providing a fertile lowland in the Bekaa, and a warm and wet semi-tropical region of luxurious vegetation in the lower Jordan Valley. And of course, the potash of the Dead Sea is beginning to play an important economic role. It has also had a psychological impact – the impression of horror and death created by the sunken salty sea, so salty that a man can float sitting in it, with bitter undrinkable waters, useless for irrigation, its barren basin thrust deep below the level of the ocean which laps against the other side of the mountain range to the west. It was this psychological impression which caused the

Hebrews to drive out to the Dead Sea the scapegoat which was supposed to carry their sins. This strange ritual so fascinated Holman Hunt that he resolved to paint a picture of it. But instead of staying in London and using a goat model and a photograph in his studio, he set off for Jerusalem, engaged a guide, secured a local and splendidly oriental-looking goat, and took it down to the banks of the Dead Sea, where he tethered it and began painting. This he did over the protests of the British Consul, who insisted that it was dangerous. And dangerous it was. He was threatened by a ruffianly brigand, but was saved by his firmness, his impressive appearance, and a pistol which he had handy: and his little procession was fired at on its way up to Jerusalem. But he painted his picture, and made a great deal of money out of it by exhibiting it all over England at a shilling a head.

The rift system has also had a great influence on human connections by sea. After all, the entire Red Sea and the Gulf of Akaba were produced by rifting, and they constituted one of the great channels of communication between Egypt, Palestine and Phoenicia and the rest of the world. Furthermore, the gap between the Red Sea and the Mediterranean was so short as to make the construction of the Suez Canal inevitable. Without the Tertiary rifts, the world would lack this great avenue of communication between west and east, and all sea traffic would still have to go round the Cape of Good Hope.

The influence of physical geography on human life is often revealed in a much more immediate manner. The same day that I first saw the Bekaa, I was given my first realization of the Middle Eastern desert. As one winds down the eastern flanks of the Anti-Lebanon it is easy to see that the country is drier and more barren, but there is water alongside in the torrent of the Barada, and just ahead is Damascus in all its fertility. It was not until just before sundown, when I was taken up into the new suburb on the slopes of the hills, that I realized the desert's enveloping presence. Below me, beyond rows of cypresses touched with evening light, lay the city, a sheet of oriental whiteness. This white centre, with its domes and minarets, was surrounded by green – the rich green of the Ghuta or Garden of Damascus. Everywhere beyond the green setting was the desert, a nondescript grey-fawn landscape of sands in which the Barada gasps itself to death, with little ranges of bare hills rising out of it. And this, though it extended out of sight over the curve of the earth, was only the northern border of the immense interior desert of Arabia.

I ought to have remembered that the desert only needs a little water to make it blossom, and that it can then, with its invigorating climate, support great towns and cities. After all, I had read of Timbuctoo, and had seen Lima, a fine capital which exists merely in virtue of Andean water discharging across the desiccated coastal strip.

Gradually it dawns on the traveller that most of the Middle East, from north-central Syria and Iraq and from near Teheran southwards to southern Arabia and Egypt, is one great piece of the world's desertic zone. This is really a commonplace of geography textbooks, but it is a very different thing to realize it by personal contact.

But this great expanse of potential desert has here and there been rendered fertile and eminently habitable by the intrusion of water. The northern fringe of foothills, through Aleppo and Mosul, has enough rainfall to take it out of the category of desert into that of fertile steppe. Along the Lebanese coast, the necessary moisture is given by the Mediterranean climate; sometimes the water enters as precipitation of rain or snow on the cool heights of mountains, as on the slopes of Elburz or the north-western half of the Zagros range, that great barrier between Iraq and Persia; but much, perhaps most of it, intrudes altogether from outside the region, having fallen in other less desertic areas and being then carried through the desert in rivers, of which the Nile and the twin rivers of Mesopotamia are the outstanding examples, not merely in the region, but in the world.

The moisture, introduced in these three main ways into the droughty region, is distributed roughly in the form of a great sickle. The handle is represented by the Nile Valley, in which practically all the water comes from outside the region, and the blade by the famous Fertile Crescent, the band of fertile, mostly steppe country that curves right up and round from coastal Palestine, Lebanon and Syria, by Aleppo and across through Assyria, backing up against the mountains of Asia Minor, and across to the Persian Gulf.

Here, I cannot forbear from quoting from Breasted's book *Conquest of Civilisation*. 'This great semicircle,' he writes, 'the Fertile Crescent, may also be likened to the shores of a desert-bay, upon which the mountains behind look down – a bay not of water, but of sandy waste, some five hundred miles across, forming a northern extension of the Arabian Desert. After the meagre winter rains, wide tracts of the northern desert-bay are clothed with scanty grass, and spring thus turns the region for a short time into grasslands. The history of Western Asia may be described as an age-long struggle between the mountain peoples of the north and the desert wanderers of the south – a struggle which is still going on – for the possession of the Fertile Crescent, the shores of the desert-bay.'

The Crescent is not only fertile, but has throughout history (and before it) provided the great through-way for human movement across the region, between the two inhospitalities of the waterless desert and the rugged mountains. Communication to the eastwards is assured by a less fertile strip running off across the Iranian plateau, just south of the Elburz and providing the main land link between India and the Mediterranean.

Another passageway for the movements of peoples runs off from the north-western corner of the crescent into the Anatolian plateau, and eventually to the fertile western coasts of Asia Minor. And much further north, on the other side of the Black Sea, are the great open steppes, the prairies of the Old World, which repeatedly gave passage for the barbarians.

The Anatolian plateau of Asia Minor was never submerged under the Tethys Sea. It constitutes a high, and on the whole rather barren but irregular tableland, consisting largely of natural steppe. It is not part of the desertic belt, but has a cooler climate, with fairly abundant moisture, although the rainfall over much of the plateau to the north is not high enough to permit the growth of natural woodland or forest. The Iranian plateau of Persia, on the other hand, is a high basin with its floor more than 5000 feet above sea-level, and surrounded on every side by mountains. The water that falls within the basin cannot escape except by evaporation, so that the plateau is dotted with salt lakes and expanses of saline mud, and even mountain domes or plugs of solid salt. Much of it is indeed so inhospitable that considerable areas remain to be properly explored geologically, or even geographically. The great civilizations that have grown up in this region have all been concentrated along the fertile slopes of the moisture-bearing mountains, though they have sometimes, like the Persian Empire, extended over the watershed of the Zagros mountains to their lower and richer western slopes.

One of the things that strikes the traveller most forcibly in the Middle East is the number of dead cities and the amount of country once fertile and cultivated but now abandoned to desert. Over large stretches of Mesopotamia, you can look down from the aeroplane and see the remains of ancient irrigation works now abandoned and silted up. In Syria, under the Romans, cultivation extended roughly 100 to 150 miles further eastward into the desert than today, as is abundantly documented by Mouterde and Poidebard in their learned work: *Le Limes de Chalcis* (Paris, 1945). Great stretches of North Africa, now more or less deserted, once not only supported large populations, but provided Rome with much of her corn. The Bekaa produced far more grain under the Romans than in recent times. Even along the Phoenician coast, towns and cities have degenerated, like Sidon, or Baniyas, or have disappeared like Tyre.

Of course, some of the cities were destroyed by conquering invaders, and some decayed because of changes in the set-up of trade and commerce. But these causes will not account for such general effects as those to be seen in Syria or North Africa. To account for this retrogression, the suggestion has often been made that the climate of the entire region has become more arid. It is of course true that climate changed drastically in prehistoric times, from the last retreat of the ice, about 12,000 B.C., to the time that agriculture began, around 6000 B.C. However, during historic times, and probably not since about 5000 B.C., I should have said that there is no evidence of major or progressive change of climate, nor of any really marked climatic fluctuations, although there have been slight fluctuations lasting a few hundred years, like that towards greater warmth in northern latitudes in the first millennium B.C., and the cool spell that started about A.D. 1300 and is now passing away. To what, then, is due the retrogression of the cities of the region and of its effective fertility?

The answer seems to be threefold. On the first, there has been widespread and indeed shocking destruction of forests, which has led to rapid runoff and dangerous erosion of mountain slopes. In the second place, there has been a pressure of population on many of the more fertile areas, such as Egypt or Tunisia, often coupled with inefficient methods of cultivation, which has led to soil erosion and soil exhaustion. And thirdly, there has repeatedly been a collapse of systems of government, which has led to the abandonment of the techniques needed for rendering arid areas cultivable.

As one flies over the Syrian-Iraqi desert, one sometimes sees strange rows of holes in the ground, each hole surrounded by a rim of sand. These mark the course of the peculiar constructions known as fogaras;* a fogara is an arrangement for draining water out of the sub-soil and taking it through arid regions without undue evaporation. It is a subterranean canal, usually

---

* Plate 70 of Mouterde and Poidebard's book gives an excellent aerial photograph. The fogara system is practised, under various names, from Morocco to Turkestan. In southern Persia, fogaras are called qanats, and provide almost the only method of supplying water.

just big enough for a small man to walk upright, beginning at a depth of 50 feet or more below the surface. It slopes gently down to where the water is needed, to emerge there into a collection basin or as a stream irrigating an oasis or supplying a settlement. A fogara is made by sinking a number of shafts to the water-bearing deposits, and then connecting their lower ends by a conduit sloping at the right angle – a highly skilled as well as a laborious operation. The holes are entries of the shafts, and their rims consist of the excavated material.

Many fogaras were made by the Roman soldier-colonists in the frontier zone, but are now abandoned. They represent an immense volume of labour, which has gone almost entirely to waste. The Romans also constructed catchment-basins to drain every drop of water falling on the surface into storage reservoirs for later use. This seems to have been the method most commonly employed in North Africa.

In general the Romans had a highly efficient system of hydraulic engineering, which enabled them to practise agriculture and to support quite large towns on the margins of the desert.

The ruined fogaras in this region, and the abandoned irrigation works to be seen all over Mesopotamia, are proofs that the retrogression is due to a collapse of human organization and a failure to utilize human skill.

It is a curious fact that civilization was born of the contact between river and desert. The desert, indeed, is a challenge to humanity. Ritchie Calder, in his book, *Men against the Desert*, has shown how Unesco has taken up the challenge, and suggests ways in which it could be met. The sight of all the abandoned areas in the Middle East is a melancholy reminder of the need for constant effort if man is to maintain his conquests over nature. But it is also an encouragement. If the ancients could make the desert blossom and could combine unruly water with barren sand as the basis for orderly and civilized human life, what can we not hope from the proper application of our greater knowledge and higher technical skill?

3

BYBLOS: DOORWAY OF MANY PASTS

Bʏʙʟos...ᴡʜʏ ᴅᴏ ɪ ғɪɴᴅ ᴍʏ-self wanting to give you pride of place when Damascus and Istanbul open a vaster sweep, and Ur has yielded richer treasures, when Isfahan is more lovely, Petra and Palmyra more fantastically wonderful, Baalbek and Karnak more grandiose and impressive? I think it is because Byblos and the region around it, comprising as they do so many and so varied layers of the past, epitomize both the enduring and the shifting qualities of the Middle East and its history.

In any case, it became for me intellectually what it was for many centuries geographically – the best gateway into and out of the region, opening doors into other countries and cultures; it is a window of vision on to the dim and distant times when man first bent the earth's fertility to his service, and in so doing came to grips, intellectually as well as practically, with the forces of life, death, and reproductive renewal.

To reach Byblos from Beirut, you drive northwards up the coast. Here is no fertile coastal plain, as in the southern half of the country, and the Lebanon breaks abruptly down to the sea in great buttresses. Among them leaps the Dog River, Nahr el Kelb. From the bridge which crosses it, you look up at a high and narrow gorge with an unusual amount of greenery, on whose rocky sides we found the little scented wild cyclamens and the narcissi flowering in November.

The main interest is in the inscriptions on the rocks. These, as Fedden writes, 'in hieroglyphics, cuneiform, Greek, Latin, and Arabic [and, he might have added, in English and French] evoke in the most striking way the long, magnificent, and depressing pageant of history'. Just south of the river mouth, the mountain juts out in a steep promontory, round which the road barely manages to crawl. This has always been a point of vantage; to pass it was always an achievement, and has been commemorated as such during four millennia.

Thus, Rameses II recorded his rounding of the promontory at the close of his expedition against the Hittites, that rather desperate campaign which for all his boasting did not save the Egyptian Empire from one of its periodic crumblings. Rameses II was not only unusually active and long-lived, but unusually set, even for a Pharaoh, on commemorating himself and his achievements. Accordingly, he had two large inscriptions carved instead of one. However, just over three millennia later, that other vainglorious (but much lesser) figure Napoleon III, obliterated one of them to commemorate the French expedition to Syria in 1860.

On those rocks, Nebuchadnezzar records his subjugation of Phoenicia; Allenby's inscription is there, very large and prominent; Tiglath-Pileser III came here from Nineveh, among other things to hunt in the forests of the Lebanon; Sennacherib, with his cohorts 'gleaming in purple and gold' also passed this way and Esarhaddon on the return from his victories in Upper Egypt. Marcus Aurelius records the building of a better road round the point, while Caracalla's mention of the third Gaulish Legion reminds us of the comprehensiveness of the Roman Empire. The Turkish conquest of Syria in 1517 is recorded by Selim I. The latest inscription, at the moment, dates from 1941; it commemorates the Anglo-French (Anglo-Free-French) occupation of Syria, although none of their forces actually passed the point.

The place is one of great sanctity. Legend has it that an enormous statue of a dog once stood on the headland, and howled and barked at the approach of an enemy. In fact, the statue seems to have represented the Egyptian jackal-god, Anubis, the divinity who presided over the initiation of human souls into the world of the dead. His special association with the Nahr el Kelb is doubtless due to the sacred awe inspired by the river's mysterious disappearance underground, and its reappearance after several miles of enormous caverns – the physical embodiment of rebirth after passage through the underworld. As Fedden suggests, it was probably the sanctity of the place,

1. The Mediterranean coast of Lebanon

as much as or more than its military importance, which set every invader chiselling his name and his exploits on the rocks.

Soon after, the road swings round the broad half-circle of a fine amphitheatral bay. The Lebanese claim that this Bay of Juni is the equal of the Bay of Naples. While this cannot be seriously entertained – Juni lacks the size and complex sweep of the Bay of Naples, lacks its islands, its volcanoes and its variety of geographical formation – it certainly is both noble and beautiful. Near by is the little port from which St Peter is said to have embarked for Rome.

Not long after, up in the hills, there lies the house where Renan lived for a number of years, writing the *Vie de Jésus*, and where his beloved sister Henriette, who urged him on with the work, died and is buried. And then, a few miles further on, we cross the mouth of another and even more famous stream, the Adonis River. Its source, where it emerges from a cave in the high Lebanon, is the scene of the legendary loves of Venus and Adonis. To that primordial legend and the significance of its focusing on this region, I shall return. Here, at the exit of its great gorge, seeing the blue sea discoloured rusty red for several miles offshore by the winter floods, laden with ferruginous particles from the iron-bearing soils of its middle course, we were able to understand the legend of the river running red with the blood of the wounded god each winter. We wished that we could also see the manifestation of that other legend, the sprouting of drops of the same divine blood to flower as the scarlet Anemone (or more properly Adonis, for it is placed botanically in another genus) which dots the hills in spring.

The modern road crosses the river just to seaward of the old Arab bridge. This, built in an early phase of the Moslem conquests, is a really beautiful structure. The complete semicircle of its opening contrasts in a most satisfying way with the straight-lined angle of the parapet, which in turn is redeemed from banal symmetry by its two limbs being of slightly unequal length and slope (pl. 5, opp. p. 41). The roadway itself, between the two walls of the parapet, is very narrow, wide enough only for a horse or pack-mule. It is one of the comparatively rare survivals from the early Arab period to be found on the coast.

And then one reaches Byblos. Byblos is the oldest continuously inhabited town in the world. 'In all probability,' add the cautious writers who have an

2. *The Obelisk Temple: the God-boxes of ancient Byblos*

academic reputation to keep up. There may just possibly be existing towns in Egypt which are older, but it is unlikely: the Egyptians had a habit of changing the sites of their towns and cities, and their oldest towns are now mere ruins. Damascus is certainly the oldest continuously inhabited large city, but that is another matter; and so is the possibility that some existing villages, perhaps along the strip under the south side of the Taurus mountains, may be still older than Byblos. But Byblos is, so far as we know, the world's oldest living town.

The first thing you see in Byblos is a square tower, a well-preserved ruin, strangely reminiscent of castle keeps in Europe. And then you discover that the resemblance is not strange at all, for it *is* an early medieval keep, built by the Crusaders when they occupied this entire coast. Then you enter the main street of modern Byblos – a narrow cobbled street, a little crooked, with shops on either side. At one point it passes through a low-arched gateway, the arch pointed in gothic fashion, set in a gothic-pointed frame coloured a surprising celestial blue, and with a modern and not very good painting of the Madonna and Child above it. The smooth blue frame in turn is set in the rugged brown of the Crusader's city walls. At the far end of the town is the church, a lovely product of the Crusader period, with some fine early gothic stone-carving and a triple set of semicircular apses rising out of a banana-orchard. There are still some Christian worshippers, though today most of the population is Moslem.

But the ruins are the focus of the place and the thread of its history. The earlier ruins even dictated the presence of the latter: the Crusaders were told to select ruined cities as sites, because they would provide plenty of stones for the castles they would have to build.

The keep is much like any other twelfth-century keep, except in one respect. Deforestation had already gone so far in Lebanon that roof-beams for a big building were hard to come by, and the Crusaders had to build their rooms with stone vaulting. This was much heavier, and so the keeps could never be as high as those of Europe.

From a window near the top, you get a view of the whole site. Along a slight rise stands a row of graceful Hellenistic columns, white between a few dark stone-pines and evergreen bushes, close to the royal cemetery of the second millennium. Through them you look at the soft but sparkling blue of the sea, like the blue of a kingfisher's wing, and the ancient harbour in a little natural bay.

It was to this harbour that the first Egyptian galleys came across the 'inhospitable sea', perhaps five thousand years ago, from it that the logs of cedar and fir were floated down the coast in great rafts to supply woodless Egypt. The sea today has smoothed out the quays and silted up the harbour, but its clear waters still protect the remains of columns, both Egyptian and Greek, which have lain there for centuries.

The slope to the left was occupied by the earliest settlement of the chalcolithic period, well before 3000 B.C. To the right, leading off from the base of the Crusader's castle, are the ancient walls. They are truly amazing – a series of huge glacis, one after another, seven of them in all. Apparently, as each wall showed signs of wear or decay, the inhabitants covered its outer side with earth and built a new wall against the old. This process went on for about 1500 years, so that each of the seven walls lasted about 200 years. Clearly revealed now by excavation, the whole series is a most impressive spectacle.

These walls were the defences of the first real town or city of Byblos, which was focused on an acropolis in the centre. It appears that the site in its original form became militarily untenable owing to the arrival of the Hyksos with their new-found engines of war, the horse and the horse-drawn chariot. At any rate, just after their arrival on the scene, the archeological evidence of occupation ceases, and we can only conclude that the defensible centre of the city was moved elsewhere. Dunand and Chehab, the French and Lebanese archeologists who escorted me on one of my visits, thought that the site might have been the Moslem cemetery. In 1932 the Lebanese Government expropriated the 27 inhabited houses on the original site, in order to proceed with the excavation; but it would be almost impossible to do anything of this sort with a Moslem graveyard.

The original acropolis was centred round the old 'King's Well'. When this deep well, with a pulley mechanism, was further excavated, stairs were found, dating from the tenth century B.C., going down into a birket – a natural reservoir formed by some fissure in the rock. This undoubtedly was the original water-supply for the whole of the walled city. Later, pipes were put in to take the water to various parts of the city. In the Hellenistic period, the birket was closed up and the well constructed.

Close by is the royal cemetery. This dates from Byblos's most prosperous period, when it was under the suzerainty of Egypt, but with a considerable measure of autonomy and a very profitable commerce. The tombs are so-called well tombs, a type which is found scarcely anywhere else. The great shafts were sunk deep into the solid rock, in an attempt to preserve the royal burials from sacrilege and plunder. One of the great stone sarcophagi which modern archeology has discovered here now stands on the open ground above, confronting the Hellenistic marble columns in the light of day. The earliest of these tombs dates from soon after 2000 B.C.; apparently, during the earlier thousand years or so of Byblos's existence as a walled city, it had no kings.

In these tombs, various interesting and beautiful objects were discovered, which are now to be seen in the Beirut museum. In the famous tomb of Ahiram, two Egyptian alabaster vases were found, together with some lovely Mycenean pots and ivories; and a silver vessel, almost exactly like a modern teapot, which appears to have been used for wine, possibly for ritual purposes. One of the early excavators found a scrap of what he thought was papyrus. He took it away and cleaned it, only to find that it was a piece of a Greek newspaper of the year 1885. How it got there is still a mystery. The fame of Ahiram's sarcophagus is due to the inscription, written in a very early script, ancestor of all our alphabets; but that I will leave till later.

On the slope to the south and west, recent excavations have revealed the earliest settlement of Byblos. This dates from the so-called chalcolithic period, that is to say the time when the use of copper had been discovered, but it was rare and only employed for ritual and luxury objects. It was not a true town, but a straggling settlement of houses built of undressed stone, with floors of hardened beaten earth, plastered over with a special clay coating. The earliest houses were mere circular stone huts, and the later ones still had rounded corners; it is only in the walled cities of later centuries that you find dressed stone and rectangular corners. This settlement began somewhere in the fifth millennium and continued right through the fourth.

Over 150 tombs have already been found here, many of them containing very interesting pottery. As often in these ancient sites, the graves and the houses are all mixed up in a way which seems rather macabre to us. In some periods, indeed, people seem to have been buried under the floors of houses after being painted with red ochre, which was supposed to have magic life-giving properties. Doubtless this was done with the express purpose of keeping their spirits in the family home, and allowing them to continue participating in its life.

It is interesting to speculate as to the reasons which caused this semi-urban settlement to become converted – it would seem quite suddenly – into a real city with defensive walls. Possibly it was the work of military conquerors imposing a new way of life on the peaceful agricultural and trading settlement.

Lucian and other classical authors mention a large and beautiful Egyptian temple at Byblos. Excavation has revealed a succession of them; the earliest, dating right back to the Second Dynasty, about 2800 B.C., is another reminder of the close connection between Byblos and Egypt.

The most striking and strange of all the monuments of antiquity that still remain standing is the so-called Obelisk Temple, southward from the Crusader castle (pl. 2, opp. p. 33). Here, in a couple of small square enclosures, into which you step down by steps cut in the solid rock, there stands a strange assortment of stone obelisks, of various shapes, sizes, and degrees of finish. Some are scarcely finished at all, looking almost like natural objects, whereas others are carefully dressed to a particular form. Some stand about irregularly, again like natural objects, whereas others are planted in series. Thus there is one series of five obelisks, a big conical one in the centre, squared-off ones to either side, and two very small cones at the two ends; the whole stands on a small dais above a stone slab. Here and there, on the interior walls of the enclosures, are the remains of niches where statuettes of gods or other holy objects may have stood.

The obelisks date from many periods, new ones constantly being dedicated by pious kings and other benefactors. One, erected at the cost of the royal secretary of one of the kings, is inscribed to the god Rechef. None of them is more than ten or eleven feet high, and the general impression is of a savage forest of primitive stone pillars, suggesting phallic worship on the one hand, and blood sacrifice on the other. In the grass, mauve anemones and yellow horned poppies were growing. The effect is astonishingly different from that produced by an Egyptian or Greek temple.

All through Semitic history, one comes across sacred stones; indeed, in many phases, stones seem to have been regarded as gods themselves, or at any rate as physical receptacles which divinities condescended to inhabit. This obelisk temple of Byblos contains, I believe, the largest collection of such stone god-receptacles still in existence.

Comparatively little is left of the buildings associated with the obelisks. These must have been elaborate, though of poor architectural style. But among the more than two thousand small objects of various sort – offerings, temple vessels, or ritual apparatus – found at the site, there are many of extraordinary beauty and still more of very fine workmanship. In one corner was a dagger, close to a jar filled with gold. In another place, the whole equipment of a temple jeweller was discovered, and can now be seen at Beirut. Then there was a sacred ritual axe, and statuettes of animals executed in very striking enamel.

The existing obelisk temple was built over the remains of an earlier temple, which perished in a great fire, when practically the whole of Byblos was destroyed. Excavations are revealing remains of building after building below the existing ones. One of the most interesting seems to have been a Hall of Purification; this contained a number of terra-cotta jars of about 2500 B.C., serving for the ablutions to be performed before entering the temple.

*

The region of Byblos was the chief centre on the Phoenician coast of the cult of Astarte and Adonis. Astarte was the patron goddess of Byblos, while Afqa, at the source of the Adonis river, was especially sacred to Adonis. The legend of the two divinities is familiar enough. Adonis, the youthful masculine god, originally sprung from a tree, is loved by Astarte. In spite of Astarte's forebodings, he goes off to hunt, and is killed by a wild boar. He is mourned and lamented by the goddess, who eventually secures his release from the underworld.

With the legend went an elaborate ritual. The marriage of the god and goddess was sometimes ritually enacted by a sacred couple, sometimes symbolized by sexual union between men and women worshippers at the annual festival in early summer. A sacred dirge was sung by women with bared breasts to commemorate the god's death, and his corpse in effigy was thrown into water; little gardens of seedlings in pots were set out, to sprout and wither in memory of his youthful vigour and premature death, and were then thrown into vivifying water to symbolize the hope of his resurrection next year. At Afqa, scarlet anemones, symbolizing the blood from his fatal wounds, were strewn on his image.

Both legend and ritual show many variations: readers can pursue the details of their somewhat bewildering transformations in the pages of Frazer's *Golden Bough*. It seems clear that the cult was one of agricultural magic, originating far back in neolithic times. Astarte is a form of the mother-goddess, symbolizing the fertility of nature. Adonis is, as so often in mythology, a composite figure. He is the masculine principle needed to fertilize the feminine element: he is the crop which withers in summer but grows again out of the dark soil next spring: and his death represents the human sacrifice which was originally made to ensure the crop's rebirth.

The boar seems to have had some connection with the spirit of the corn (the pig was sacred or tabu in many parts of the region). The tree from which Adonis was born must have some connection with the sacred tree which in many parts of the world is the chief symbol of vegetation and its annual renewal – a symbol which survived in Europe in the guise of the maypole. The ritual union of the sexes is a piece of fertility magic, and the sacred lament for the god is part of the rite for securing his resurrection.

The centring of the cult at Byblos was, we may conjecture, due to its being situated where

> *Smooth Adonis from his native rock*
> *Ran purple to the sea.*

The river's annual red floods could be taken as nature's symbolization of the wounded god's blood, and its source at Afqa was a fit spot in which to place his rash hunting expedition and his death, as well as having a 'holy and enchanted' quality in its own right.

We spent a memorable day exploring the valley to its source. The final gorge through which the river makes its exit is impassable: the road from Byblos has to wind up over an outer shoulder on to its southern margin. Far below, the river is seen in the steep-sided gorge it has cut for itself in the grey limestone. On the gentler slopes above its rim, every inch of available soil is terraced, the precise narrow terraces following the exacting contours of the steep valley. From above, they look like part of an enormously enlarged finger-print. The terrace system, representing the slow toil of centuries, is in some regions being neglected by an impatient modern generation.

Beyond, on a shoulder ridge, a ruined temple, small and primitive, stands like a sentinel, its gateway scarcely distinguishable from the great limestone blocks protruding from the mountain-side. This temple marks the half-way stage in the pilgrimage from Byblos to Afqa. Beyond this point, after a solitary Moslem grave by the roadside, the valley steepens, its flanks grow more barren, and patches of snow appear on the summits. Only with an effort can one visualize the immense processions of worshippers that annually ascended it. In a modern car on a modern road the journey took us over three hours: on foot on a rough mountain track the crowds must have taken a couple of days.

Some way further on, the main road swings out of the valley, to reach mountain resorts where summer coolness and winter sports can be enjoyed; only a branch keeps on towards Afqa. Suddenly the end of the valley is revealed – a blank limestone precipice, the backdrop of a final grim cirque gouged out of the backbone of the range. At the base of the rock-wall is a great cave; and out of the cave gushes the Adonis river from its subterranean sources within the mountain, to plunge over a series of fine waterfalls into its narrow gorge. The floor of the cirque is a tiny green plain, unexpectedly flat and fertile in the midst of the stupendous cliffs. Among the steep chaos of boulders just across the torrent can be seen the jumbled blocks of a sadly ruined temple of the Roman period. For this, the latest temple to be erected here, Assuan granite was brought all the way from Upper Egypt – a proof of the importance of the Afqa celebrations even in imperial times.

Passing the last few hovels, we scrambled down the rough path from the end of the road. One of the local inhabitants had provided us with a rickety ladder, up which we climbed with some difficulty to reach the cave. On the stage of sward below, three thousand feet above sea-level, crowds of worshippers had gathered every year for over thirty centuries to compel nature's fertility with magic, to celebrate her rhythms with ritual art, to lose themselves by identification with the forces of nature which they at the same time worshipped – an astonishing phenomenon, enacted in an astonishing setting.

For fifteen hundred years now, the ritual has not been enacted. The ancient religions of the region were submerged by the new tide of Christianity. As Milton wrote, both learnedly and beautifully, in his immortal Hymn on the Nativity,

> *Peor and Baalim*
> *Forsake their temples dim,*
> *With that twice-batter'd god of Palestine;*
> *And moonèd Ashtaroth*
> *Heaven's queen and mother both,*
> *Now sits not girt with tapers' holy shine;*
> *The Lybic Hammon shrinks his horn,*
> *In vain the Tyrian maids their wounded Thammuz mourn.*

Today in Russia the Christian God is being driven out of his temples, and in many other countries his ritual is fading. Is the world heading for another

3. The Bekaa, the northern end of the Great Rift Valley of East Africa

4. Cultivation terraces in the Adonis valley, product of the slow toil of centuries

5. *The Arab bridge over the Adonis river: a rare survival of early Islamic building in Lebanon*

6. *The Riviera coast of southern Turkey*

religious revolution, as drastic as the passage from paganism to Christianity? We returned down the valley with our minds full of strange thoughts.

★

The divine protagonists of the neolithic sacred drama took on different names in different regions. Adonis is also Thammuz, and Osiris, and Attis. Astarte is also Ishtar, and Atargatis, and Cybele, and Isis, and of course Aphrodite and Venus. The cult in its typical form seems to have developed in Sumeria, with Ishtar and Thammuz as its divine personages. But it originated through the amalgamation of two earlier elements, the cult of the mother-goddess and the sacrificial ritual associated with the death and resurrection of the masculine corn-spirit. The two were linked by means of a ritual marriage.

As Toynbee points out in his *Study of History*, the emphasis on the male and female partners varied a great deal in different cultures. For the Hittites, the mother-goddess in the guise of Cybele remained dominant. For the Egyptians, Osiris and his resurrection were more important than Isis and her fertility. Later, however, when Egyptian influence spread westwards, the cult of Isis had much greater appeal to the Romans. And the cult of the Virgin Mary represents a reinstatement of the mother-goddess within the masculine theology of early Christianity, which in turn was grounded in the exclusive masculinity of Jehovah.

Isis and Osiris as well as Astarte and Adonis have a connection with Byblos. In the Egyptian legend, Osiris, the husband and brother of Isis, was killed by his brother Seth; his coffin was thrown into the Nile, and floated ashore at Byblos. There it became lodged in the branches of a tree, which then grew round it, and was later cut down by the King of Byblos to serve as a pillar in his palace. Isis, mourning and searching for her husband's body, discovered its whereabouts, and became a maidservant of the Queen in the palace. Then follows a curious interlude in which she tried, as nurse of the royal babe, to confer immortality on him by burning away his mortality in the fire, but was prevented by his horrified mother. Upon this, she revealed herself and begged for her husband's coffin. This was granted her, and she sailed away to Egypt, leaving the tree-trunk to become a sacred pillar in the temple dedicated to her in Byblos. In Egypt, Osiris was resurrected (but again dismembered by his jealous brother).

The legend is interpreted by some scholars as meaning that the cult of Adonis in Byblos sprang from that of Osiris, and was an importation from

Egypt. Personally I feel that the influence is more likely to have been in the other direction. The imprisonment of Osiris's body in a tree recalls the legendary birth of Adonis; and the leaving of the tree-trunk in Byblos implies the migration of the god from the wooded regions where the vegetation-spirit originated, to the treeless plains of the delta. Osiris is then Adonis transplanted from his original home of temperate neolithic barbarism to a subtropical treeless civilization. Here he gradually suffered a metamorphosis, to become the symbol not of vegetable but of human resurrection, and his cult developed into the main religion of the Egyptian masses.

Be that as it may, the cult of the Phoenician Adonis eventually spread all over the eastern Mediterranean, co-existing with that of Osiris in places like Alexandria; and his festival continued to be celebrated into late imperial times.

All three of the triad of Greek elegiac poets have left a dirge for Adonis. The most beautiful is that of Bion, with its recurrent refrain, 'Woe, I cry for Adonis and the Loves cry again'; and the most poignant also, with its emphasis on the passionate grief of his goddess-lover. As she sees the blood welling out of the great wound in his thigh, she lifts up her hands and wails 'O dearest and sweetest, thou diest and my dear love is sped like a dream.' She snatches a kiss from his dying mouth, unties her hair and wanders lamenting barefoot through the wild wood.

Bion's dirge goes on to describe the laying-out of the effigy of the corpse on a golden bed, anointed with Syrian perfumes and unguents. 'Fling garlands and flowers upon him; now that he is dead let them die too, let every flower die' – a sentiment ritualized in the gardens of Adonis. The Levantine origin of the rite, hinted at by the mention of Syrian unguents, is definitely indicated by Aphrodite lamenting Adonis as 'her Assyrian lord'.

Moschus's briefer dirge is almost entirely concerned with the murderous wild boar. The boar, captured by the Loves and upbraided by Aphrodite, becomes unexpectedly touching. He explains that when he saw Adonis 'beautiful as a statue', he became irresistibly possessed by 'the burning mad desire to give his naked thigh a kiss'. And now he is bitterly repentant, and begs to have his tusks cut off – 'for why should I possess teeth so passionate? And if they suffice not, take my chaps also, for why dare they kiss?' And Aphrodite had compassion on him and released him. And he voluntarily burnt off his tusks in the fire, and ever after 'went not to the woods' but followed her about.

Theocritus's famous and delightful idyll, like Bion's, is concerned with the festival at Alexandria. It describes the adventures of two women of Peloponnesian extraction, Gorgo and Praxinoa, in the crowd converging on the festival, and the dirge they listened to. The singer, as Gorgo tells us, is 'that Argive person's daughter; you know, the "accomplished vocalist" that was chosen to sing the dirge last year.' The dirge is by no means a gloomy one: it stresses Adonis's marriage with Aphrodite even more than his death.

After describing the marriage feast – the silver platters of cress and salad, the golden vessels of Syrian balm, and the scented honey-cakes of bolted meal made in the forms of animals and birds – and the marriage-bed, the dirge continues

> *And now she's in her husband's arms, and so we'll say goodnight;*
> *But tomorrow we'll come with the dew, the dew, and take hands and bear him*
>   *away*
> *Where plashing wave the shore doth lave, and there with locks undight*
> *And bosoms bare all shining fair we'll raise this shrilling lay:*
> *'O sweet Adonis, none but thee of the children of gods and men*
> *'Twixt overworld and underworld doth pass and pass again.'*

A huge crowd is pressing to see the Festival, and the Royal Horse are out to make a display and help in keeping order. The festival takes place inside a big public building. On a dais hung with embroideries ('how fine the work is, and *such* good taste!') is a silver bed with the holy boy Adonis lying on it.

The dirge makes it clear that the traditional mourning rite was still carried out, with bare-breasted women throwing Adonis's effigy into the water: and the Gardens of Adonis were still in vogue. But the two women's talk shows that in Alexandria in Hellenistic times the festival had been largely diverted from its original function of canalizing the religious feelings and magic rituals of an agricultural society, to serve as a gigantic show, staged by the state for urban delectation.

For a somewhat later account, we have Lucian's *The Syrian Goddess*. This was written in his middle twenties as a record of his travels through Egypt, Syria, and Phoenicia in A.D. 148 and 149, during which he visited both Byblos and Afqa. Lucian himself was of Syrian origin, having been born at Samosata on the upper Euphrates. His account is thus of special interest, since he was looking at Syrian religion with the eyes of a Syrian, but through the spectacles of an education in Greek literature and philosophy and Roman law.

At Byblos, he saw 'a large temple, sacred to the Byblian Aphrodite [i.e. Astarte]: this is the scene of the sacred rites of Adonis: I mastered these' – but, alas, he says nothing more about them! This temple is represented on an almost contemporary coin from Byblos, figured in the British Museum catalogue. Steps led up to an open forecourt, bordered with something apparently intended to symbolize a pillared cloister. Just inside the main gate, a big sugar-loaf obelisk (perhaps a phallic symbol combined with a tree symbol) towers above the façade. The sacred sanctuary was approached by a further flight of steps.

The people of Byblos, Lucian continues, 'assert that the legend about Adonis and the wild boar is true, and that the facts occurred in their country'. This assertion of the primacy of Byblos is somewhat weakened by the further statement that 'some of the inhabitants of Byblos maintain that the Egyptian Osiris is buried in their town, and that the public mourning and secret rites are performed in memory not of Adonis, but of Osiris.' This, however, might well be the natural reflection of the long millennia during which Phoenicia had become of secondary importance to Egypt. The prevalent view in classical antiquity was to make Egypt the origin of all things, the *Urmutter* of civilization. This was the attitude of Herodotus, and also that of Lucian, who begins *The Syrian Goddess* by the sweeping statement that 'the first men on earth to receive knowledge of the gods, and to build temples and shrines and to summon meetings for religious observances are said to have been the Egyptians.' Such is the power of a long-established and physically well-preserved civilization over later ones.

Lucian cites the following 'fact' in support of the Osirian primacy. 'A human head comes every year from Egypt to Byblos, floating on its seven days' journey thence. . . . It never varies on its course but goes straight to Byblos.' This clearly is part and parcel of the ancient legend of Osiris's corpse being miraculously floated to Byblos, there to be recovered by the questing Isis, a legend which as we have seen is really one of the strongest supports for the Byblian primacy of the festival, and for the origin of Osiris from Adonis.

The trouble is that Lucian ends the story by saying that the arrival of the head 'came to pass while I was myself in Byblos, and I saw the head in that city'. This is as disconcerting as Benvenuto Cellini's story in his autobiography of how, when a mere child, he saw a live Salamander in the fire, and of how he remembered it so vividly because his father beat him to impress the interesting event for ever on his youthful memory! Both, I fear, are among the innumerable examples of the fallibility of human testimony concerning marvels, of which there are still all too many, even in these soulless modern days – we need only recall the Angels of Mons, the three Portuguese children who 'saw' the Virgin Mary six times at Fatima in 1917, the snow on the (non-existent) Russian soldiers' boots in England in August, 1914, or the Bronx apparition of the Virgin in 1945. We must also remember that Lucian, though he wrote the *Vera Historia* as a satire on credulous travellers' tales, liked a little mystery himself as a sauce to the dull facts.

Lucian also mentions a place that must be Afqa. 'I went up also from Byblos into the Lebanon, one day's journey, as I had heard that there was an ancient temple of Aphrodite there founded by Cinyras. I saw the temple, and it was indeed old.' He tells us nothing more. What would we not give for a picture from his accomplished pen of the great annual procession!

At Afqa, the sacred prostitutions and ritual copulations that marked the festival of Adonis incurred the Christian displeasure of Constantine, who sent troops to demolish the temple and remove its priests and priestesses. However, the cult was later revived, and dragged on into the 5th century, while sacred promiscuity persisted in the recesses of the Lebanon until modern times. Even today, a remnant of sanctity clings to Afqa. The old fig-tree that has grown out of the ruined temple is still festooned with rags of clothing, tied on by local pilgrims of various religious faiths, who believe that this substitute sacrifice on a substitute sacred grove will restore health to the sick from whose garments the strips have been torn. They are unwittingly carrying on a tradition which links present-day Afqa with the neolithic past.

★

Byblos is among the many places which have given their names to objects. Our little party whiled away some of the time spent in planes and trains in thinking of examples from the region. There are a fair number of them, mostly concerned with adornment like *turquoise*, derived from though not produced in Turkey; with special kinds of material, *damascene metal* and *damask* from Damascus; *muslin* from Mosul; or with eating or drinking – like *damson*, also from Damascus (which thus holds the record for three different derived objects); *mocha*, especially in French; and *turkey*, though this last is a double confusion. Turkeys were first confused with guinea-fowl, and the fact that guinea-fowl were introduced to the West through the Turkish dominions was then confused with the country of their origin; the real African origin of guinea-fowl was only indicated in their name when the Portuguese began bringing them back from the Gulf of Guinea (and by the way, a guinea is yet another derived object). Most curious of all, *tabby* is derived from the Attabiy quarter of Baghdad (itself named after Attab, a grandson of the Prophet), and came to mean first a striped taffeta, then a striped cat, and finally (I suppose by conflation with *Tabitha*), a spiteful female gossip!

Among the most interesting examples are *babel* and *bible*. The former is, of course, a reminder of the time when Sumerian civilization was the most advanced in the world, and the great Ziggurat of Babylon, probably the tallest and certainly the most elaborate building as yet built by man, was a focus for legendary admiration and envy.

And bible is from Byblos. I cannot do better than quote again from Breasted's *Conquest of Civilisation*. After reminding us that pens, ink, and paper reached Europe from the Middle East, and that the word *paper* is directly derived from *papyrus*, he continues: 'Much of the papyrus used by the Greeks was delivered to them by Phoenician merchants from Byblos. Just as we apply the word "china" to the special fine tableware which first came to us from China, so the Greeks often called papyrus "byblos", after the Phoenician city from which it came. Thus when they began to write books on such rolls of paper, they called them *biblia*.' And as the Holy Scriptures were *the* book (or rather, books) par excellence, they were called the biblia, first in the plural, and then as a collective singular noun, the Bible.

Writing on paper was certainly one of the great cultural inventions. Clay tablets had their advantages, especially in countries which had plenty of clay but little or no papyrus. Clay epistles even show a parallel evolution to paper ones, in the development of envelopes against inquisitive eyes en route: in the Baghdad museum, you may see how tablets, after being written on and baked (part-equivalent of being blotted with blotting-paper) were enclosed in a fresh sheet of clay on which the address was written, before it too was baked. But it would be very difficult for the Post Office to handle 560 million clay missives at Christmas, as it did last year with paper missives in England; and as for clay libraries, their bulk would have exerted a powerful brake on the progress of learning. The great libraries of the world are now finding the bulk of paper books unmanageable, and are experimenting with materials more economical of space, like microfilm and tape-recordings; the unmanageability of a clay library would have set in at a bulk of words perhaps a hundred thousand times smaller.

As I wrote this, I realized that here was another place-derived word. For, of course, parchment is derived from Pergamon, the famous kingdom in Asia Minor. Here in the 2nd century B.C., according to Pliny, King Eumenes, who prided himself on the possession of one of the great libraries of the ancient world, was confronted by the hostile Ptolemies with an embargo on the export of papyrus from Egypt. He therefore had to revert to skins as writing material, but introduced a new method of preparation so that both sides could be written on, instead of only one. Such double-sided writing skins came to be called *pergamena* or *pergamentum*, which later evolved into *parchemin* and *parchment*.

Bible and parchment – can any other region rival the Middle East in having two place-names immortalized in words concerned with man's intellectual activities?

In any case, it was the use of parchment, with its superior toughness, which facilitated the change from the rolled to the paged book. Papyrus was not strong enough, and it was not until the introduction in the 10th century of a new method of making paper out of linen rags, that the main vehicle of the written word switched back from an animal to a vegetable material.

The substitution of paged books for rolled volumes seems at first sight merely a small technical improvement, but one has only to think of consulting the *Encyclopaedia Britannica* or *Bradshaw* in roll form to realize its importance.

The first paged books were called *codices* (from the Latin word for a block of wood, and thence for the three-leaved tablets into which small blocks were sawn), and began coming into use in Rome late in the 1st century A.D. The earliest codices had three or four narrow columns on each page, and it was not till the 5th century that the number was reduced to two, while the first whole-page codex dates from the 6th. This at first sight meaningless fact is an illustration of the almost invariable tendency for a new invention to take over some of the characters of the invention which it replaced, whether useful or not in their new setting. Rolled books had to be written in a series of narrow columns parallel to the rollers, the breadth of each being adapted to the space available for reading as the book was unrolled; and the codices simply took over this arrangement as railway carriages and automobiles took over many details of horse-drawn vehicles.

The new form also took over the old terminology. *Volume* really means *roll* – something wound, as the papyrus scroll was wound round the wooden rollers to which it was fastened. But it has been appropriated, without demur even from etymologists, for the unit-book of the new paged type.

But to revert to Byblos: Byblos is intimately concerned not merely with the history of paper and books, but with an even greater cultural invention, alphabetical writing.

I have already spoken of the great shaft-graves of the Byblian kings. At the bottom of these shafts were the royal sarcophagi, which are now among the most precious exhibits of the Beirut Museum.

The latest of the five sarcophagi so far discovered was that of King Ahiram, dating probably from the 12th century B.C. On it is an inscription, not in hieroglyphic but in alphabetic script. What is more, the script is unquestionably ancestral to all the alphabets of the modern world. There is also a *graffito* on the wall of the tomb, in the same script but a different 'handwriting'.

The inscription is readily decipherable, because of the resemblance of the letters to those of later developments of the alphabet. It tells how King Ítobaal of Byblos made the sarcophagus for his father, King Ahiram, and invokes threats and curses upon anyone who might disturb this 'dwelling-place for eternity'. Unfortunately the threats were unavailing, and robbers had disturbed it long before organized science did so. But though they had rifled the tomb, they left the sarcophagus with its infinitely precious lettering.

The sight of those three lines of letters, talking directly to us from over three thousand years ago, was very impressive. Most people, I imagine, take the alphabet more or less for granted. Actually the alphabet is one of the major human inventions, worthy to rank with the invention of writing itself. Indeed it can properly rank higher, as one of the major human discoveries, for while early writing, by means of pictographs, hieroglyphs, and the like, was a series of inventions which gradually improved a practical technique, alphabetic writing involved what is in the true sense a scientific discovery – the discovery that although words are the best units for spoken thoughts, yet for purposes of transposing thoughts into a material form which will have some independent persistence in time, the best units are not words but letters.*

The inventors of alphabetic writing did not bother their heads about providing separate letter-units for all the different units of sound into which spoken words could possibly be analysed. This was lucky, since otherwise the practical advantage of having a really small number of units would have been sacrificed to the ideals of theoretical completeness.

There were only twenty-two letters in the alphabet used for the Ahiram inscription. A major economy was secured by having no letters for vowels. Presumably, the early Phoenician language, like all Semitic languages, was essentially consonantal, the roots being groups of consonants, with vowels serving mainly to denote grammatical variations like the inflexions of nouns or the moods of verbs.

Indo-European languages, on the other hand, are not so rigidly consonantal, and indeed cannot be efficiently reduced to alphabetic writing without the use of true letters for vowel-sounds. Accordingly we find that as soon as the Indo-European-speaking Greeks realized the value of writing, which by then, about 1000 B.C., meant alphabetic writing, they introduced letters for vowels – or rather the principle of having letters for vowels, since they took five Semitic letters for consonants and simply turned them into vowels.

Obviously Ahiram's alphabet was not the beginning of alphabetic writing, and equally obviously alphabetic writing must have originated from some form or other of the non-alphabetic writing which had been in use for close on two thousand years before Ahiram's time. One interesting fact that soon emerges is that while true alphabetic writing was invented once and only once in human history, non-alphabetic writing developed on several separate occasions in different areas. We can leave out of account the quipu, the curious method of sending messages by means of knotted strings, a cross between a memoria technica and an elaborate tally: this originated once only, in pre-Columbian Peru, and never reached a stage to which the term *writing* could properly be applied.

All kinds of true writing appear to have originated from a system of pictographs, though in the course of time many other types of written signs might be added.

* See D. Diringer's monumental work, *The Alphabet*, London, 1946; B. Ogg's *The Twenty-six Letters* (London, 1949) can also be consulted with profit, and the summary account in R. Turner's *The Great Cultural Traditions*, vol. I. p. 261.

We can be fairly certain, with only the faintest trace of question, that pictographic systems of writing were invented independently in the Old World and in the New. Thus we have in Central America some elaborate (and largely undeciphered) scripts, using highly conventionalized pictographs but with some phonetic signs added, all apparently derived from some form of Mayan writing; and it is very unlikely that the Mayans should have been able to borrow or import the idea, let alone the actual system.

In the Old World, there are three very early but very different-looking scripts – the hieroglyphic or Egyptian, the cuneiform or Sumerian, and the as yet undeciphered Indus Valley system. The first two were already in existence before 3000 B.C., cuneiform being probably the earlier, reaching back perhaps to 3500 B.C. The precise dating of the Indus Valley civilization is still rather obscure, but the script certainly goes back to the early part of the 3rd millennium. Cuneiform died out just at the beginning of the Christian era; hieroglyphic writing was used until the 5th century A.D.; at present, the Indus Valley writings are not known later than about 2000 B.C., though this may well be due to the fragmentary nature of our knowledge.

A hundred and fifty years ago, the Indus Valley script (and indeed the entire civilization) had not even been discovered; and though abundant writings in both the other two scripts were known, not one word had been deciphered, even of the thousands of perfectly-preserved inscriptions that crowd the walls of Egyptian temples. However, thanks to the Rosetta Stone (now in the British Museum) for hieroglyphic, and the trilingual inscriptions of ancient Persia for cuneiform, both these scripts can now be read, and their messages, after millennia of unintelligibility, can be incorporated in the world's storehouse of knowledge.

The three types of writing are very different to look at, and may possibly be separate creations as scripts: but they are probably not independent in origin. The likelihood is that they are all dependent on a single idea – the realization that simple picture-symbols could be used as the basis for an organized system of written communication. If so, the *idea* of true writing arose only once in the Middle East (probably in Mesopotamia); but as knowledge of the existence of writing spread to other peoples in the region, they too grasped the idea and put it into practice, but by other methods. Certainly this process of 'idea-diffusion', as Kroeber calls it by way of distinction from the material diffusion of objects and products, has been of great importance in man's cultural evolution.

The systems of pictographic writing had to adapt themselves to the needs of more varied communication, and became extremely elaborate. The business of learning to write was thus an arduous and lengthy one, and the scribes formed a restricted and highly specialized professional group in the population. What is surprising at first sight is that the immense simplification conferred by an alphabetic system had to wait for nearly two thousand years – until one realizes that the unit-letter principle in language was a difficult discovery, almost as revolutionary as the discovery of the unit-atom principle in chemistry.

With non-alphabetic writing, many hundred separate signs had to be learnt, without even the advantage of a single underlying principle. For in all such scripts not one but several different principles were confusedly at work. There was first the pictographic principle – the representation of words for objects by means of pictorial symbols. As time went on, these symbols became steadily more conventionalized until often no obvious pictorial association remained. Then there was the ideographic principle. This was a natural extension of the pictographic: ideographs are word-signs, evolved by taking a straightforward pictograph like that for 'sun', and adapting it to mean something less directly objective, like 'day', or something more abstract and general, like 'time'. Next there was the quite different phonogram principle, of using pictographs to indicate not words, but the sounds of words. By thus having sound-signs available, it was possible to put into writing all sorts of words that escaped the pictographic and even the ideographic principle, like adverbs, prepositions, and proper names. This was in essence a rebus method like that which amused our childhoods with pictures of a little boy and a child's bed for *boycott*, and the like. But it gradually developed into an elaborate subsystem, in which the sounds of syllables and even of single consonants were represented by signs which had lost all connection with their pictorial originals, and where certain signs were used as determinatives, to denote grammatical inflexions of case, tense or mood, or different applications of the basic ideographs. No pictographic or ideographic script can manage with less than five or six hundred signs, and their number may easily run into thousands, or, as in Chinese, even exceed ten thousand.

Once phonograms were introduced, it was theoretically possible to decompose words into syllables. If this principle is rigidly applied, the result is a syllabary instead of an alphabet, and the total number of units required drops to a hundred or less.

Syllabic systems of writing occur in various parts of the world, but have never spread very widely. In the Middle East, the inhabitants of Cyprus used a syllabary, first for an as yet untranslated language, and later, from the 6th down to the 3rd or 2nd century B.C., for Greek. How this originated, and why the Greek-speaking Cypriots used it instead of an alphabet, is still a mystery: but the fact of its existence is of great interest as showing the independent evolution in one and the same region of two radically different simplifying principles in regard to writing.

As regards the origin of the alphabet, two important discoveries have been made in recent times, one in Sinai, the other at Latakia. Sinai was the great source of copper for Egypt, and many hieroglyphic inscriptions are found among its barren mountains; but since 1927, some fifty brief inscriptions have been found there, confirming Flinders Petrie's suspicion in 1905 that certain Sinaitic inscriptions, the earliest dating from about the 18th century B.C., were in an alphabetic script, for the total number of signs is less than thirty. In spite of two inscriptions being bilingual, with a hieroglyphic version, all attempts at decipherment have so far failed, except for one word. One hieroglyphic version refers to Hathor as the protecting goddess of those desert establishments; and in the alphabetic version one word has provisionally been identified as the Semitic equivalent of *goddess* – Baalat, the feminine of Baal or Lord.

The actual letters are not very similar to those of the Ahiram inscription; but it seems clear that this Sinaitic script was the basis out of which the Phoenicians developed their more efficient alphabet two or three hundred years later. The Sinaitic signs are almost certainly adaptations of Egyptian hieroglyphs, though used for the writing of a Semitic language. An Egyptian idea has been taken over, and then used in new ways, by those in charge of the mines of Sinai.

The process of idea-diffusion certainly operated in northern Phoenicia. Here in 1929, at Ras Shamra, large numbers of clay tablets were found with writing in an unknown cuneiform script. Analysis at once showed this to be alphabetic, since it used only 32 signs; and it was speedily deciphered, on the correct assumption that the underlying language was a Semitic one. The language is not true Phoenician, but another of the Canaanitic group. However, the same alphabet was also used for the non-Semitic language, Hurrian; and this probably accounts for the fact that it contains extra letters for sounds not necessary in Semitic.

The documents are mainly of the 14th century B.C., with perhaps a few of the 15th. The script seems to have gone out of use in the 13th century, and cannot well have originated earlier than the 16th. The signs, though cuneiform in the purely morphological sense of consisting of wedge-shaped or arrow-headed marks made by impressing a broad-headed stylus on wet clay, are quite different from those used in the ideographic cuneiform of Mesopotamia.

The explanation seems to be that the alphabet had already been invented in Phoenicia, that the Kings and merchants of Ugarit had heard of it and decided to take advantage of the idea, but that they did not wish to utilize the actual proto-Semitic letters, and therefore invented cuneiform signs in their stead. It has been suggested that this was motivated by the abundance of clay near Ugarit. But while this may have been a contributory cause, we may suspect that there was also a political reason. Possibly there was hostility between Phoenicia proper and the power that exercised suzerainty over northern Syria, and so, in order to show their cultural independence, the Ugarites rejected the proto-Semitic alphabet and produced one of their own, based on clay as the most convenient alternative material.

There is one further rather obscure clue – the existence, in that same Byblos which produced the earliest prototype of our alphabet, of ten documents written in a previously unknown script, the so-called pseudo-hieroglyphic script of Byblos, dating from somewhere around 2000 B.C. The script contains about 100 signs, and must therefore be primarily a syllabary, though some of the signs may have been purely consonantal and therefore alphabetic. Many of them are either borrowed or adapted from Egyptian hieroglyphs; but the language they expressed was a Semitic one. Thus it looks as if this were really a stage in the conversion of a non-alphabetic into an alphabetic system.

It seems clear that the alphabetic principle was discovered by Semitic-speaking people somewhere in the first half of the second millennium, using for the most part adaptations of Egyptian hieroglyphs as letters. The discovery was not a single event, but took several centuries for its full accomplishment.

The Egyptian system of writing was very flexible, but it was so elaborate that it needed professional training to learn and use it. And though we may be sure that individual Egyptians here and there realized that simplification would be useful, the bureaucratic traditionalism of the country was an insuperable barrier to any radical change.

The Phoenicians, on the other hand, were not hampered by any such prejudices or vested interests. They were traders first and foremost: what is more, they did not carry on trade by means of elaborate official expeditions, but individualistically, as private individuals or firms. They needed written documents to conduct their business – invoices, bills of lading, instructions to foreign representatives; but they did not want to be bothered with professional scribes if they could manage with what we would call clerks, nor with the traditional hieroglyphic script if they could find a handier system. And so they set about the job, producing first the pseudo-hieroglyphic script, and then the true alphabet. The world certainly owes an immense debt to them; for without an alphabet the diffusion of knowledge would be immeasurably slower, and general education would be impossible.

It is interesting that this notable new invention sprang from the material needs of trade, not from the claims of pure knowledge or literary record. Indeed it seems that even the Greeks were much slower to use alphabetic writing for recording their poems and dramas than for commercial transactions.

Once the alphabetic principle had been fully grasped and rigorously applied, and once it had been adapted to Indo-European languages by the addition of letters for vowels, it remained essentially unchanged. There is only one small point in which we have tightened up the alphabetic principle beyond that which the ancients had reached, and that concerns the names of the letters. We call them by words primarily symbolizing their sounds – A, B, C and the rest. But the Greeks continued to call them by the names of the words which the signs originally denoted. The very word *Alphabet* comes from alpha and beta, and alpha and beta are the Greek corruptions of the Semitic *aleph* and *beth*, which mean *ox* and *house* respectively. It is rather as if, instead of calling our letters A, B, C, D, we were to call them Apple, Bed, Cat, Dog.

But the actual alphabets which were the results of its application did change, and did so to an almost bewildering extent. The accompanying pedigree of the alphabet, a simplified version of a diagram in the *Encyclopaedia Britannica,* is very similar to the family trees of evolutionary biology: the similarity is not surprising, for what it records is the evolutionary differentiation of the alphabet. The main difference is that, in addition to the ordinary process whereby one alphabet is actually transformed into another in the course of time, a wholly or largely new script may sometimes arise by idea-diffusion;

another difference is that sometimes a new alphabet may have been influenced by more than one 'ancestral' alphabet – a process analogous to
so-called introgressive hybridization in plants, where crossing introduces a
limited number of genes from a strange species.

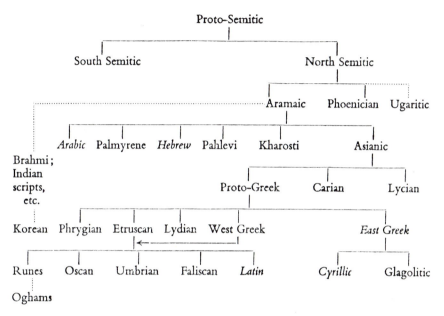

A summary genealogy of western alphabets: the South Semitic group is omitted, as are
many minor offshoots of the North Semitic. Dotted lines indicate idea-diffusion, not transformation of one script into another. Those alphabets still in use today are italicized; the
rest are extinct. The arrow from the West Greek alphabet indicates that it probably influenced the other alphabets in the Italian peninsula. The Indian and neighbouring scripts
were probably induced by idea-diffusion from Aramaic, and the Korean by further idea-
diffusion from one of them, probably Tibetan.

Alphabetic evolution thus began by leading to an exaggerated differentiation of a large number of distinct alphabets, often in quite a small area. As
time went on, most of these died out, and the comparatively few survivors
like the Latin, the Arabic, and the Cyrillic Greek, enlarged their sway. This
was sometimes due merely to an extension of the languages which utilized
them; but sometimes to their jumping the barrier into a new language
where they ousted some quite different script. As example of the former we
have the huge spread of English and Spanish due to colonization: of the latter,

the recent adoption of a Latin script for Turkish; many people regret that the architects of the Russian revolution did not do the same for Russian. I should imagine that within two or three centuries at the outside, our descendants will see a single alphabet in use all over the world, perhaps as the script of the universal second language (on present form English, but who can foresee the future?) which will by then have come into general use.

This pursuit of the alphabet up and down the corridors of history illustrates what seems to be a general characteristic of human life – namely the inseparability of the twin tendencies, towards differentiation and towards integration.

It also shows that history is neither a regular cyclical order nor just a chaos of events, neither recurrence nor mere disorder, but an irreversible process in which novelty appears. It shows that the most important novelties are new ideas, and that if they are good ones, they persist and spread and influence the further course of the process. It also shows how rare good new ideas are, and how the diffusion of ideas is just as important as the diffusion of material things. And finally it shows that history is not merely irreversible but directional, with tendencies that may be impeded but in the long run have their way: and that one of its most important tendencies is in the direction of greater knowledge. Once writing had been invented it was bound to spread; once alphabetic writing was invented, it too was bound to spread. And its spread facilitated the trend towards more knowledge.

So Byblos is proving to be a gateway not merely into the Middle East, but into the process of History itself.

7. *Baalbek: six golden-brown pillars of the Temple of Jupiter, the tallest columns in the world*

8. *An inspiration of eighteenth-century European architecture: one of the chapel-like exedrae in the court of the Temple of Jupiter at Baalbek*

9. *The Tower of Hermel, a first-century hunting lodge in the Great Rift*

4

BAALBEK
AND THE PROLIFERATION OF DIVINITY

$\mathbf{B}$AALBEK IS THE SHOW-PLACE OF
the Lebanon. Its stupendous ruins have been described and figured over
and over again, from Robert Wood's great folio in the middle of the
eighteenth century, to Hoyningen-Huene's superb post-war photographs.*

Some purists profess to find Baalbek vulgar. That is unfair: the proper
adjective is grandiose. It is grandiose as St Peter is grandiose, or the great
temple at Karnak, exhaling a sense of power, size, and glorious magnificence,
and through its design and setting achieving beauty.

In addition, it sets one thinking about the power of Rome, which could
create such magnificence in Coele-Syria – the hollow trough of the Bekaa;
and it brings up some of the bewildering problems of early religion.

For Baalbek, you fork northwards from the Damascus road at Shtora.
Here there is a celebrated hotel, much frequented by honeymoon couples.
On my second visit, the proprietor astonished me by remembering my name
from my brief passage seven months earlier. He also charmed me: on my
mentioning how beautiful we had found the table decoration at a presidential
dinner-party in Beirut a few days before – deep rose-coloured wild tulips
thickly scattered down the centre of the white table-cloth – he sent out a man

* Robert Wood, *The Ruins of Baalbek, otherwise Heliopolis in Syria* (in one volume with
The Ruins of Palmyra), London, 1857 (original issue 1753); Hoyningen-Huene (photographs) and D. M. Robinson (text), *Baalbek ; Palmyra*. New York, 1946.

into the nearby fields, and had a big bunch of the lovely things ready to present to us as we drove off.

According to some scholars, Baalbek means The Lord of the Bekaa.* The Bekaa rift is grand, but it goes on and on between its two flanking scarps, until you feel there is no reason why it should ever stop or change its character. Gertrude Bell complained bitterly of the monotony of travelling up the Bekaa – but that was on horseback: in a car the time-scale is happily altered.

The Bekaa, and the neighbouring regions of Coele-Syria, were once one of the great granaries of Rome. For that, organized irrigation and large-scale farming were necessary. Under Turkish rule, the system collapsed, and the valley sank back into unproductive poverty. There had been plenty of poverty in Roman times; the bulk of the population were either slaves or mere agricultural labourers, working for a miserable wage on the latifundia, large and small, private and imperial, on which the great bulk of the farming was done. But at least the poverty of the many was productive. As well as producing riches for the few, it produced Baalbek for all posterity. Today, the Bekaa is, in parts, not unproductive; but the irrigation schemes now being planned should increase its productivity greatly – perhaps to a level close to that of eighteen centuries ago.

The first sight of Baalbek is memorable. Through the bare boughs of poplars the great columns are seen, standing surprisingly high above the plain. This elevation is due to the entire complex of buildings being raised on a huge substructure, nearly 300 yards in length. Although this provided space in its bowels for storage and stabling, its primary function was a psychological one – to serve as an artificial acropolis and to render the temples more imposing by lifting them high above the neighbouring landscape. The medieval cathedral-builders could provide their main structures with a greater impressiveness of height through the new gothic methods of building and buttressing, and could add a further soaring quality by means of their towers and spires. The Romans, in their religious architecture at least, were still confined to the methods of building which had been adapted from wood construction: the height of their temples was limited by the possible height of the supporting columns. Even though the columns of the temple of Jupiter at Baalbek are the tallest in the world, the building would never have become

* Others think it means Lord of the Sun – an idea taken over by the Greeks, who called Baalbek 'Sun City' – Heliopolis.

a landmark and cynosure for the region, as has Salisbury Cathedral, for instance, without the aid of the substructure.

The substructure contains some of the largest single blocks of stone in the world – much larger than anything I had imagined possible. The largest block of all, however, is not there – we saw it in the quarry near by, still not completely cut away from the underlying rock at one end. According to *Whitaker's Almanack*, it is the largest cut block in the world, measuring 60 feet in length, and 17 by 14 feet in cross-section. That means over 500 cubic yards of stone – the dense white crystalline stone which in the ruins has weathered to various shades of grey and fawn tinged with gold: and that means a weight of around 1500 tons.

Some of the stones actually built into the substructure are almost as big: three of them measure 14 by 11 by over 62 feet, and each must weigh at least 1000 tons. What is more, their joints are accurate to the width of a knife-blade, and they are up twenty feet and more above ground-level. How even Roman engineers got them into place is a mystery. Leonard Woolley told me that his native overseer sat silent for a long time gazing at the great stones, and then walked away shaking his head and muttering 'What a foreman they had! It gives *me* a headache.'

The most obvious marvel of Baalbek is the row of six golden-brown pillars of the Temple of Jupiter that still stand erect, surmounted by their fragment of entablature – architrave, frieze and cornice – which rises for over 16 feet above the 65 feet of the columns (pl. 7, opp. p. 56). They are made of three huge drums, the drums having been cemented together by pouring in molten lead along grooves on their surface. The Arabs stripped the Roman ruins of every fragment of metal they could find. Gilded bronze, as on the capitals of the temple of Bel at Palmyra, was their special prize; but they did not despise baser metals, and the columns at Baalbek show the holes they drilled to extract the lead jointings.

Others of the fifty-four original columns lie in fragments on the ground · and some were transported to form parts of later buildings, such as Santa Sophia at Constantinople, dedicated to other religions. The columns them-selves are a quintessence of imperial Rome; but the frieze above them, with its rich palmettes and its series of bulls' and lions' heads, is a reminder that Rome here was near its eastern limit, with oriental influences seeping in.

The second obvious glory of the place is the so-called Temple of Bacchus. This was ironically called the Little Temple in antiquity, because (though actually larger than the Parthenon) it was smaller than the enormous Temple of Jupiter next door.

The temple is beautifully preserved, its stone weathered to a glowing golden fawn, and is probably the finest and assuredly the richest Corinthian building of the entire Roman world (pl. 11, opp. p. 61). Certainly the impression of disciplined luxuriance given by the first sight of the interior is unrivalled. Many of the columns are fluted, and many still show *entasis*, that extraordinary invention of Greek architects which the Hellenistic and Roman period largely abandoned, its subtle swelling designed to give a more satisfying effect to the upward-looking eye. As for the capitals and entablature, the carvings of foliage and fruits and birds, the swags and garlands, the bacchantes and other dionysiac figures, they are of a glorious richness. One can mount to the top of the walls by means of an interior 'square spiral' stair: this, it seems, was a local peculiarity. From above, the beauty and the lovely proportions of the roofless interior are revealed from a new angle, and are seen against the wide background of the Lebanon's snow-capped scarp, running away southward into blue distance. (The building was originally roofed with stone slabs over three square yards in area.)

The little round Temple of Venus, lying off some two or three hundred yards from the elevated main group of buildings, is a marvel, not of grandeur, but of delicacy and originality. Its central stone-domed *cella* is encircled by a peristyle of cornices and columns, whose circumference is indented by five semicircular bays. The freedom of the plan and the charm of the carved decorations make me think now of Renaissance pavilions, now of baroque chapels. In the famous eighteenth-century gardens of Stourhead in Wiltshire, the little circular temple was copied from Wood's description of this ancient masterpiece at Baalbek.

The influence of Roman architecture on that of north-western Europe becomes very evident when we look at the main court of the great temple, the Court of the Altar. This had a colonnade running round three sides; and in the walls behind the colonnade are four large semicircular chapel-like recesses or exedrae, their semicircles crowned with half-domes (pl. 8, opp. p. 57). These bring to mind some of the handsomest achievements of French and British architects. Many details of the windows and the decoration also have a strangely familiar look. Certainly Baalbek, through the intermediary

10. Gigantic columns of the Temple of Jupiter at Baalbek

of the Englishman Robert Wood, contributed directly to the later development of Europe's classical style, just as Diocletian's palace at Spalato did
through the intermediary of the Scotsman Robert Adam, though much was
of course taken over earlier from the antiquities of Rome itself.

The final glory of Baalbek is its superb planning. The temple complex on
its elevated substructure was approached by a grand stairway, mounting to
a colonnaded portico flanked by a pair of towers. From this the worshipper
passed into a hexagonal forecourt, this unusual plan being perhaps due to
Semitic influence; and from this into the aforementioned Court of the Altar,
a vast colonnaded place whose far side was largely occupied by another flight
of steps, leading very impressively up to the further platform on which,
still on the same axis, was laid out the great Temple of Jupiter.

There are many other interesting points – the use of arches between
columns instead of flat architraves, which was rare in the first century A.D.,
and may have been due to the brittle limestone; the way the Christians
spoilt the looks of the Court of the Altar by building a big church at one end
of it, and making another smaller church out of the Temple of Venus; the
addition of a mosque by the Moslems near the Temple of Bacchus; the
'hitching bars' for camels, made by piercing a double eyelet round a piece
of the solid wall (we had seen similar attachments cut out of the living rock
by the Upper Paleolithic people in the Dordogne); the sad evidences of
destruction by man and nature – by the Mongol invaders in the thirteenth
century, by earthquakes in the twelfth and again in the eighteenth; the
transformation of the site into a fortress by the Arabs, who built their fortifications on top of the Roman wall.

But I have no space for details: what I want to bring out is the huge scale
of the place, the tangible evidence of the security and prosperity that Roman
rule had restored to Syria. The Romans took over the cult of Baal or Bel by
identifying him with Jupiter, but a Jupiter with special local attributes, whom
they called Jupiter Heliopolitanus. Doubtless the inhabitants of Syria continued to think of the local divinity as Baal; and in the 3rd century that *outré*
character, the Emperor Heliogabalus, officiated here as Baal's High Priest.

The so-called 'Temple of Venus' was perhaps in reality dedicated to that
very Roman divinity, Fortuna. But the assignment of the other great

---

*11. The Temple of Bacchus at Baalbek, probably the finest and assuredly the richest Corinthian
building of the Roman world.*

Temple to Bacchus is incorrect: it was probably the shrine of the great female divinity of the ancient world. Her local manifestation was the goddess Atargatis, whom the Romans then fused with Venus. The result of this policy of amalgamating their own religion with those of the peoples they had conquered, instead of enforcing it as the one true system, was that Baalbek became one of the largest centres of religious pilgrimage in the entire Syrian region. The busy town that once surrounded the great shrine has now vanished, and no attempt to excavate its remains has yet been made.

In the excellent hotel, wood-burning stoves contributed much-needed heat (for it was late November, and Baalbek, though in the Bekaa trough, is 3800 feet above sea-level, close to the watershed between Orontes and Litani). After dinner we visited the ruins once more: the half-moon gave them a desolate beauty, and it was difficult to evoke the bustling life with which the place once seethed.

Next day we were on our way northwards by seven. Some of the scenery was fine; but the general impression was one of bareness, of geological formations on an outsize, inhuman scale. High up in the air we saw some eleven big birds – really big birds – steadily coming towards us. My companion, who knew Africa, was willing to bet that they were cranes. But when we finally got our field-glasses on them, they turned out to be pelicans – 'pelicans in the wilderness', many miles from the nearest water, the Lake of Homs to the north. I do not know what they were doing, but I shall always remember their grotesque yet strong flight headed southwards along the great trough, soon to look down on Baalbek, and then on to the Sea of Galilee.

Prompted by Fedden's description, we took a side road towards Hermel, a little white town in an oasis of deep green on the foot of the huge slopes of the Lebanon, and then branched off again on a rough track across a stony steppe, studded with little plants of an inedible prickliness, to the springs of the Orontes.

The Orontes is invisible until you are right upon it: it runs in a narrow gorge (I would guess, along the actual fault-line of the rift) between the flat valley-bottom and the Lebanon slopes. The gorge had cliffs up to a hundred feet high, all in light ochreous rock, with an exquisite pale green-blue stream, very clear, bordered by green grass, trees, and occasional cornfields. The only sign of life was a group of coal-black sheep, moving up a track beyond. We made our way down to the 'Source of the Orontes' – a spring welling out from beneath the cliff into a limpid pool, six or seven feet deep, its lucid aquamarine transparency set in a border of emerald-green water-weeds, and overhung by a solitary plane-tree. The pool slips into the main stream by a narrow channel – a lovely origin for a famous river.

Round a corner is the remains of a rock-cut monastery, hewn out of the cliff above the river. So far as I can make out, it was an offshoot of the great monastery at Ribleh, a few miles to the north, established in the fifth century by St Maron, who disputes with the later patriarch John Maron the honour of giving the Maronites their name. This monastic stronghold was destroyed by Justinian II in the seventh century, and hundreds of its inmates were put to death as heretics. The offshoot that we visited was a small one: even so, there were several storeys of cells in the cliff. From the main hall we looked up to see the remains of a spiral staircase piercing upwards through the rock, but now quite inaccessible. It was from this area that the persecuted Maronites withdrew into the heights of the Mountain.

A little way off, on a small rise on the valley floor, stands the enigmatic building, the Tower of Hermel (pl. 9, opp. p. 57). This is strange both in its solitude and in its architecture. It is a square tower of heavy stone construction, probably of the first century A.D., surmounted by a pyramid; Ionic pilasters decorate the upper storey, while on the walls of the main storey are reliefs of weapons and animals of the chase, and one panel of a wild bull attacked by wolves.

The pyramidal top recalls some of the tower-graves of the Palmyran desert further east, and there is a curiously un-Roman look about the place. Perhaps it was the hunting lodge of some local potentate who aimed at combining Semitic tradition with the new Hellenistic ideas.

Further north, we caught glimpses of the Lake of Homs. Unfortunately we had no time to turn aside to see the ruins of Qadisha: and it was only afterwards that I realized that Qadisha is Kadesh, scene of the famous battle between Rameses II and the Hittites about 1300 B.C., which we later saw portrayed on Rameses' temple at Luxor.

The lake is reputed to be the earliest large artificial reservoir in the world, its dam having been built well over three thousand years ago. There is a much-ruined Hittite fortress on an island in its centre.

Homs is a rather disappointing town, mostly second-rate and shabby, though with one good mosque. In the souks there was a particular abundance of American sun-glasses, styled 'Hollywood', 'Palm Beach', and the like. There was also abundance of silk – men carrying raw silk in lovely rich

yellow skeins, shopkeepers with silken stuffs for sale. The local silk is all
yellow, but some white is imported from Italy to make up into fabrics.

From Homs to the coast we made our way through the gap between the
north end of the Lebanon and the south end of the Alawit range – rather
depressing brown country, like a desiccated version of the least attractive
type of Scottish moor. At one spot, the Lebanon revealed a valley strangely
like one in the North Wales mountains, with great sheets of rain drifting
across between it and the distant sea. Later on, we ran into a violent storm,
with thunder and lightning incessant on all sides, and at one place a 'demi-
water-spout', a short truncated cone with a serrated lower border,
protruding down from the heavy cloud above, and visibly rotating.

After a tantalizing glimpse of the greatest of all Crusader castles, the Krak
des Chevaliers, perched on the foothills to northwards, we left the storm
behind us and reached the sea in sunshine. All round us marvellously active
little racing-crabs rushed over the sand. It is remarkable that any animal can
achieve such speed in a sideways direction. When held in the hand, at the
advance of a threatening finger they lower their long eye-stalks sideways
into protective grooves, at the same time lifting their two big claws over
them for further protection. When running, their bodies are lifted high
above the sand, and their long legs give them a very thoroughbred look.

High up on the beach were some beautiful shells – sea-snails like our
Natica in shape, but pale violet above, intense violet below; the lip was so
fragile that I found none unbroken.

★

Baalbek was the first obvious and large-scale manifestation to come my way
of that efflorescence of divinity which spreads over the Middle East. And I
do not mean just an efflorescence of religion: that existed, for instance, in
medieval Christendom, but was concerned with one god only. I mean an
efflorescence of variety in divinity, producing a veritable rash of gods and
goddesses.

At Baalbek itself there was Baal (who was also Hadad and also Jupiter);
and there was Bacchus (who perhaps had a touch of Adonis or Attis about
him); there was also Venus (who is certainly in part Atargatis and to a lesser
extent all the other avatars of the Mother Goddess); there was Christ in the
remains of the Churches, and Allah in the Mosque. At Byblos there were, as
we have seen, Osiris and Isis, Adonis and Ashtaroth, besides the Phoenician

gods imprisoned in their stone obelisks, and the Christian Trinity in the beautiful church. Jehovah existed in Solomon's Temple, long ruined, and in all the synagogues of the region. Jerash had Artemis as well as many other divinities; Petra had Roman gods, as well as Nabataean ones in their 'god-boxes' on the High Place. From Tyre to Carthage Moloch received his offering of infants; Bel and Bel-Shamin flourished in Palmyra; Allah succeeded Christ in Santa Sophia; and ancient Egypt fairly pullulated with divinities.

As for the gods of the Hittites, and the Assyrians, and the Babylonians, and the Sumerians, it is difficult for a layman in these matters even to remember their names; but there they were, widely dispersed, and often extending their sway by a process of religious imperialism. The crumbling ziggurats on the flat plains of Mesopotamia are the ruined homes of a Sumerian pantheon; and there are Layard's spoils in the British Museum to remind us of the curious developments which the gods of Babylon underwent in Assyria.

Most of the ancient divinities are now dead as doornails. But within the region we can also see how Jehovah was spiritualized by the Jewish Captivity and given the force to survive centuries of persecution, and how new and powerful divinities like Christ and Allah emerged on to the religious scene.

This multiplicity of gods is an invitation to study the relations between religion and civilization – or should I say between religions and civilizations? The Middle East is the ideal laboratory for a study of the development of religions regarded as functions of society, for it generated the earliest civilizations and witnessed the struggles between them, and it gave birth to the two most powerful higher religions of today, Christianity and Islam, as well as to Judaism. It also produced a number of other new religions, like Zoroastrianism and Mithraism, which after a vigorous youth, died out or relapsed into unimportance.

It is a commonplace to say that religions are a recognition of the element of sacredness in the world. But they are also formulations of men's beliefs about their destiny. Toynbee has noted how the breakdown of civilizations, and the frustration of men's efforts to achieve spiritual satisfaction within the existing social framework, will lead to the radical reformulation of old religions, or often to the rise of new ones.

Many social historians have pointed out how the increase of knowledge (not only science, but all kinds of knowledge) makes new formulations desirable or inevitable. Xenophon was a civilized Greek: but his decisions were guided by the omens derived from inspection of the entrails of sacrificed animals, in a way that is incomprehensible to a modern European. The discovery by the Babylonian astronomer-priests of the laws underlying the apparently irregular movements of the planets, led to a reformulation of human destiny in the fatalistic terms of astrology. The multiplicity of gods and religions within the early Roman Empire led the Romans to superimpose the cult of the Emperor as symbolizing the unity of the empire; but at the same time it led St Paul to find a new unifying principle in the unity of the human species and the universality of the new doctrines of Christianity.

The Middle East shows us how man began by projecting divinity into local and partial aspects of reality; how religions grew up expressing the sacred destinies of distinct and competing societies; and how ignorance often led to the ascription of supernatural sacred power to purely natural phenomena. It demonstrates the inevitable supersession of primitive religions, however elaborated, by systems more universal and more adequately expressing the state of knowledge. Meanwhile the modern world shows how traditional types of religion may be supplanted by new systems like Nazism or Communism. These are often called pseudo-religions; I would rather say that they are primitive specimens of religions of a new type, with a social or non-supernatural basis and inspired with hostility towards their predecessors. But religion of some sort, in the sense of beliefs about human destiny, and involving the sense of sacredness, is bound to exist in any active human community. Furthermore, religions of all types can be bad just as well as good: it is not true that religion *per se* is always a good thing (or, as Lucretius and the Marxists maintain, always a bad thing!). Nazism was evil; and so were some of the barbaric religions of the ancient world.

Such facts and thoughts pose crucial questions. How can the religious spirit cope with the crisis and chaos of the modern world, save by a new vision of man's role on earth? Is not humanity engaged in the stupendous adventure of realizing new and fuller possibilities for evolving life? And is it not the task of religion to formulate and express this new vision of sacred destiny in new ways, ways that are consonant with scientific knowledge and psychological fact? In the crisis and chaos of the ancient world the old gods died, but the new unifying religions of Christianity and Islam were born. I would prophesy that the next hundred years will see equally drastic changes of religion, quite new expressions of the religious spirit, and novel developments of its social functions.

5

LEBANON: PHOENICIAN LAND

My SECOND ARRIVAL IN BEIRUT was by air from Constantinople, in November 1948. Unexpectedly bad weather, with snow flurries and icy winds, put off our departure through a dreary Sunday; but on the Monday we were up at 5.45 and out to the aerodrome, past domes and minarets still with a powdering of snow on them, in a cold greyish dawn. Our journey was far from comfortable; but we had a memorable geographical experience. To the south of the Sea of Marmara rose fine mountains, snow-capped, the resort of skiers from Constantinople. After that, rolling upland basins with green lakes, and limestone hills strangely pitted with sink-holes. Then down over the steep southern rim of Asia Minor to the Gulf of Adalia, across the fifty miles of sea to Cyprus and over the steep-sided mountain ridge which shelters its central plain from the north. In a few minutes we were looking down on Famagusta, with its harbour, its medieval walls, its Gothic cathedral and its memories of Othello.

In Cyprus, 'Dame Venus, Love's Lady, was born of the sea'. The legend is, I suppose, a reminder of her oriental origin. The fertility goddess of the ancient Middle East is transported by the early seafarers of the Phoenician coast to Cyprus. She becomes Aphrodite the foam-born of the Greek mariners, and Venus to the Romans. It is a curious reflection that her legendary birthplace is now a British colony.

The British have two special achievements to their credit in Cyprus. Malaria and the goat are two of the worst scourges of the Middle East: in Cyprus the British have eradicated the first and brought the second under control. But we never succeeded in dealing with the violent nationalist spirit of the Enosis movement. I wonder what would have happened if we had provided a first-class centre of higher education on the island. We might have prevented much violence and hatred, and have made possible a bloodless development to self-government and independence as has happened in Nigeria. We might have diverted the enthusiasm of young Cypriots from a sterile political nationalism to the constructive aim of a fuller life for their country. We might even have provided a much-needed focus for the entire Middle East, where future professional men from different countries could learn to think in regional instead of merely national terms. Something of the sort is now (1961) being provided by the new Middle East Technical University in Ankara, though this is primarily concerned with the C.E.N.T.O. (Baghdad Pact) countries, and more limited in scope.

★

My first arrival in Beirut was also by air, but from Ankara, and in spring. The part of the Turkish plateau that we traversed was less fertile: at one place extraordinary craters protruded their circular eyes from the barren landscape. The mountainous rim we flew over was much higher – the ten-thousand-foot mountains of the main Taurus chain. Its northern slopes were marked with a curious patchwork, an alternation of narrow parallel strips of snow and outcropping rock, darkly dotted with sparse pines.

The southern slope of the great plateau was here more fertile, more obviously Mediterranean than by Adalia. The mountain buttresses descended, one beyond the other, in wooded slopes, with towns and villages along their base. Rivers gleamed in the green plain below them, on their way to the glittering blue of the sea (pl. 6, opp. p. 41), in smiling contrast to the sternness of the Anatolian upland.

★

The Lebanese coast continues to show a smiling Mediterranean face, though here and there the landscape reminds us of the proximity of the desert. There is a wonderful wood of umbrella pines between the airport and Beirut, and the same lovely Mediterranean tree abounds on the slopes above the city; minified by distance, in the deceiving brilliance of morning light, they look like plantations where all the green umbrellas needed by the world are fantastically being grown.

The main portion of ancient Phoenicia is roughly equivalent to Lebanon;

its northern extension, from the Homs gap to Ras Shamra, is now assigned to Syria. Lebanon consists first and foremost of a narrow but fertile seaboard wedged in between the sea and the mountains. Then comes the Mountain – the Lebanon range, rising to over ten thousand feet; its lower continuation, the Alawit range to the north, rising between Latakia and the lower Orontes, is in Syria. And then the Bekaa, the Lebanese section of the great rift valley, which I have already described, succeeded by the second mountain rampart, the Anti-Lebanon, rising between Lebanon and Syria.

The Mountain is almost entirely limestone. Its seaward slopes, and the sides of the long profound valleys that run down westwards from its high crest, are covered with wonderful cultivation terraces (pl. 4, opp. p. 40), which support the surprising number of villages concealed in its recesses.

The entire range was once forested, densely covered with trees, not only the famous cedars, but also innumerable pines. Today there is nothing left which can be called a forest, and only two ageing remnants of the cedars, a few hundred trees in all. I urged on the authorities the desirability of creating a National Park, which should be centred on a real cedar forest. Everyone has heard of the Cedars of Lebanon, and every visitor to the country would want to see a forest of them. But so far as I know, nothing has been done.

Freya Stark once told me a story about the cedars which was current during the French mandate. Whether true or not, at least it illustrates the complexity of the religious situation. The French, anxious to secure the natural regeneration of the cedars, appealed to the religious authorities to restrain the villagers from pasturing their goats in the groves. After six months a French officer called on the Maronite bishop to ask how the regulations were being carried out by his flock. 'Excellently,' was the reply, 'but I think I ought to tell you, Sir, that the Orthodox goats still persist in eating the seedlings.'

We can hardly wonder at the denudation when we remember that the large-scale export of timber from the Mountain began over five thousand years ago. It was almost the only source of wood for ancient Egypt; boatloads of timber and great rafts of logs travelled down the coast and up the Nile. Cedars of Lebanon provided some of the largest beams in the Achaemenid Kings' great palace at Persepolis, a thousand miles away across Mesopotamia. When Solomon decided to build his Temple, he appealed to Hiram, King of Tyre, for help. 'Now therefore command them that they hew me cedar trees out of Lebanon; . . . for thou knowest that there is not among us any that can skill to hew timber like unto the Sidonians.' Hiram agreed, and Solomon sent three lots of ten thousand men to Lebanon to fell cedars and fir-trees under Hiram's instructions; while Hiram arranged to 'convey them by sea in floats' to Palestine.

The Romans continued the destruction, which extended northwards far into what is now Syria. In their day, the port of Baniyas lost much of its importance as the timber within easy reach of it was cut out* : still today the slopes above it are brown and treeless. Indeed, in most of the range, few trees are now left except for the sacred groves of the pagan Alawit religion, direct descendants of the sacred groves of the Old Testament, that are still venerated by the primitive villagers.

Reforestation has been begun in some areas, but it will be a long time before the Mountain recovers from its denudation and regains its moisture-conserving mantle.

*

The ancient Phoenicians, with only a narrow strip of fertile land between the coast and the great mountains behind, inevitably looked seawards. They seem to have arrived relatively late in the region, pushing westwards from their earlier home in south-eastern Arabia to reach the Mediterranean soon after the middle of the second millennium. It was doubtless the collapse of the Minoan Thalassocracy which encouraged them to extend their trading activities ever further afield. In any case, the sea became their empire, and maritime trade the chief source of their fortunes. They developed the few ports of the region into powerful industrial and trading cities – Tyre, Sidon, Byblos, Arvad, with Beirut and Ras Shamra as subsidiary centres. None of these enjoyed a dominant advantage, and so they remained as separate independent kingdoms; like the Greek city-states, they never combined into a single strong political entity. They frequently came under foreign suzerainty, but were content so long as they could pursue their commercial destiny. Soldiering they regarded as an inferior occupation, and preferred to employ mercenaries. They were not interested in conquest, but built up a commercial system on an imperial scale, by establishing settlements all over the region. These were not so much colonies, like those of the Greeks, as

* Baniyas should regain some of its prosperity now that it has become the terminus for a new pipeline from the oilfields of Iraq.

trading posts and counters. The one exception was Carthage, founded by a discontented group from Tyre in the ninth century B.C. Carthage was also exceptional in that it set its foot on the path of imperial conquest, with the Punic Wars as disastrous result.

Before the classical period, the Phoenicians had pushed as far afield as Cornwall in search of tin, and had established trading posts in Sardinia, southern France and even beyond the Pillars of Hercules, in the biblical Tarshish near modern Cadiz. Matthew Arnold epitomized this long-range commercial network in his lines on the Phoenician skipper of a later century, who, confronted with the Greeks, 'the young light-hearted masters of the waves' in the Eastern Mediterranean, held on westward

> to where the Atlantic raves
> Outside the Western Straits, and unbent sails
> There, where down cloudy cliffs, through sheets of foam,
> Shy traffickers, the dark Iberians come;
> And on the beach undid his corded bales.

From Tarshish, the Phoenicians seem to have ventured some way down the Atlantic coast of Africa; the Egyptian Pharaoh Necho in 596 B.C. sent a Phoenician expedition down the east coast of Africa, and they may have circumnavigated the entire continent: one would give a great deal for a fuller account of their voyage. And about 500 B.C., their Carthaginian descendants under Hanno extended the limits of the known world to the Ivory Coast and even beyond, an extraordinary achievement.

D. S. Harden * considers it certain that Hanno established a trading post at the mouth of the Senegal river, and probable that he reached the Cameroon mountains. The exact evaluation of his voyage is difficult, because of the extreme brevity of the only surviving account – only 600 Greek words in all!

When the first gorilla skull was found by a missionary in the Gaboon in 1847, he suggested the name *Gorilla* for the animal on the basis of Hanno's statements. Hanno said that they came across 'women' with shaggy bodies whom his interpreters called 'Gorillas'. Three were killed, flayed, and their skins brought back to Carthage. They were almost certainly not gorillas, but either chimpanzees or possibly baboons.

The Phoenicians never organized overland traffic themselves; but they had their posts and missions on established trade-routes, at places like

* *Antiquity*, 1948; 22, 141.

Damascus and Hama for the eastern caravans, and Memphis for the trade of Egypt.

Tyre (and its offshoot Carthage) was the home of the famous or infamous god Moloch, with his 'burning Idol all of blackest hue', in whose 'furnace blue' children were sacrificially committed to the flames. In Carthage, the nobility are said to have offered low-born children as substitutes for their own, fattening them up in order to render them more acceptable. It is probable that the usual horrific descriptions of the rite, culminating in Flaubert's *Salammbô*, are exaggerated, and that the children were killed before being 'passed through the fire'. But certainly the worship of Moloch demanded organized child sacrifice, and its persistence into classical times is a remarkable and ghastly survival from barbarism.

Today the four chief centres of ancient Phoenicia have dwindled into insignificance. Proud Tyre is now a broken-down fishing port, and Byblos no longer a port at all. Arvad we saw from the mainland – a little island (Ruad is its modern name) with a little fishing town huddled on it, a reminder of the small scale on which ancient economy was organized. The entire island is less than half a mile long; yet it was once a powerful fortress city, with satellite towns on the mainland and commercial tentacles extending all over the Mediterranean.

We spent a morning in Sidon, and found that it has at least kept its charm. The ancient harbour is still used by the fishing fleet, and you have only to walk a few steps from the main street to come across little ships being built on the shore, right up against the houses. On the tip of the sheltering spit across the harbour is the Crusader Castle, alas now in ruins after a bombardment in 1840. A camel in a small caravanserai struck a surprising note among the luxuriant gardens for which Sidon is famous above all other Lebanese towns.

Another surprise was the two-storeyed arcaded French Hostel, erected by the great Emir Fakr-ed-Din early in the seventeenth century to encourage trade with the West. In this handsome *Khan*, French merchants could be comfortable and safe from religious fanaticism. The gate is like a College Gate in Oxford, but more formidable. Studded with nails, furnished with a set of huge bolts and bars, and with an exceedingly small night postern, it kept the foreigners secure. Today the arcades have become cloisters round a green central court: the building has been taken over for an orphanage by the Sœurs de St Joseph, so that it is still an outpost of French civilization.

Almost the only remains from Sidon's Phoenician greatness are in the Beirut Museum. The most striking are a series of no less than twenty-six white marble sarcophagi from the ancient cemetery. They are obviously adaptations of Egyptian 'anthropoid' coffins, with second-rate portrait heads, in which the formality of Egyptian style has been vulgarized by Phoenician bad taste. The Phoenicians had not developed a style of their own; nor, it seems, did they bother overmuch about art. But the expressions of the faces are interesting: as Fedden says, 'Company directors are buried in these sarcophagi.'

The one tangible memorial of Phoenician times is the enormous shell-mound by the city walls. This, over 150 feet high at one point, is entirely composed of the waste from the purple industry, in the shape of millions of Murex shells. At the sight of it, questions about purple began to stir in my brain. 'Who fished the Tyrian Murex up?' – not Browning's metaphorical Keatsian murex, but the real gastropod mollusc? Did the industry die of over-fishing? When did the use of murex purple begin, and when and why did it stop? – and so on and so forth.

It was surprisingly difficult to find any comprehensive account of the subject. Neither Girardin's *Pourpre du Tyr* nor von Martens's *Purpur und Perlen* is in the London Library. D'Arcy Thompson's *Glossary of Greek Fishes* is invaluable but incomplete; and the masses of facts in Pauly-Wissowa's *Real-Enzyklopaedie,* in Johnson's *Introduction to Conchology,* and in Otto Keller's formidable *Tiere des Klassischen Altertums* are sadly disconnected. Here is an admirable subject ready to the hand of some classical historian.

However, I have managed to dig out some of the answers, and here they are: murex purple was the most prized dye of antiquity because it was one of the few sources of brilliant reds and violets, and because it was exceedingly 'fast' (some of the enormous hoard of purple cloth that Alexander found in Darius's treasury was 190 years old, but quite unfaded). It was so valuable that early in the Roman Empire its manufacture was made an imperial monopoly, and great purple factories were established all over the Mediterranean. For, although the Phoenician coast was famous for the quality of its purple (indeed the very name Phoenicia means Land of Purple), it gradually ceased to be the only or even the main source of the dye.

Purple is produced by two species of the large sea-snail Murex inhabiting the Mediterranean. Curiously enough, the other genera of the family

Muricidae seem not to produce it, while our common Dog-whelk, though assignable to another family, produces enough purplish dye for it to have been used for ornamental writing by medieval scribes in regions where Murex is absent. The creatures are voracious carnivores, boring holes with their toothed tongue-ribbons through the shells of other molluscs. But not being averse to saving time and trouble, they will also eat dead meat, and were accordingly trapped in baited wicker creels laid out along a ground-rope like lobster-pots.

The source of the dye is the hypobranchial gland, a glandular mass of obscure function in the wall of the mantle-cavity. Its secretion is colourless, but rapidly changes colour on exposure to air and light: it is chemically related to indigo, and contains bromine. Though colourless, it is not odourless, but stinks. Cole, writing about 'the purple fish' in an early volume of the Philosophical Transactions of the Royal Society, says that the dye has 'a very strong smell (which divers who have smelt it could not endure) as if *Garlick* and *Assa-foetida* were mixt together'. The purple-factories must have been unpleasant to work in.

The purple of the ancients was not all purple in the restricted colour-sense in which we use the word today. It ranged through intense red, rose, heliotrope, violet, and a deep sea-blue, to almost blackish-purple, and, with special treatment, even to green. Amethyst was the most prized shade of all, at least in certain periods. The different shades were produced by using different techniques in the boiling and dyeing vats. Some legends ascribe its discovery to Hercules and others to Bacchus; but all we really know of its origin is that it must lie far back in antiquity. It was in wide use by the fifteenth century B.C., and Phoenicia was the site of a well-established purple industry before the thirteenth.

Later, there were purple-factories in many parts of the Mediterranean, mostly in its eastern half. The purple of the Peloponnese was considered second only to that of the Tyrian coast. Tarentum has Murex-mounds almost as big as those of Tyre and Sidon, but composed of the shells of a different species of Murex. There were purple-fisheries in northern Syria, Asia Minor, the Greek Islands, off Crete, at Carthage and elsewhere on the North African coast, Thessalonica, Constantinople, and various places in Italy and Sicily. The Murex shell was used as an emblem on the coins of various towns on the Phoenician coast, and of Tarentum. In many places there were guilds of purple-makers.

The word 'purple' originally meant 'crimson'. Crimson was used in the earliest times to stain the hands and faces of sacred persons and the bones of the dead, being a magical colour. The wearing of purple which grew out of this tradition was later confined to the powerful and the wealthy. Later still, attempts were made to restrict its use by law to certain classes, and to award the wearing of it as a distinction. In some periods of Roman history, the wearing of the most expensive kind of purple by unsuitable people was punishable by imprisonment; but even before our era it was widely used by the rich bourgeoisie in Rome.

Various Emperors preferred not to wear it on occasions when they wanted to court popular favour. However, it always remained a symbol of power and luxury – the royal ships of the Ptolemies had purple borders on their sails, and at Actium only Cleopatra's sails were purple. The later Emperors managed to keep an economic grip on the precious substance, by making it an imperial monopoly – and a very profitable one too: Justinian's Code contains elaborate regulations on the subject.

While the dyeing of cloth was far and away its main use, purple was employed also by painters and by the writers of manuscripts (there is a famous purple codex in Sweden, and a purple-and-gold gospel of Charlemagne in Paris); and there is a queer reference in Pliny to its use in dyeing live sheep.

Purple cloth was of course a valuable article of trade. Long before Darius's time, the caravans took it across the desert to Babylonia and Persia, and some may have travelled all the way to India. In the Byzantine Empire, purple was so much the imperial symbol that *Porphyrogenitus* was added to the title of those actually 'born in the purple'; though whether the term refers to the imperial infant being wrapped in a purple garment, or to his birth taking place in a special room hung with purple tapestries, is obscure.

And then came 1453 and the Turks and the fall of Constantinople; and purple was no longer available to Christendom. It is on record that already by 1464 Pope Paul II had to fall back on cochineal, and therefore on scarlet, for his Cardinals' robes.

There are some questions still asking themselves in my mind. Were Cardinals' robes purple and not scarlet before 1453? Why had the purple industry already begun to go downhill long before the capture of Constantinople? Why did the Moslems not keep the precious industry going for their own use, and for trade by caravan or by ship to the East? Why is murex purple no longer used at all?

Perhaps one day I shall light on the answers. Meanwhile the great shell-heaps remain in my memory as relics of a huge industry which has now entirely perished, but which was the precursor of even greater giants like I. G. Farben and I.C.I. There are no shell-heaps at the I.C.I. dye factories; but perhaps some traveller of the fortieth century will be impressed by remains of our twentieth-century dyestuff industry, by then superseded by some new source of material as thoroughly as Sidon and the Murex have been superseded by us.

*

Lebanon still has an oversea orientation: it sends its surplus population abroad. There are plenty of Lebanese in New York, in parts of South America, in Egypt. The Lebanese colony in Mexico is large enough to warrant a Lebanese Ambassador; in West Africa it is the so-called Syrians (mainly Lebanese Christians) who take the place of the Indians in East Africa and the Jews in various medieval countries: they are the small traders and shopkeepers and moneylenders of the region.

I had the surprise of my life when serving on the Commission for Higher Education in West Africa in 1943. In Kumasi, capital of Ashanti, one of the few barbaric militarist societies to survive into the modern world, I wanted to buy some Ashanti gold rings from a Lebanese pawnbroker. The pawnbroker insisted on presenting them to me, so I naturally offered to make a return gift. When I asked him what he would like, he replied 'the *Life* of your celebrated grandfather, T. H. Huxley'! The President of the Lebanon was delighted with this evidence of Lebanese culture when I told him the story five years later.

The emigrants generally send money home, and often return themselves in their old age, so that emigration renders the country more cosmopolitan in outlook as well as richer.

Lebanon today is unique among Middle Eastern countries in having a Christian majority. However, when the French, after World War I, decided to split off Lebanon as an independent State from the rest of Syria, they thought to favour it by including the Bekaa and other mainly Moslem areas in its new boundaries. By an irony of fate, the Moslems are multiplying faster than the rest of the population, so that the predominantly Christian state that the French hoped to encourage is likely to turn into a predominantly Moslem one.

The country is a religious patchwork, comprising many sects which have survived only in the Middle East. The Maronites, the strongest Church in the Lebanon, remind us of the violent religious disputes of the fifth to seventh centuries. They originated as monothelites, believers in a single will in Christ. I am not competent to expound the subtleties of early theological controversy, but will only recall that monothelism was supported by the Emperor Heraclius as a compromise designed to heal the bitter schism between the monophysites, believers in a single nature for Christ, and the upholders of the orthodox doctrine of his two natures, laid down at the Council of Chalcedon. These metaphysical or metatheological differences seem trivial today, but at the time were associated with violent religious power-politics. Monophysite doctrine, for instance, was the focus for anti-imperial movements, especially in Egypt.

Monothelism was rejected as a heresy, and the persecuted Maronites eventually found refuge in the mountain recesses of the Lebanon. In the fifteenth century they became affiliated with the Church of Rome, but preserved their own Eastern ritual and liturgy. One of the most surprising of their peculiarities, mixed monasteries of monks and nuns, has only recently come to an end.

Then there are other Uniate sects, also loosely affiliated to Rome: some true Roman Catholics; and a number of Orthodox churches – Greek Orthodox, Syrian Orthodox, and Armenian Orthodox. The Moslems include a large block of Shias in the south as well as Sunnis scattered through the country; and there are strange religions like that of the Druzes in the Mountain above Sidon, and the Alawis in the hills north of Tripoli (though these latter fall almost entirely within the boundaries of Syria).

If it is a miracle that Switzerland has achieved national unity out of a diversity of distinct language groups, it is equally miraculous that the Lebanon has achieved national unity out of a diversity of religious groups. Admittedly the unity is not so well integrated; but then the number of distinct groups is greater and their diversity more striking. Lebanon's problem is aggravated by the small size of the country. Its total area is only some 4300 square miles, as against nearly 16,000 for Switzerland, and all its diverse religious and cultural groups add up to less than a million and a half people.

*

I find it impossible to arrange my remaining impressions of Lebanon in an orderly sequence, and must be content with a mosaic of snapshots.

The Hotel St Georges at Beirut stands on a little promontory jutting out into the sea. Its name and site remind us that St George early became mixed up with Perseus, who slew his marine dragon somewhere along the southern Phoenician coast.

Beirut was in Roman times the seat of the famous Academy of Law, for three centuries the most frequented school of higher education in the empire. Today it has two institutions of university rank, both of them established by foreign initiative – the American University and the French Jesuit Université St Joseph. Each of them in its own way has done great things for the country, both in promoting scholarship and humanistic research, and in the training of men for professional and administrative service.

One by-product of the Université St Joseph is the existence of a group of young writers and painters imbued with the French spirit. This educational set-up is in marked contrast with that of Syria. Politically cut off from the Lebanon, Syria decided to establish a National University at Damascus, which would be housed in a converted barracks. There was immense enthusiasm for this new national venture. Sometimes enthusiasm seemed to outrun competence: I was a little surprised when the Professor due to take charge of biology revealed his incomprehension of the genetics he said would be included in the curriculum. But the institution will assuredly develop into an important national organ.

Can the Lebanon dispense with a national university, and be content with foreign institutions of higher education, however admirable? I do not know. One possible solution might be to convert the handsome buildings erected for the Unesco Conference into a government College of some sort, and then affiliate this with the existing universities into a University of the Lebanon, somewhat after the pattern of the University of London – a loose federation bound together by a common title and a common degree. But whether such an illogical arrangement would ever commend itself outside Britain, I am not at all sure.

★

Beirut is a rambling city, without any specially striking features. It swarms with large cars, mostly of American make, and some of its citizens shake their heads and say, half-sadly, half-proudly, that it's just one big garage. But alongside a Cadillac you may see a barefooted man carrying two bunches of bananas on a pole over his shoulders. The port is now the largest on the coast, full of shipping, from liners and big cargo boats down to gaily-painted schooners and brigantines for the coastal trade.

There are some exceedingly rich families in Beirut and if some of them owed their fortunes to feudal exploitation or cornering grain during a famine in the past, nobody worries much about that sort of thing. On the other hand, corruption in the present led, in 1952, to the fall of the President.

We were invited to some beautiful houses. Madame S.'s, for instance, was built round a large main room with a fountain in the centre, and filled with priceless and magnificent carpets, some on the floor, some hung on the walls as decoration, some even used as curtains. Another room had been reconstructed in the style of 13th-century Damascus, with lovely panels of painted wood, carved cupboards for the cushions and bedding, and a dais for the masters. A modern little bar opened out of the main room; with its chromium and its cocktails it seemed at first sight anachronistic, until one remembered that Beirut society lives half in the international western world, half in the orient.

Madame S. is a striking and interesting woman. Her pearls were prodigious, as big as the proverbial pigeons' eggs, and getting on for the little local hens' eggs. Carpets are as much prized here as in Persia and most other countries of the region. At a lunch given by a wealthy citizen of Beirut, a lady of the Unesco party, confusing her host with someone else, enquired whether he was not interested in horses. 'Horses? Oh no,' he said. 'They give trouble and expense, and then they get old and die. What I like are carpets. Carpets are beautiful; they don't give any trouble; they cost nothing to keep; and' (with a nudge of his elbow in the lady's ribs) 'they appreciate ten per cent every year.' The Phoenician spirit is still alive.

I have one socio-ornithological recollection – a party in Beirut where small song-birds were among the delicacies provided. Piles of the pathetic little brown carcases were handed round, like plates of little sausages at a London cocktail party. You eat them whole, bones and all, and most of the guests crunched away at them with every sign of enjoyment. My wife tried one, and confessed it was delicious; I found I could not bring myself to take any. I suppose they were mostly what the Italians eat under the name of *beccafichi* – little warblers on migration, grown fat on autumnal fruit and insects; but they may have included small finches.

Our ancestors in the Middle Ages habitually ate small birds, as George Trevelyan records in his *English Social History*; and skylarks for the London market were trapped in hundreds on the Downs, well on into the 19th century. It is a good thing that a combination of law and sentiment has brought this slaughter to an end in Britain, and it would be a good thing if it could be checked in the Middle East. The Lebanese, situated on one of the great migration routes, run the risk of depleting the bird stock of other countries as well as their own.

★

The Unesco Conference occupied all my working energies for three weeks. I don't propose to say very much about it, with its endless meetings and working committees and behind-the-scenes lobbying. So long as the world is content to get its international work done by an organization of independent sovereign nations, so long will the cumbersome business of conferences of official national delegations continue. But useful work does get accomplished. At Beirut, to take a few examples, the foundations were laid for the universal copyright convention signed in 1952 by the delegates of 43 nations; Unesco's work in promoting fundamental education among the illiterate masses was put on a firm and agreed footing; and the idea of a world scientific and cultural history, to be sponsored by Unesco, was formally accepted.

I believe firmly in the value of holding alternate Unesco Conferences away from Paris. This does involve some extra expense; but it brings home to the people of the region the reality and value of Unesco, and is also highly educative for the delegates from other regions and for the secretariat from headquarters, in showing them something of the problems of world education, science and culture in actuality instead of merely on paper.

I do not think that any of us will forget the Mass, celebrated according to the Greek rite, in the Maronite Cathedral, which marked the opening of the Conference. The service began with a slow procession of bearded black-robed priests, wearing strange black headgear like stove-pipe hats with a brim at the top instead of the bottom. They were followed by other priests in stiff cloth-of-gold vestments, with long bands of black stuff hanging down from their small square hats. The chief among them (I suppose the bishop) wore what I noted as 'a sort of filigree turban', and a truly magnificent embroidered robe. Then there were singing priests in silver and white and blue, each carrying a set of three candles, twined round each other and secured with coloured braid, and little choirboys in pale blue and white, shepherded by a regular *Suisse* with beadle's staff, such as you may see in a French cathedral. As the consecrated bread and wine was ceremonially brought up, two priests vibrated a square of gold cloth over the bowed head of the bishop before the altar, with dramatic and indeed thrilling effect.

The strange and beautiful music combined with the visual drama of the rite to give an impression of ancient mystery, surprisingly surviving into the modern world. Enthroned to one side, the Renaissance figure of the shaven papal representative in his scarlet robes was in sharp contrast with the Byzantine feel of the Maronite service and the black-bearded Maronite priests, impassive like mosaics against the wall.

Nationalism has its cultural as well as its political aspects; and one of the troubles of an organization like Unesco is the constant pressure to increase the number of its official languages. The Beirut Conference was naturally the occasion for pressure in favour of Arabic. The miracle of simultaneous translation can obviate some of the dreary waiting when speeches have to be translated successively into two or three other languages, but the technical facilities cannot be installed in every committee room; and formidable extra work and expense is involved in circulating documents in three or four languages instead of two. If and when Chinese and Hindi and Russian and Malay are added, the burden of Babel will become overwhelming.

The interpreters and translators have a hard job, always working against time, and inevitably making occasional slips. Thus in one document concerning Mass Communications, 'the sound track' had been rendered in French as 'la bonne voie' – suggesting that the translator was unconsciously following his religious preoccupations. Mistranslations may even on occasion be helpful. I remember a rather sticky meeting in which 'the technical sub-committee' was translated 'la commission sous-technique', which raised a laugh that happily lubricated the further proceedings. Sometimes the trouble is in the ear of the hearer. In an Executive Board meeting, a Latin-American member, wishing to be idiomatic in his English, said of another and very distinguished member, 'Mr X is O.K.' This, literally translated into French, sounded like 'Monsieur X est toqué', which caused some surprise until an explanation was forthcoming.

But the difficulties must not make us forget the achievements. Thus it was a very positive achievement of the Lebanon to have built the Conference buildings. When I visited Beirut in the spring there was little on the site but some holes in the ground, and workmen busily laying foundations in them.

By November Beirut had been provided with a splendid central hall, flanked by committee rooms, two large ranges of offices, and a pleasant restaurant to one side. The processional steps from the main entry down to the central building were gay with the flags of all the member-states, with the United Nations flag between them.

In passing, I wish the U.N. could have chosen a better flag. The present world map in pallid blue and white had the sad and uninspiring look of something designed by intellectuals in a study. It has no emotive force as a visual symbol. I must confess, however, that this matter of visual symbols is a difficult one. After much discussion, we in Unesco adopted a letterhead in the form of a Greek temple with its pediment supported by the letters UNESCO, elongated to represent pillars. We had never reflected on the fact that when the word was translated into Arabic, the letters could no longer be made to serve as supports, but looked like a broken-down jumble of ruins. Here is a problem in applied semantics.

Some of my most pleasant memories of those three weeks are of a place for lunch which my secretary discovered. With a few friends, I could sometimes slip away, past the magnificent limestone rocks in the Bay of the Pigeons, to a sandy beach with a view of the coast range down towards Sidon. A quick bathe inside a rocky reef was followed by a meal in a ramshackle restaurant, of delicious fish straight out of the sea, with a sup of local red wine. Thus fortified, we could better face the long afternoon sessions, the planning of next day's work, and the inevitable official entertainments of the evening. You can't do that in an English November.

★

The traveller in Lebanon acquires a new sense of the Crusades – perhaps the most dramatic of the many encounters between east and west that has taken place on this coast. In the Musée des Monuments Historiques at Paris there is a splendid model of the famous Krak des Chevaliers, the largest and finest flower of Western medieval military architecture. T. E. Lawrence, in his big book on Crusader castles, calls it 'perhaps the best preserved and most wholly admirable castle in the world'. Time forced me to choose between a visit to the Krak and a visit to Palmyra; and I chose Palmyra. But through my field-glasses I saw its walls and towers in the Syrian foot-hills to the north of the Homs gap; and with the sight gained a fresh realization. Here was the feudal West spilling over into the occupancy of a large strip of the distant

Levant, partly animated by religious motives, partly by the need to check the westward advance of Islam, and partly by the desire of princes and nobles to carve out for themselves a better domain than they were likely to find at home.

The occupancy went on for two centuries. It was made possible by the size and number of the castles.* In our own brief stay we saw the Crusader ruins at Byblos and Sidon; the citadel dominating Tripoli; Tortosa, with a unique little French Gothic cathedral in addition to its castle still dipping its feet into the sea, but condemned to accommodate a ragged cluster of Moslem houses and huts; Baniyas on its spur; Kerak in Jordan (though only from a plane); and a glimpse of Sahyun up in the Alawit Mountains (we had no time to turn aside and see its amazing rock-hewn moat, 110 feet deep, with a central pillar of rock left to support the drawbridge); and Beaufort, in its impregnable position above the gorge of the Litani, now used as a military post. But there are dozens of others.

The Crusaders were quick to learn: they took over some of the features of Byzantine and Arab fortifications, while some of what they brought from Europe were adapted to eastern conditions: the result was the development of military architecture to a pitch beyond anything previously known in the West. (Château Gaillard, Richard Cœur-de-Lion's famous stronghold on the Seine, was the result of his experience in Syria and Palestine.)

Without the castles, the handful of Christian Counts and Kings could not have maintained their rule over a population of alien race and religion, or safeguarded themselves against hostile invasion from the East. However, most of the greater castles were not manned by the rulers but by the soldier-monks of those extraordinary organizations, the two military orders, the Hospitallers (The Order of St John of Jerusalem) and the Templars. The Crusades created the Hospitallers by converting them from their original task of looking after pilgrims in Palestine, the Templars with a fighting function *ab initio*. The mind's eye pursues the Orders in their fabulous rise to wealth and power in every country of Europe, in the later metamorphoses of the Hospitallers into Knights of Rhodes and then into Knights of Malta, and in the ghastly downfall of the Templars, as soon as their original occupation of fighting for the Holy Land had gone with the final expulsion of the Franks. The Templar trials in France, with their confessions and recantations, their tortures and burnings, are alarmingly prophetic of the staged trials of

* R. Fedden's recent *Crusader Castles* is an admirable brief study of the subject.

our own generation in Communist countries: the great historian-theologian Döllinger considered them a major disaster for Western Christendom. Napoleon drove the Hospitallers from Malta in 1798, and loaded their fantastic treasures into the great ship *L'Orient*, which Nelson sank later at the Battle of the Nile; and there at the bottom of Aboukir Bay the treasures remain.

In their heyday the Frankish kingdoms of the Levant seem to have been reasonably successful, with their rulers adopting various Eastern habits and according a wide tolerance and a fair measure of justice, administered through mixed courts, to their subjects. In fact a number of Moslems emigrated from Saracen territory to enjoy the greater security to be found under the Franks.

One is tempted to ask what would have happened if jealousies and quarrels in the Western ranks had not brought the experiment to an end. Would a new kind of nation, a fusion of Eastern and Western culture, have established itself along the coast of the Levant? I expect not: it would in all probability have been as impossible for Christian rulers to establish themselves permanently within the fringes of Islam as it was for Moslem rulers to establish themselves permanently in Spain, within the fringes of Christendom.

Richard Cœur-de-Lion, and Frederick II after him, tentatively explored another possibility – of making Jerusalem an international holy place. Our generation has had another opportunity of doing this: but the opportunity has so far been missed, and there is as much of an Iron Curtain between the two parts of Jerusalem, and between Israel and the Arab countries, as between Eastern and Western Europe. Indeed, if you want to visit Palestine *and* the Arab countries, you must have two passports!

*

Now for a snapshot of the Druze country. With typical Eastern hospitality, Kemal Jumblatt, the young Druze leader, had invited us and a large number of other Unesco people to a celebration at his Castle-home in Mukhtara. Up we climbed from the coast near Sidon, past the place where that extraordinary woman, Lady Hester Stanhope, settled when her task of looking after her uncle William Pitt came to an end with his death. We shall run across her tracks again in Palmyra: here I can only refer my readers to books like Miss Haslip's *Lady Hester Stanhope*, with the assurance that they will find much to entertain and astonish them.

Then up a steep gorge into more open terraced country, and so to Beit-ed-Din, of which more later. And from Beit-ed-Din over a bare shoulder 2500 feet above sea-level, to a steep-sided valley, with terraced side-branches in all directions, and little villages among poplars and plane-trees. Near the shoulder the strata were so level and so regular that the ledges looked as if artificially fortified. Across the valley lay Mukhtara, chief centre of the Lebanon Druzes.

The castle of Mukhtara stands on a projecting cliff. We were ushered into a gateway in the rock, from which a passage-stairway led to the great hall above. From this an external staircase led in turn to the main open courtyard, with a central fountain and a superb view. The arched passage and the hall were lined by Druzes armed with swords, who burst into song and hand-clapping as we passed between their ranks, while buglers welcomed us with ear-splitting blasts – the most impressive reception I have ever experienced.

Jumblatt I had met before – a tall, lean young man, the best type of practical intellectual, he had been for a while in the Government, but had become disillusioned and had resigned. Later, he became the leader of the Socialist party. I was interested to see that in August of 1952 he had presided over a much larger crowd at Mukhtara, met to demand the resignation of the President and the reform of Government corruption and mismanagement. When I read that he was associated with Hamid Franjie, the cultivated and sincere man whom I had got to know and respect as Minister for Education at the Conference four years earlier, I realized that here was a powerful reform movement. Within the next few months, there was a peaceful revolution, and the old Government and President both disappeared from the scene.

But in 1948 all this was remote: we were meeting a clan chief in retirement, together with his beautiful wife and his mother. His marriage had been a Montague-Capulet affair – the young people belonged to clan families in feud with each other. Madame Jumblatt senior was a most impressive figure. Handsome, intelligent, with piercing eyes, aquiline nose, and great force of character, she was like a Roman matron in the Lebanese landscape. We both fell under her spell, and were sadly grieved to hear of her death three years later.

The great courtyard was full of people. The Druzes are still organized on a clan system, rather like the Scottish Highlanders in the 18th century. Jumblatt had summoned his clans for the celebration and here they were assembled in force to do honour to Unesco and to enjoy a feast. The fleet of motor-buses that had brought them, some from right down on the coast, was parked outside the castle.

The younger men, strong mountaineers in jackboots, some with tarbooshes, others with white keffias on their heads, still others entirely in Western dress, began a monotonous but impressive dance. The groups from the various villages or sub-clans joined hands, and began to move slowly, stamping two steps in one direction, then one in the other – two, one, two, one, in a sideways-rotating half-circle. A small but particularly cheerful and sturdy fellow carried a huge flagpole.

Meanwhile we had been introduced to a group of Druze sages – learned initiates in turbans. One in particular I shall always remember (pl. 12, opp. p. 88). He wore a large bulbous all-white turban, in virtue of having reached the highest grade of wisdom; his face perfectly expressed the scholarly dignity and calm saintliness of the ideal Druze initiate, and with the most beautiful features to boot. He knew 'les sept livres de la sagesse' by heart.

We got to talking of philosophy. He asked me if we in England venerated Plato and Aristotle as they did here, especially Plato – only he called them Aflatoun and Aristo. Yes, I said, we know quite a lot about them, though I had to confess that, as a scientist, I preferred Aristo. 'Ah, you are wrong, Sir,' he said. 'Aflatoun knew everything that was to be known, and wrote no fewer than seventy-seven volumes about it: Aristo merely took his knowledge from Aflatoun.'

Our philosophical conversation was interrupted by my host, who informed me that the climax of a Druze welcome was for the visitor to be chaired on Druze shoulders round the courtyard. This was somewhat of an ordeal. It is not easy to preserve a dignified or indeed an approximately erect position with one's two feet on two separate shoulders, even with the aid of two swords whose hilts are thrust into one's hands by a couple of supporters. The stone pavement looked very hard from my swaying perch, and I was glad when my precarious progress through the cheering crowd was over. Kemal Jumblatt then had to submit to the same ordeal, and I experienced a slight satisfaction at finding that he wobbled even worse than I.

So ended a memorable visit.

★

The Druze community has a strange history. The Druze religion is a secret one, and our knowledge of it far from perfect.* As in other cases, secrecy has led to accusations of blasphemous and immoral practices; but these appear to be without foundation. But what we do know is strange and interesting. According to the Druzes, God has revealed himself to man in a series of incarnations – seventy is the number usually mentioned – of which the latest was the 11th-century Caliph Hakim. It is an irony of history that this tyrannical and megalomaniac creature, who claimed to hold direct communion with the Deity, and was almost certainly insane, should be regarded as the final revelation of God to man. It is another irony that the name *Druze* should be derived from one of Hakim's ministers, Darazi, who, after proclaiming the new faith based on Hakim's divinity, was later repudiated as a heretic.

The new faith seems to have incorporated a good deal of an earlier nature-worship. The religion is a messianic one: Hakim will in due course come again on earth and conquer the world for his religion.

Strangely enough, proselytization was early forbidden, and no new converts were admitted to the closed community. There seems to be nothing in the nature of public worship for the community. On the contrary, the Druze religion is an esoteric one, with an emphasis on grades of perfection. Initiation is reserved for those – probably not more than a seventh of the adult population – who are willing to submit to a special rule of life and assume the responsibilities of their fuller knowledge. They are called the Intelligent Ones, in contradistinction to the Ignorant Ones, who make up the bulk of the community. Among their privileges is the wearing of the special turbans I have mentioned. There is a further grade of initiation, confined to a handful of Sages such as the one we met.

In the 16th century, Druze rule (though not the Druze religion) extended over the whole Phoenician coast, and inland as far as Palmyra; but today the Druzes exist only in two groups, one in the Hauran Mountains (the Jebel Druze) south of Damascus, the other in the Lebanon massif. Toynbee calls them and their religion 'a fossil in a fastness'. However, the metaphor is misleading. They are very much alive inside their shell of tradition, and might at any moment crack it to embark on new evolutionary adventures.

It would be interesting to make a study of the forces that have enabled the Druzes to persist as a distinctive people – what they owe to their secret

* G. de Gaury gives some account of it in his *Rulers of Mecca*, and Toynbee's *Study of History* has an illuminating passage on the subject.

religion, what to their feudal organization; how much they have been consolidated by persecution, how many of their virtues are due to their mountain environment. All I can do is to testify to their vigour and attractiveness,
and to the honour paid by them to learning. They are clearly an important
element in the Lebanon, and much will depend on the extent to which they
and their traditions can be integrated into its modern life.

★

Beit-ed-Din was for a time the capital of the Little Lebanon when it was a
province of the Turkish Empire. It lies in a magnificent valley with the main
backbone of the Mountain at its head. On the way to it we stopped at the
small palace erected in the 7th century by the Emir Fakr-ed-Din, the same
who built the French merchant hostel at Sidon. It had some lovely painted
ceilings and cupboards, and a handsome gateway with two rather comic lions
carved in the yellow stone.

17th

Beit-ed-Din was just across the deep valley, but to reach it we had to make
a loop of some eight miles. It is one of the show places of the Lebanon, built
by the powerful Emir Bechir in the early 19th century. It is the last example
of the palatial Damascus style, but a little decadent and heavy.

But there are some lovely things about it. The gardens are very fine, with
magnificent cypresses and planes, and a tree I had never seen before, bearing a
fruit rather like a spindle-berry, but with an even more vivid colour-contrast,
of scarlet and vivid green, instead of the spindle-berry's cerise and orange.

I liked the Emir's private room, with its pretty painted flower-panels and
its low window overlooking the courtyard, where he installed himself of a
morning to smoke and think in peace. And I particularly liked the hammam
or Turkish bath. Our first sight of it was from above – a series of white domes
of various sizes and forms, from circular to elliptical and stumpy sausage-
shaped, stuck over with protruding bottle-ends, looking like almonds stuck
in a trifle (pl. 13, opposite): these serve to keep out the glare and to admit
only a grateful and soothing illumination.

The rooms below are charmingly designed and decorated (very different
from a London Turkish bath!). The cold plunge was screened by a delightful
asymmetrical pair of pointed arches, and the big cool room was as pleasant a
club as one could hope to find.

I liked also the story of the Emir's second wife, which was told to us by
Emir Chehab, a descendant of the first wife, and now in charge of the

12. *The saintly and scholarly sage, expert in the Seven Books of Druze wisdom*

13. *The roof of the Turkish bath at Beit-ed-Din; the bottle-ends serve to admit a grateful and soothing illumination*

14. *Dancing dervishes at Tripoli, their skirts flaring out into great white cones*

15. *The Sheikh of the Dervishery at Tripoli, with his assistant to the left, and to the right the policeman with a weak heart whose deepest desire was to die while dancing*

Antiquities Service of the country. The Emir wanted to raise a beautiful Circassian slave to the status of lawful wife; but she did not like the responsibility which official marriage would involve. So the Emir took her to the great kitchen (a flat-vaulted room with central pillar, where they regularly cooked for 150 people) and said 'You smell this smell of onions? Either you marry me, or you shall smell it always, for you will have to work here all the rest of your life.' She married him.

*

One last snapshot – Tripoli and the Dancing Dervishes. A friendly Moslem lawyer we met in Beirut offered to arrange for us to see the dervishes dance. This was an offer not to be refused, and after the Conference we duly set out for Tripoli. Under his guidance, we saw the Crusader castle on its rocky acropolis; and the modern harbour; and the river running through the very middle of the old city, a narrow strip of water between two rows of old Moslem houses; and the souks; and the little white mosques tucked away in side-streets; and the public hammam. This last was not so beautiful as the Emir Bechir's bath at Beit-ed-Din, but much older, and had provided generations of citizens with cleanliness and relaxation. In it were two gigantic half-naked men drying the wet floor by rolling a heavy cylinder of white felt before them with their bare feet: their rhythmical stamping gave the impression of a technique as ancient as the baths themselves.

Then to the dervishery. There are very few dancing dervisheries left in the region. The one at Tripoli stands among olive groves just outside the city, on the banks of the Kadesha river. The Sheikh of the community, a dignified little man with a greying beard, led us through the various domed dwellings to the separate building set aside for the ceremonial dancings, or turnings as they might better be called. This was a square hall, open on the valley side, with balconies round the other three, supported on wide white arches. We took our places to the left of the sheikh, with the musicians on his right. The rest of the seats were soon filled up with privileged spectators. After a time the dozen or so dervishes walked in slowly with folded hands, and sat down cross-legged on carpets. They were wearing tall khaki fezzes protruding from small turbans, and brown abbas – sleeved robes like heavy dressing-gowns, but without a belt, and made of camel's hair. The musicians began chanting chants full of semi-tones, and prayers were intoned. The dancers rose and began to walk slowly round and round in a heavy ritualized step, with a solemn pause at each forward pace, and a turn and a bow each time they passed one corner of the hall. A flute and drums struck up, and after some twenty minutes the dervishes took off their abbas, disclosing full white skirts with weighted hems, reaching from waist to feet. Then, each in his appointed spot, they began their turning.

Turning consists essentially in pivoting on the left foot, with two or three steps of the right foot to each full turn. As the speed of turning increases, the white skirt flares out into a great rotating cone. One handsome young dervish elaborated the movement by making a graceful dip during each turn, and by varying the position of head and arms. His most beautiful pose was one with arms and hands fully extended in line, one diagonally upwards, the other downward, with head inclined against the upward arm, and a serene, absorbed, prayer-like expression on his face. Then there was a stoutish middle-aged little turner, who spun round with head thrown back. He lacked the effortless grace of the young man, but achieved the same look of rapt serenity. He was a policeman by profession.

The turning went on for an hour or more, its monotony remaining strangely beautiful and fascinating instead of becoming boring. Most of the dancers stopped at intervals for a short rest, but the policeman and the graceful young dervish never broke their turning. The Sheikh later told us that the policeman had a weak heart, and that his deepest desire was that he might die while dancing.

At the private ceremonies of the community, turning may go on for many hours, until the dancers fall immobile on the floor in a state of exalted and complete exhaustion. The Sheikh covers them with their abbas, and there they lie until they recover.

I had got it into my head that the dances we were to see would be orgies of violent and frenzied motion, but I had been confusing the dancing dervishes with a quite different confraternity, the howling dervishes. The turning ritual seems designed to give a sense of liberation and ecstasy, but a serene and orderly one. It was clear that the turners could, through their controlled and long-continued rotation, spin themselves into a state in which the world of everyday was transcended. We are apt to look down on such simple physical methods of achieving a sense of ecstasy or transcendence as barbarous or childish. I can only say that, to the casual visitor like myself, it looked like a satisfying form of ritual and, for some of the participants at least, seemed to provide a quality of real fulfilment.

Dancing dervisheries are one among the many kinds of religious or semi-religious communities and associations that grew up as Islam developed. They were designed to satisfy men's needs for associating with his fellows out of business hours, and participating in activities other than those concerned with making a living. Professor Carleton Coon gives an interesting account of their role in his book *Caravan*. Some of them developed into institutions not unlike monasteries, while others more nearly resembled our clubs or societies. They constituted an important part of the framework of social life in Moslem countries, but are tending to disappear under the influence of westernization. What will emerge to take their place is difficult to prophesy.

6

TURKEY: PAST AND PRESENT

Constantinople – I should of course write the official name, Istanbul. But I remember being told as a boy at school that Istanbul was merely a corruption of εἰς τὴν πόλιν – 'into town', a phrase coined when there was no other city than Constantinople which could have been simply called 'the Town'. Istanbul is the same city as Constantinople; but has never attained such greatness as under its earlier name.

The first – and the last – impression of Istanbul is the wonder of the site – the steep slopes covered with houses, dominated by striking buildings; the waterways in various directions, all busy with shipping, north to the Black Sea, south to the Sea of Marmara and the Mediterranean, and the Golden Horn curving round to its blind end up a side valley: above this last, the col over which in 1453 the Turks dragged their galleys (a portentous feat!) so as to get them inside the great chain the Byzantines had stretched across the straits.

At first the geography of the place is confusing; but the map brings realization. Constantinople proper, the original city, is built on a tongue or rather snout of land, for the area within the great walls bears a strong resemblance to the profile of a dog's head with small prick-ears. This snout sticks out eastward, looking across towards Scutari on the Asiatic side. The Bosporus stretches away a little east of north, and to the south-east lie the fashionable Prince's Islands. Above the imaginary dog's head lies the Golden Horn, debouching at right angles into the Bosporus, and across the Golden Horn are Galata and Pera, originally suburbs outside the walls, but for long the chief residential parts of the modern city.

Byzantium originally occupied only the very tip of the dog's snout, the high ground where the Grand Seraglio of the Turkish Sultans still stands. From there, high above the water, you have an amazing prospect, not only a geographical prospect to the four points of the compass, but an historical prospect to innumerable quarters of the human past – Constantine and the establishment of Christianity; Florence Nightingale in the muddle and misery of the British Army hospital at Scutari; the wicked diversion of the Fourth Crusade against Constantinople; Xenophon arriving with the remnants of the Ten Thousand; Jason and the Argonauts on their adventurous passage; Sultan Abdul Hamid cowering in his new palace in Pera; the serpent column brought from far-off Delphi to preside over the chariot races; the conquest of the city by the Turks, with all its repercussions on the West; the creation of that miracle of architectural achievement, Santa Sophia. . . .

The steep slope below our hotel was laid out in narrow streets of rough cobbles with muddy earth sidewalks, flanked by little wooden houses, each storey projecting a little further over the street than the one below. Vines were sometimes trained right across the narrower streets, which must be very agreeable in summer. At the bottom was a small harbour, with a few ships and plenty of rowboats, charmingly painted. Men, sometimes barefoot, were carrying baulks on their backs down the gangplanks and stacking them in huge piles on the quayside. None of the women was veiled.

The unveiling of women was one of Atatürk's great achievements. Another, of course, was the forcible imposition of the cloth cap in place of the fez for men. This has meant the general (though not yet universal) abandonment of traditional costume, especially in the towns, with the loss of a great deal of colour, picturesqueness, and indeed beauty. These results of his policy have been much deplored. However, one is driven to admit that something of the sort was necessary if Atatürk was to succeed in his great ambition. That ambition was to raise the country rapidly out of its low political, economic, and intellectual level, a level due to a mixture of backwardness and degeneration, fatalism and sloth, and to transform it from a non-industrial 'Oriental' to an industrial 'Western' nation. Such transformations require their visible symbols, and it is hard to see what other symbol than the western worker's cap could have been so effective.

The effectiveness of the transformation was very evident in the academic and educational field. A gathering of University professors in Turkey today is very much like a gathering of University professors in Central or Eastern Europe, or at least what such a gathering used to be like before the War. You converse in German or English, you discuss research or curricula, you indulge in philosophic small-talk or academic gossip.

Now and again, however, some phrase will remind the foreigner of the background difference. For instance, one day a cultivated Turkish civil servant, speaking English fluently, and as 'European' as Atatürk could have wished, apologized for not being able to show me round the city next day – 'My niece is getting married, and though I don't normally go to mosque, I think I ought to on this occasion.' 'Go to mosque' – it brought up with a shock the fact of Turkey's completely different religious background.

And as one explores the city, new aspects of basic difference show themselves. The Great Bazaar, for instance, is wholly un-European. It is an oriental habit to do your shopping in this sort of rabbit-warren of covered passageways, with little shops built into their sides, and cups of coffee much in evidence. The whole set-up is different from that of a big Western market, or from that of a European shopping street. It is all very picturesque, except for the objects; for, alas, a great many of the goods exposed for sale are all too western – mass-produced stuff, trinkets and gadgets, a combination of Woolworth's and the Marché aux Puces, though with a certain oriental accent.

The law says that nothing may be sold *in* the streets. Actually, a great deal of street selling goes on: the Great Bazaar is virtually continued in all the nearby busy little streets. But the goods are all on little folding tables, or on pieces of cloth on the ground, so that they may be easily whisked indoors at the sight or suspicion of a policeman. Close by is the Egyptian Market, once a Spice Market, now merely another bazaar, but distinguished by its really fine architecture, high and spacious.

Turkish is now spelt phonetically, in western characters. The phonetic transcription of foreign words and names provides an amusing exercise for the western visitor. Our party entertained itself on its trips through the city by seeing who could spot the highest number of these transcriptions. Of course one has to know the rules of the game, such as the fact that *s* stands for *sh*, and *ç* for *ch*. *Futbol* is easy enough. *Otobus* is of course Autobus, *Perukar* was revealed as standing for *Perruquier* by being blazoned on hairdressing establishments; and a picture of a vast American car gave the clue to *Lükso-*

tomobil Sevrole – a luxury model Chevrolet. A photograph of a well-known face and cigar in a bookseller's window made it easy to identify *Çerçil*; and, once the unwary Englishman has realized that the transliteration may be from French or German as well as English, it was not too difficult to translate *Vatman* into that mysterious being *le Wattman*, to whom one is forbidden to speak in French trams, and *Vagonli Kook* into *Wagonlits Cook*.

But even so it took a certain degree of cerebration to cope with *Abajur*, *Trençkot, Peyzaj, Fuar,* and *Liberonion*. The last, on the menu of a restaurant where we lunched, was liver and onions; *peyzaj* is a landscape; *Trençkot is,* of course, Trench-coat; and *Abajur* I was quite proud of deciphering as *abat-jour*.

But I find in my diary one phrase which has relapsed into untranslatability – *Dram Tiyatzone*. And I don't think we should have ever picked out *Klotfarel* and *Piyerloti* as transliterations among the hundreds of street-names, unless we had been told that they commemorated two French writers, Claude Farrel and Pierre Loti.

Pigeons are everywhere in Istanbul. They abound on the railway terminus at Scutari and especially round the mosques, where they are fed by the devout as an act of merit.

Santa Sophia both is and deserves to be the most famous building in the city. It is not particularly outstanding in external view; but its interior is superbly beautiful and satisfying. Nor is it so very large – only 250 by 235 feet, as against such vastnesses as the 555-foot length of Winchester, and with the main dome only 107 feet in diameter, as against the 140 feet of St Peter's; but no other building has given me the same sense of space. The space is not cluttered up with objects or constructions that interfere with the sweep of eye or mind; nor is there any of that exaggerated monumentality of orna-mentation, which in St Peter's with its false scale reduces the effective grandeur of the whole. Justinian's architects were men of genius who achieved that supreme task of great architecture, the enclosure of space in a harmonious pattern, in such a way that the enclosed space, far from appear-ing imprisoned, reveals its inherent qualities of spaciousness, and seems almost to live, through the organic way in which its separate volumes are related into a whole.

The dome, supported on four noble piers in the centre of the nave, is a masterpiece. The mind of the beholder, in that act of love and unison which great art compels, ascends into its sublimity, not drawn painfully up and ever up as by the tension of even the greatest Gothic, but floating, aerial yet secure, within its bounding curve. It achieves this effect by virtue of its construction, on which, as I am no architect, I quote from the *Encyclopaedia Britannica*, 'From the cornice of the dome stretches eastwards and westwards a semi-dome, which in its turn rests upon three small semi-domes. The nave is thus covered completely by a domical canopy, which, in its ascent, swells larger and larger, mounts higher and higher, as though a miniature heaven rose overhead.'

The great galleries constitute a separate storey all round the building; their recesses, seen through a range of supporting columns, and only half explorable by the eye from below, add a sense of intricacy to the construction without detracting from its central spaciousness. The galleries were reserved for women: here the Empress Theodora sat when she attended service in her husband's masterpiece.

Though there is no great expanse of glass as in the later Gothic cathedrals, there is an adequate and lovely illumination: you feel that it is just what the architects wanted for their great church.

The walls are lined with a varied revetment of marble, and there are no less than a hundred splendid columns in the interior, many of them with very beautiful capitals. The four pairs of porphyry columns in the bays at the four corners of the nave are the most magnificent; they came from that most grandiose of temples, the Temple of the Sun at Baalbek, after having first been taken to Rome by Aurelian as booty from one of his Syrian campaigns.

It is curious to reflect that Santa Sophia would never have been built but for a riot. In the Nika rising, which almost caused Justinian to seek safety in flight, the mob burnt the existing cathedral to the ground. A new church had to be built: and it is to the everlasting credit of Justinian that he encouraged his architects in their revolutionary designs.

The interior of Santa Sophia was covered with mosaics, ranging in date from Justinian's time to the 14th century. When the Turks converted the church into a mosque, the mosaics were covered with hangings so as not to offend the eyes of the faithful; and in the 19th century they were plastered over. In the inter-war period, Mr Whittemore of Boston obtained permission to begin uncovering and cleaning them. He was a Henry James sort of American, with a superbly one-track mind interested only in Byzantine antiquity. He showed us round with an unforgettable combination of learning and enthusiasm in spite of his seventy-eight years, so that the news of his death in 1950 came as a personal shock.

Some of the mosaics are extremely fine, though none comes up to the best of those in Ravenna. Their untarnished brilliance brings back the past in a more direct way than any other form of art. There is one very strange representation of Christ – 'The Christ with the Angry Eyes'. And there is a good deal of history embodied in them: for instance, the portrait of the first husband of one Empress has been furnished with the head and name of her second.

For nearly five centuries Santa Sophia had been used as a mosque, symbolizing the triumph of the Crescent over the Cross, when in 1935 Atatürk took the bold step of converting it into a museum. This was one of his most spectacular gestures of breaking with the past and launching Turkey into the modern world; and it has been abundantly justified.

Santa Sophia is remarkable in another way: as a building erected for the purposes of one religion which served as prototype for the sacred edifices of another faith. A great many mosques in Turkey and Egypt are modelled on Justinian's church. The addition of slender minarets marks them as Islamic, and this, together with their more prominent domes, often adds appreciably to their external appearance. Internally, however, none of them rivals its prototype in beauty.

The 16th-century mosque of Sultan Ahmed is nevertheless very fine, and its stained glass is in some ways better than glass of the same period in Europe. Here an imam was intoning the Koran to some thirty women in a strange and rather beautiful chant, sounding rather like an oriental version of Gregorian plain-song, but with many grace-notes. He kept on taking pieces of paper from one pile and putting them on another: these were the texts he was chanting. On ceremonial occasions, I was told, the Koran is recited in Arabic, although it is understood by no one in the congregation, and sometimes not even by the imam himself – a good example of the fossilization of ritual so often found in long-established religions.

Among the strangest places in Istanbul are the huge underground water-cisterns, built in the early days of Byzantine power as a reserve of water against a prolonged siege. The one we saw was an enormous place, the roof supported by over 400 columns. Rising out of the dark water illuminated by electric light, the dark pillars, with their beautiful capitals and arches, were an impressive and awe-inspiring spectacle.

The Unesco Executive Board met in the Yildiz palace, in a room where unpopular viziers were once given poisoned coffee. It was an unattractive 19th-century building, externally in a magnified Swiss Chalet style, and with overabundant interior decoration. Architecturally, the famous Serail is also disappointing. It resembles a collection of over-large and over-decorated summer-houses thrown down higgledy-piggledy in a spacious enclosure.

It is now a museum. The old kitchen, with its rows of cones topped by chimneys, was capable of cooking for 7000 people, or 10,000 on very special occasions. It now houses a huge museum of porcelain, including the most astonishing collection of green celadon ware, as well as many horrors of later centuries. The gift of the Emperor of Japan to Abdul Hamid was a miniature palace of gold filigree, complete with gold trees and people – an emblem of conspicuous waste.

Another fascinating exhibit was the equipage provided for the Sultan's pilgrimage to Mecca – a superbly caparisoned camel, a large tent whose interior was all embroidery of the richest kind, and a vast and gorgeous cloth windbreak in whose shelter the royal tent could be pitched.

Then there was the room where the Council of Viziers met, with a barred window in one wall, through which the Sultan could listen unobserved. And the untidy harem, with half a dozen styles round its court. And the main gate, with a sort of grilled cage into which a vizier would be put when deposed by a palace revolution of the janissaries. There he would wait until the janissaries cut his head off; and then, as our guide said, 'the revolution would be over'.

The janissary corps was part of an extraordinary system whereby the Ottoman empire was run by slaves – infidels from outside, conscripted children from within – while the Ottoman aristocracy was shut out. This topsy-turvy arrangement was surprisingly efficient, owing to the elaborate education given to promising boys, the rigid discipline, and the glittering prizes open to the ambitious.

The eunuchs' quarter had a mosque in it, and all the windows were heavily barred. Our guide pointed to an inscription which he said had been put up by his great-grandfather when an inmate of the place – though how this was compatible with his being a great-grandfather was a delicate question we did not venture to ask.

Occasionally castration was not effectively carried out, and the men had the opportunity of illicit enjoyment on the grand scale. One such favoured person was also a favourite of the Sultan. When he was given away by a jealous colleague, the Sultan instead of having him executed merely ordered him re-operated: but the operation proved fatal.

Across the water was the pretentious palace in which the last Sultan, Abdul Hamid, secluded himself miserably for years in morbid fear of assassination.

Not far from the Serail is the so-called Baghdad Kiosk, built in the 17th century by the violent Sultan Murad IV, who died at the age of 29, it is said from excessive drinking – a vice in which he certainly indulged in spite of his strictness against the same offence in others. He is said to have had over 100,000 people executed in a space of little over ten years. In addition, so our guide assured us, he liked some more personal outlet for his sadistic impulses, and used to indulge in archery practice on the passers-by from the corner window of the Kiosk. Though he rationed himself to a maximum of four victims a day, the habit must have discouraged traffic along this important thoroughfare.

Also close to the Serail is the Hippodrome, where chariot-racing became the focal point of popular passion, and political faction expressed itself in the rivalries of sport. For the 'axis of the Byzantine world', as it has been described, it was smaller than I had imagined; but one could visualize the excited factions, sporting their rival colours and cheering their favourites, or the crowds assembled to shout insults at an unpopular emperor. One curious monument struck my eye – a pillar composed of upward twining serpents, the spiral loosening towards the top. It was symptomatic of the nationalist spirit of modern Turkey that our guide concentrated on Ottoman monuments, and passed over this object in silence. It was only when I later visited Greece that I discovered what it was – the famous Serpent Column from Delphi, erected in 479 B.C. to commemorate the great victory over the Persians at Plataea.

The triple walls of the city still stand for much of their extent – a formidable fortification which kept barbarian assaults at bay for over a thousand years. It is impossible not to be moved by the sight of the great breach made in 1453 with the aid of Hungarian artillery, through which the Turks stormed into the city, killing the last emperor on the way.*

The famous Golden Gate still stands, the gate through which the Emperors returned after a victory. It is very handsome, with two great cubical

* See the excellent article, 'Constantinople, 1453', by Dr Malcolm Burr in the *Geographical Magazine* for May 1953.

blocks, faced with marble, projecting on either side, and a propylaeum in front.

In a big tower on the wall near by is the old execution-room, kept in its pristine state as a museum. Overlooking its centre are two wooden tiers supported by a meshwork of beams, to which the prisoners were chained (those of them who were not shut up in stone dungeons below), and could see all the incidents going on in the central space. These incidents included men being decapitated, and their heads being thrown down a narrow stone tube to the water below; and prisoners strapped to a post for the executioners to practise on, with scimitars, or pistols, or axes – the post is pitted and pocked with blows and bullet-marks. It is one of the most grisly museums in the world – a place of real horror.

Another memorial of that time is the fortress of Rumli Hissar, a few miles up the Bosporus, quite different from any western castle, with its vast round towers and its oriental plan of construction. This was built by Mahomet II when he had finally closed in on the city. Together with the smaller castle on the Asiatic shore built by his grandfather, it dominated the Bosporus and blocked all passage to or from the north. It must have been appalling for the Christians cooped up in Constantinople to have to wait helplessly while their encirclement was being completed.

The Bosporus is a strange geographical phenomenon. It is essentially a short river serving as outflow from the gigantic brackish lake we call the Black Sea. Its surface current flows out at an average of 3 miles an hour. But it is also, though to a lesser degree, a 'reverse river', for in its depths there is a counter-flow of more saline water into the Black Sea.

The Black Sea basin was produced in geologically recent times by the dropping of a large area of the crust inside a series of fault-cracks. Parts of it have dropped over a vertical mile since the Pliocene; and some of its edges must have been submerged since the early neolithic. It is unique in its lifeless depths: below 100 fathoms no higher organisms exist and the water is charged with sulphuretted hydrogen. This may very likely be due to the deep 'reverse river' when connection was first established between the two seas, probably in late Tertiary times: the saltier and therefore heavier Mediterranean water inevitably flowed down to the depths of the brackish Black Sea, there to kill the fauna which was adapted to less saline conditions. And the sulphuretted hydrogen is presumably the result of this mass destruction of life.

The guidebooks expatiate on the beauties of the Bosporus. It certainly is very lovely, and remarkably unspoilt, in spite of the villas along its banks. Some of them are abominably pretentious, some merely funny, in their attempts to adapt the 17th-century Turkish style of wooden construction with corbelling and roomy balconies, to 19th-century ideas of suburban luxury: but they somehow blend into the general landscape of dense woods and grassy slopes. The old wooden fishing villages, like all the older wooden buildings in the city itself, seem to have been burned down. But there are still plenty of fishermen: the Bosporus at night is alive with boats fishing (largely for swordfish) with powerful acetylene lights. The north end of the Bosporus is a military zone – mined and with a boom across it: even looking through field-glasses is prohibited.

All along the Bosporus, every day for most of the year, files of dark gull-like creatures are constantly winging their way low over the water in both directions. They turned out to be shearwaters, of the same species (though not the same subspecies) as our Manx Shearwater, with which I had become familiar on the islands off the Pembrokeshire coast.

There, the great experiences are two, one of sight, the other of sound. The visual experience is to see the huge evening raft of birds, running into many thousands, between Skomer and Skokholm. It is the silent gathering of the shearwaters, after they return from their oceanic feeding journeys (which often last for several days), and before they rejoin their mates in the nesting burrows with the approach of dark. Only after this does the auditory experience begin, to last all through the night. The shearwater's call is one of the most peculiar sounds in nature: it is like an unholy cross between a cock crowing and a witch laughing. And this truly fantastic sound not only fills the air, but the upper layers of the ground as well, for the birds give it as part of their greeting and love-making in the breeding burrows, so that you can lean your ear to within a dozen inches of it.

But I had never seen shearwaters behaving as they did here in Istanbul, and the constant passage of these small parties on their purposeful journeys remains a puzzle. The local naturalists knew very little about the breeding habits of the birds. They thought that the shearwaters might well nest on a group of islands in the Black Sea: but there was little prospect of finding this out, since the islands are in a military area. A military area means something serious in Turkey: a man I met was very nearly shot because he was geologizing in one.

On the banks of the Bosporus lies the American foundation, Robert College. Such foreign-sponsored institutions as this in Turkey, Aleppo College in Syria, or the American University in Beirut, have been important agencies in promoting the transition from an ancient to a modern way of life in the Middle East.

My final view of Constantinople was an unusual one. After a heavy fall of snow, the waters of the Golden Horn and the Bosporus were steaming, and the domes and minarets and roofs of the great city were outlined in white against a sky of dark grey-blue.

The visitor may find it sad that Istanbul is no longer the capital of a great empire, or even of a single nation. But it is perhaps better that it should remain as living witness to an incomparably eventful past, while yielding its functions as headquarters of a modern state to the more centrally placed Ankara.

★

In Turkey I had two encounters with familiar birds. On arriving in Constantinople in April, we passed through thousands of white wagtails, presumably on their northward migration – even more abundant, though less orderly, than the great procession of 'water wagtails' in Edward Lear's story of the Four Children who went round the world. They are members of the main race of Linnaeus's *Motacilla alba*, of which our pied wagtail is a darker insular subspecies. On the overnight train journey to Ankara, I awoke in the sleeping car to hear a succession of corn buntings give their absurd but distinctive song, like a fisherman's reel running out: and at this sound, the undulating steppe of the Turkish plateau immediately became linked in my mind with the Downs behind Brighton, where I first learnt the corn bunting's song nearly fifty years ago.

The country near Ankara is rolling and open, with large orchards here and there in the valley. The Scottish geologist at the University confirmed my supposition that this north-central area of the plateau is true grass-steppe, never forested during historic times, a region where grass and not woodland is the natural ecological climax. Alas, I saw none of the typical steppe fauna, such as the squirrel-like burrowing susliks (*gophers* in America) which swarm in some areas, or the jerboas, or the cranes and bustards.

While on the subject of natural vegetation, I must recall the interesting fact told me by Dr Malcolm Burr of Istanbul, that a species of *Liquidambar*, the sweet-gum of America, grows wild in a small area of south-western Turkey. *Liquidambar* is here a relict. It was one of the common components of the great warm-temperate forest which encircled the northern hemisphere in mid-Tertiary times. Over most of Eurasia, such of the sweet-gums and other warmth-loving trees that survived the mountain-building uplift of the Miocene were crushed out of existence during the glacial period, between the ice-sheets extending from the north and the glaciers advancing from the east-and-west mountain ranges further south. But in North America, where the mountain-axes run north and south, and in China, the forest could simply move southward with the cold and northward again with the return of warmth.

So far as I know, south-west Turkey is the only place in the Old World west of China where a good sample of the Miocene forest survives – not only *Liquidambar*, but wild grapes and other plant genera. Why this small area has been spared is an interesting field for research. But meanwhile the *Liquidambar* and the rest of the relict vegetation is in danger from felling and clearing: there is a strong case for establishing a nature reserve to save this unique ecological community, just as the Nature Conservancy is now establishing reserves for the various kinds of ecological community in Britain.

★

Ankara is really three cities in one. There is the old town with its castle, towering over the rest rather like the old town and its castle in Edinburgh; below it lies what we may call the middle-aged town, from Augustus to Atatürk; and finally there is the new town stretching out into the flatter country, begun when Ankara became the capital, and still a-building.

The old town is a fortified acropolis, surrounded by a splendid wall, with towers at short intervals (pl. 16, opp. p. 108). Before the First World War, houses had crept up the steep slope below, so as almost to hide the walls. Luckily, a conflagration destroyed them, and the slope has been left free.

There has been a great housing shortage in the rapidly growing city. The hill to the west of the acropolis is now covered with thousands of shacks, many of them constructed overnight by squatters who cannot legally be evicted. It is a deplorable sight, calling for drastic action. But town-planning has been so busy with the official new town that this unplanned excrescence has by now firmly established itself on the city's back doorstep.

A really good piece of planning has been realized in the Ankara Dam, which secures the capital its water (pl. 18, opp. p. 109). The strong curve of the dam stands out boldly in the deep gorge. Above, the man-made lake extends in two arms, far into the rolling mountains, with soil-conserving plantations of planes and pines reflected in its water, and prickly bushes of pink-flowering wild almond on the barren slopes. Below, by the power-house, is a restaurant and casino, built in an attractive modern style, where the inhabitants of Ankara can repair in summer.

The old town has a single gate piercing the medieval walls; these are made of every conceivable material – sometimes cyclopean masonry at the base, and then rubble; here a group of statues laid sideways, there a row of mill-stones, with occasional drums of columns or bits of Roman decoration among the stonework.

In the open space before the gate was a busy market – huge lemons, nuts, melon-seeds, various kinds of peas; water-sellers with brass ewers and cups; women selling cream cheese or yoghourt; stalls with scrap-metal and stalls with bright scarlet powder (was it henna?). Some of the women were finely dressed: their yellow and orange-red stuffs were particularly handsome. Here was a group in head-kerchiefs and coloured trousers; there an old lady in very bright but rather ragged kerchief, shawl and skirt.

The little boys and girls were just coming out of school. They wore black blouses with wide soft collars, which gave their olive black-eyed faces a great charm. Most of them looked very healthy; the adults generally have a powerful physique, based on strength of bony framework rather than bulk of flesh. Some of the old men gossiping in the market were grand-looking, with hawk noses and white beards.

Inside the walls, the houses are crowded pell-mell. One morning I deter-mined to find my way into the castle itself: but I never got there – every new turn I took led into a cul-de-sac smaller and dirtier than the last, until I felt like the hero of a Kafka novel. The poverty of the smaller houses and the general slummy effect were lamentable. But the site is a glorious one; it would be a great enterprise to convert the best houses to use for civilized living, while pulling down the rest. Some of the houses are half-timbered: curiously enough, the half-timbering is very like what one sees in Nor-mandy.

The 'middle-aged town' below the acropolis, besides containing interest-ing 17th-century houses with projecting upper storeys, has some good Roman remains. The entrance portal of the Temple of Augustus is truly magnificent, very high, with carved jambs and lintel. Near by stands the tall Jovian Column, which is now crowned with a storks' nest instead of a statue of Jupiter. I wondered whether it would not be a good bargain if we could replace one of our high-placed London statues with a flourishing storks' nest – the Stork's Column instead of the Duke of York's Column, perhaps. But I fear that there would be difficulties both with the storks and with the Office of Works.

A friend of mine who spent some time in Ankara as a prisoner of war during World War I tells me that this Jovian storks' nest was then enormous, several yards in height, as the result of successive annual additions. The earlier additions had all been made on one side, so that the nest had become a Leaning Tower, in considerable danger of falling: whereupon the birds had begun to build inwards again, until the top was once more centred over the foundations. I wish I could have seen the great flight-procession of migrating storks on their way from Africa to their nesting-grounds, but I was too late in the season for that.

On one main street, a professional letter-writer was taking down a letter from a client at a little table on the sidewalk. There is nothing very remarkable about this, you will say: but the letter-writer was in European clothes, and was using a typewriter: nothing could have better typified the rapid transition in which Turkey now finds herself.

In the new town is the Park of Youth, with a lake; and beyond it a handsome modern theatre and concert hall. Here I heard a concert of English and Turkish music, played by the local orchestra with Arthur Bliss as conductor. This joint venture, organized by the British Council, seemed an admirable method of promoting good cultural relations between two countries, and of demonstrating that each side has something to give and something to receive. On the other hand, the reliefs on the base of Atatürk's statue, commemorating the Turkish victory over the Greeks in 1922, are not calculated to promote international understanding. Indeed, they are highly provocative. The Greeks are all contemptuously represented as cowering down under the savage bayonet lunges in which the Turkish soldiers are obviously glorying. It seemed more in the spirit of ancient Assyria than that of a nation aspiring to modern civilization.

The Archeological Museum, housed in a beautiful old bazaar, is largely devoted to Hittite material. There are hunting scenes; a couple of grand bulls; some fine reliefs of Hittite cavalry and infantry; fascinating scenes of royal domesticity – two men playing a game; a mother with her baby; leading an animal to sacrifice; two children spinning tops; and a curious sacred procession, some of the people carrying ears of wheat, others mirrors. However, it must be confessed that some of the gods were grim, and some of the art distinctly heavy and forbidding.

The Hittites have now been more or less adopted by the Turks as their cultural ancestors or historic predecessors. There is a great deal to be said in favour of stressing cultural instead of racial ancestry, though in this case the continuity of cultural history was in fact almost completely broken.

Until recently we knew extremely little about the Hittites, except for the references in the Old Testament and the Egyptian accounts of battles. Then in 1906, a large number of cuneiform tablets were discovered at Hattusas, the ancient capital of the Hittite Empire, on the Anatolian plateau east of Ankara. Some of these were in an unknown language; but modern techniques of decipherment were able to cope with it, and revealed that it was essentially Aryan or Indo-European both in structure and vocabulary. The Hittites were in fact the first of the Aryan-speaking peoples to arrive on the stage of documented history, reaching Anatolia from east of the Black Sea soon after 2000 B.C.

Leonard Woolley, in his *Forgotten Kingdom* (1953), has recently suggested that the Hittites' westward migration from the region of the southern Caucasus first took them along the northern edge of the fertile crescent to settle in the region of Antioch. Driven thence after a couple of centuries by fresh invaders, some took refuge in Palestine, to become the Children of Heth of Abraham's time, while the majority moved northwards to establish the Hittite kingdom in Anatolia. Whatever their actual route, the time of their arrival in Asia Minor is confirmed from other sources. As the physical anthropologist at Ankara told me, the very brachycephalic type with exaggerated 'Jewish' nose and flat back of the cranium, characteristic of the Hittite aristocracy and the Hittite gods, and now so widespread in Anatolia and Armenia, has not been discovered here before 2000 B.C.

The Hittites' culture was largely built out of elements from neighbouring cultures – Sumerian, Akkadian, Hurrian, Egyptian – but it had a distinctive basis in the shape of their Indo-European language, and was operated, through a distinctive system of rule, by a conquering élite of priests and military knights.

The Hittites produced a system of law in many ways in advance of its time; and under their aegis the new technique of iron-working, which had its centre on the Anatolian-Armenian plateau, developed rapidly. By an irony of fate, the new metal did not become decisively available until their empire had come to an abrupt and violent close in about 1230 B.C. Hittite power seems to have been destroyed by the irruption of the Phrygians; and with its collapse, Hittite culture disappeared, not to be rediscovered for over 3000 years.

A great deal of archeological work is being carried out in Turkey – partly by the Turks themselves through their Archeological Institute, appropriately lodged in an old caravanserai, partly by other nations. When I was there, Professor Garstang at the age of 72 was gallantly holding the fort for Britain in this field. Since then, the British Institute of Archeology in Ankara has launched out on a bold programme, under the direction of Seton Lloyd. Work in this area is certain to shed light on the turbulent development of civilization during the crucial second millennium, in particular on the Danaans and the Achaeans, and on the factual basis for immortal legends like those of Jason's Argonauts.

The official encouragement of archeological research is one symptom of Turkey's transformation into a modern nation. The encouragement of education at all levels is another. The University of Ankara is a well-equipped university of modern Western type, with a number of Europeans on its staff. It fought hard for its autonomy, which was granted in 1946. There is also a Middle East Technical University in Ankara, founded primarily by U.S. initiative. It was founded in 1957 and is planned eventually to take five thousand students. Though it is open to Arabs, it hopes to draw most of its students from the C.E.N.T.O. countries.

However, one foreign observer who has lived for some time in the country made the friendly criticism that the Turkish academic world was too self-complacent, too inclined to believe that Turkey had become sublimely self-sufficient, and that, though an immense amount had been achieved, the universities and research institutes still fell somewhat short of good western standards.

Turkey's transitional state itself was well illustrated in the field of social anthropology. A Turkish woman anthropologist was being trained in the U.S.A. under Margaret Mead: but, according to my informants, it was doubtful if any woman could hope to do effective anthropological field-work in Turkey before the attitude to educated women had changed in the remoter areas. Further, the Government authorities seemed unaware of the value of social-anthropological studies: presumably they preferred propaganda to science. This is a pity, for Turkey would provide a unique field for studying the acculturation (horrible but useful word!) of semi-primitive societies to a modern way of life.

However, education certainly bulks large in Turkey's programme. The Minister for Education was a keen, youngish man, obviously concerned to get things done. Rather to my surprise, I found him particularly interested in Unesco's scheme for the wider translation of the classics of different countries. Nowhere else was I received with such a degree of official politeness: after I had paid my official call at the Ministry at 10.30, the Minister returned the call at my hotel at 11.30. As showing the Government's pre-occupation with applied science, one of his two under-secretaries is exclusively concerned with Technical Education.

In the Technical Training College, 1600 boys are being trained. The curriculum is centred round design and engineering draughtsmanship. But the emphasis is on making things: they turn out electrical apparatus, glassware, furniture, metal-work (from designs prepared by the girls' training college), and radios, and do motor repairs (even occasionally making an engine). It was fascinating to see little Turkish boys of 13, with cropped hair and a serious energetic expression on their broad faces, thoroughly enjoying themselves banging away at red-hot iron in the big forge; or slightly older lads, half-way from primitive village life to the modern industrial world, clustered earnestly round the radio instructor.

The boys make furniture and scientific apparatus for all Government schools; if there is anything over, the College can sell it and put the profit in its revolving fund. Clearly the feeling that they were actually making things for use was a great incentive to the boys.

The corresponding institution for girls was smaller, and restricted to feminine arts such as embroidery, decorative design, or dressmaking. It has been a great step forward to provide any sort of technical education for girls; and we may expect that, as time goes on and opinion changes, its scope will be broadened.

One day we set out across the rolling steppe to see the training school for rural teachers at Hassanoglan. Teachers for the remoter districts are urgently needed if the educational transformation of the country is to go forward, and these rural training schools have been set up to meet the need. Very rightly,

The Citadel of Ankara above the Old Town

Ancient and modern in Ankara: a concrete check-point flanked by a Hittite lion

18. *Modern Turkish planning: the Ankara dam*

19. *Turkish student-teachers rehearsing a play in th*
auditorium at the rural training-school at Hassanoglan

they have not been established in or even near the cities, but in the heart of the countryside. Hassanoglan is a little cluster of old houses, like thousands of other Turkish villages: it is in striking and instructive contrast with the spacious new buildings of the rural training school on its outskirts.

The boys get their training free, but must pledge themselves to return to teach in their native villages, or at least in their home areas, for a number of years. Their training is an interesting blend of theoretical and practical (pl. 19, opposite). At the time of my visit, the boys were building their own theatre. One group was rehearsing a play in the unfinished open-air auditorium; fifty yards away, another was excavating new foundations for its walls. Behind the diggers was a marble replica of a fine Greek statue in the museum at Istanbul.

Later, a team gave a performance of Turkish folk-dances. The dances were interesting, often employing staves or batons in their rhythmic ritual. The boys' close-cropped hair and tight-fitting blue uniforms were in curious contrast with the age-old figures and chants. To western eyes the trainees' existence seemed rather regimented: but probably a regime is a necessity to accustom boys from primitive areas to a totally new mode of life and thought.

*

Though there has recently been an unfortunate recrudescence of traditional religious influence, the trend of Turkey towards modern secularism can never be reversed. In particular, the dervish orders, whose suppression was somewhat analogous to Henry VIII's suppression of the monasteries, will assuredly not be re-established, and the State will remain a secular one. Much of the population, especially in the remoter areas, still lives in pre-revolutionary primitiveness; but there is a general sense of achievement, and, what is more, a sense of movement towards further achievement. It was the only one of the countries I visited which gave me the feeling of having achieved a new and effective national dynamism.

One man I met had been concerned with the elections of 1946. Since 1925 there had been only one legal political party – the Republican People's Party – but Atatürk had always expressed the view that an official Opposition was in principle a good thing. In 1946 the formation of new parties was allowed; and my informant had to help in supervising some of the resultant elections. I gathered that some of the officials at headquarters considered that he had allowed the new Democratic Party to win too many seats: but the fact remains that an Opposition had come into being with the approval of the party in sole power; and that in subsequent elections it has itself come to power. I wonder whether any of the one-party States beyond the Iron Curtain will ever plan an Opposition in this way.

Kemal Atatürk seems to have been one of those statistically improbable individuals who, by virtue of their exceptional peculiarities, affect the course of history, and introduce an element of unpredictability into the statistical determinism of mass social and economic trends. Some sort of revolutionary transformation would in any event have occurred in Turkey during the first half of this century, but without Atatürk it would have run a less vigorous course and produced different and less successful results.

His 'improbable' genetic constitution was reflected in his exceptional energy. Not one man in a million is capable of living as he did, working for 12 or 16 hours a day, and then plunging into the enjoyment of violent pleasures, with only a few hours left for sleep. He once made a speech in the Assembly which went on non-stop for two (or was it three?) entire days.

Turkey has certainly moved far and fast in the revolutionary decades since the end of the First World War. Even after a few days, the visitor realizes that the country has set its feet firmly and inevitably on the road of modernization.

7

MODERN JORDAN AND ANCIENT PETRA

Tᴴᴇ ᴛʜʀᴇᴇ ᴛʜɪɴɢꜱ ᴛʜᴀᴛ ᴍᴏꜱᴛ impressed me during my visit to Jordan, or Transjordan as it then was (a visit, as usual, quite impossibly short, but during which I was able to see improbably much), were Petra, King Abdullah, and Jerash, in that order. Petra is unique, Jerash is remarkable; King Abdullah was outstanding.

He received me three times during my short stay. He was a smallish man, bearded, and bright-eyed, with obvious dignity and force of character. While talking, he used his hands in a beautiful and expressive way. He gave the impression of a peculiar shrewdness, sometimes rising to wisdom, a shrewdness compounded of native intelligence, a certain naïveté, and a rational cunning, which was very characteristic and could not well have developed except in some such circumstances as his – a position of power, yet played upon by still more powerful outer forces, a man caught between two worlds, the modern world of armed technology and the world of the desert and Arabian Islam. And he had outstanding charm. When he laid his hand on my arm and said 'the conversation of learned men is the highest pleasure', he was irresistible; and again when he took my hand to lead me to lunch.

His study was a pleasant, spacious, rather low room, wood-panelled, to which a couple of steps ascended from the main hall of the palace. This was a modest building of low construction, more like a semi-western country-house than a palace, oriental or otherwise. After I had explained the purpose of my visit, which was to secure the adherence of Transjordan as a Member-

State of Unesco, and the presence of a strong Transjordanian delegation to the forthcoming General Conference of Unesco in Beirut, he asked a number of questions in which his particular type of shrewdness was very manifest. One of my arguments was that the fact of the General Conference being held in the Middle East provided a great opportunity for the countries of the region to demonstrate their solidarity, their pride in their own culture, and their international good will. However, he seemed much less interested in this than in the general point that Unesco represented world education, science, and culture. This clearly appealed to his traditional Arab respect for learning and learned men, and he concluded by saying that since Unesco wished to promote learning and education, it must be a good thing.

The King also asked me a number of questions about myself. When I told him that I was a zoologist by original profession, he inscribed and presented to me an Arabic book on zoology from his library. The book is actually a reprint of an older volume on Animals rather than on Zoology – a very curious work, illustrated by marginal woodcuts, in which real and fabulous creatures, scientific observation and mythology, are uncritically mixed.

I cherish one of his utterances at luncheon. The King, though his Turkish was as fluent as his Arabic, spoke no European language; accordingly our conversation was carried on through the Chef de Protocole, an amiable diplomat who spoke an excellent French. At one moment the subject of women was mentioned, in what connection I have forgotten. The King thereupon delivered himself of a forcible utterance, accompanied by considerable gesticulation and a final thump of his fist on the table. 'Qu'est-ce que dit Sa Majesté?' I enquired of the Chef de Protocole; who with the utmost suavity replied, 'Sa Majesté dit que les femmes sont un mal nécessaire.' This memorable remark was, I gathered through discreet enquiry, very true for the King, to judge from the harem which he found necessary to maintain, its numbers, and the variety of race and age of its members.

King Abdullah was easily the most outstanding personality in high places whom I met in the Middle East. His assassination, in the holiest place of the area he had incorporated into his kingdom, was a grave blow, both in the loss of a remarkable personality, and as a frightening demonstration of the obstacles erected by political and religious fanaticism to the constructive development of the region.

King Abdullah was also a reminder that the Middle East is still partly in a political phase which Western Europe and North America have left behind – the dynastic phase, in which political power is centred in the institution of monarchy, and can be extended over alien areas by dynastic marriages and other personal arrangements. Where the dynastic pattern has collapsed, power tends to become concentrated in the hands of a wealthy oligarchy, or of a military leader. Turkey is an exception in having made a considerable advance towards a parliamentary democracy of Western type.

In Israel there is a unique situation: a democracy consciously based on modern science and its technological applications, consciously inspired by the ancient dream of a promised land, and supported by contributions from world Jewry. It has to struggle with the problem of assimilating immigrants from many backgrounds and from every level of culture; to guard against impending overpopulation, while menaced by Arab hostility from without and by the contrary forces of reactionary orthodoxy and ultra-modern terrorism from within. Time alone will show whether the result will be merely another jealously nationalistic little country in the Middle East, or whether the constructive ideas and energies at its core become a stimulus instead of a stumbling-block to its neighbours, a stimulus to the real job of recreating a high civilization in the region, and taking a constructive hand in the human adventure as a whole.

Meanwhile, regional politics operates under the shadow of oil and the rivalry of the two great power blocs, so that development is constantly being distorted by pressures from without and resentful reactions from within. Can the relation between the great powers, with their resources of capital and technical expertise, on the one hand, and the countries of the Middle East on the other, be converted from the primarily exploitative activities of the Western world in the past and the ultra-nationalist and sometimes dog-in-the-manger (or dog-in-the-oil-trough) reaction of some Middle Eastern countries in the present, into one of mutually advantageous and complementary participation in a common enterprise? That is the overriding question for the Middle East.

But I have strayed from Jordan, and must retrace my steps. The elderly guard outside the palace was handsome in a rugged and non-Semitic way, finely dressed in a black tunic and breeches with scarlet embroidery, and a sheepskin cap (pl. 20, opp. p. 116). *Circassian* was the thought which rose in my mind: and I was right. In the 60's and 70's of last century, as the result of the spread of Russian power in the Caucasus and of the Russo-Turkish war of 1877, many Circassians moved into Turkey to find refuge in a Moslem country; and considerable groups of them were established by the Turks as colonies in what is now Jordan, to reinforce the settled population relatively to the nomad Beduin.

Amman is an amusing little town, situated at the bottom of a steep valley, and spreading somewhat up one or two side valleys. Fifty years ago it was little more than a Circassian village of some 2000 people. Today it boasts about 40,000 inhabitants, including large numbers of Arabs. The Western invasion has begun, and there are shops where one can buy European and American goods – trinkets and gadgets, textiles and toilet articles, mostly of rather cheap quality. Though it has a very provincial air, it is full of life and bustle, without any of that sense of decay which is all too frequent in the region.

In the valleys which lead out of Amman to the level desert plateau, I saw my first Beduin encampment. The long low black tents, the 'houses of hair' made of black goats' wool, are very impressive, especially when the whole pattern of them is seen from above, as here in a hollow of grey limestone made bright by patches of blue bugloss (pl. 21, opp. p. 116).

Just opposite the only hotel is a Roman theatre, scooped out of the steep side of the valley. It was built when Amman, called Philadelphus, was a provincial city of the Roman Empire instead of the capital of a small Arab nation. It is a handsome construction, with tier above tier of seats, surmounted by what appear to be special boxes, and with galleries which must have served as a foyer. Today it is a showpiece for tourists, deserted save for a few black goats which jump from tier to tier in search of the grass that sprouts between the stones. It seems a pity that this superb theatre should not be used: a concert or a dramatic performance staged in it would be a memorable event.

But this is merely one detail in the neglect of cultural resources which obtains in Jordan (and to a lesser extent in other countries of the Middle East) – a neglect all the more lamentable because the resources are so rich. To reach Jerash is not so difficult; but there is no hotel nor even any eating-place when you get there. To reach Petra, on the other hand, is both arduous and expensive: when you have reached it, there is nowhere to stay, not even the camp in one of the rock-hewn tombs which was run by Cook's before the Second World War.

In some ways worst of all, the country has no Museum. As a result, the remarkable collections made by the Department of Antiquities (which when

I was there consisted of one young Englishman with a handful of non-professional helpers) are all in crates in one of the Government buildings. The Nabataean kingdom was a unique phenomenon; yet our knowledge of it and its works is largely shut away in that storage basement in Amman.

Overhanging modern Amman is the ancient fortified acropolis, a place full of history. In it are the arched ruins of El Qasr, a Moslem palace from the 8th or 9th century; on the very rim, with a superb view over the valley below, are the earthquake-shattered remains of a great Roman temple; and here and there are traces of the Ammonite fortress of Rabbah or Rabboth Ammon. It was below these walls that Uriah the Hittite met his death, and in so doing left the way open for Bathsheba's marriage to David.

An expedition to Jerash, kindly arranged for us, gave an opportunity of seeing some of the more fertile northern part of Jordan. Flowers were everywhere, for it was the season of the rains. The asphodel was over, and the oleanders not yet out; but along the valley out of Amman the rocks were smoky blue with a kind of borage, and all along the way a fine *Anchusa* was growing, almost up to the Dropmore variety. Then there was a spectacular giant viper's bugloss; scarlet anemones; glorious red poppies rather larger than ours; and wild pink hollyhocks, surprising on the barren limestone slopes. At one place a sort of cuckoo-flower covered a field with a sheet of bluish-mauve. Scabiouses were a dominant feature; both a charming pale primrose-yellow one, and a taller more solitary species, with frilly white flowers. A sea-lavender with curious papery bracts was a reminder that not every *Statice* lives in salt-marshes. And I must not forget the exquisite sky-blue geranium, or the yellow and mauve-pink rock-roses, or the superb and peculiar thistles. There was one very unpleasant plant, a piluliferous nettle, much larger than ours, and much more painfully urticant.

Halfway to Jerash, we came upon scattered gnarled ilex, and then to the edge of the still extensive pine-forest. Reforestation was being done where needed, not so much for timber but as a measure to check erosion.* Here we began to see the cistuses, both mauve and white, so characteristic of Mediterranean hillsides. The region here was of great beauty, with flower-carpeted clearings running up among the pines.

Among birds, there were the lovely bee-eaters that I speak of elsewhere, and a large and handsome jay, boldly marked in black and white, among the

* In December 1952 Jordan was the scene of a regional conference on forest problems, sponsored by Unesco – an important first step towards restoring its lost trees to the region.

pines. Near here I had my first view of the great black-and-white vultures, *Neophron*, which the English in Egypt have dubbed Pharaoh's Chickens. They were very puzzling at first sight, for they looked so different from all the other vultures I knew, which for the most part are just dingy black or brown. Like other vultures, they are ugly at close quarters, but of great beauty in flight, soaring effortlessly over the bare hills.

Claude Berkeley was in the front seat of the car going to Jerash; he was startled out of his wits by a violent explosion close to his right ear. A distinguished Lebanese who was accompanying our party had been so excited by the sight of a Neophron floating along close to the road that he had drawn his army pistol and fired at it past Berkeley's head. The bird was unhurt: but Berkeley suffered from deafness and shattered nerves for the next twenty-four hours.

After a few more miles, we came down into more open country, with Jerash in the distance. Jerash, under its ancient name of Gerasa, was an important caravan centre on the inland route from Petra to Damascus, and a fine representative of the Romano-Syrian culture of the region.

One of the characteristic features of the towns in this cultural province of the Roman Empire was the building of colonnades (sometimes covered, as at Antioch) along the main streets. These are seen at their most splendid and extraordinary in Palmyra, but are impressive enough at Jerash. Jerash has one unique feature – the so-called Forum, a large and not quite regular ellipse, paved, and surrounded by a handsome colonnade (pl. 22, opp. p. 117).

But the most beautiful buildings of Jerash were the Temple of Artemis and the Propylaea. The Temple of Artemis stands on a height above the city, its slender and elegant columns dominating the skyline. We approached from the main street through a field of marigolds, whose brilliant yellow set off the dark grey of the temple, the soft grey of the limestone foreground, and the hazy blue of the distant hills. Skylarks and desert-larks sang overhead, and goldfinches dipped and twittered musically among the ruins.

The Propylaea was an elaborate construction, designed primarily for its architectural effect at the city's central cross-roads. The triumphal arch, with its curious feature of large 'wind-blown' acanthus leaves carved at the base of its principal columns, was also designed for its architectural effect at the city entrance.

Buildings like this remind one of the unique contribution made to architecture by imperial Rome. No other culture has so successfully managed to

20. *A member of King Abdullah's Circassian bodyguard at Amman*

21. *Beduin 'houses of hair', made of black goat's wool, in a valley outside Amman*

create such urban dignity. Other cities may be more romantic, other styles produce more outstanding or more beautiful buildings; but no other culture has given rise to such a combination of splendour and restraint. Certainly Rome has nothing to show which can compare with the best Greek buildings in beauty and wonder – the Parthenon, the superb temple of Neptune at Paestum, and a score of others; but equally certainly Greece can show nothing comparable to the general town-planning effect of Roman cities – including, let it be remembered, such outlying spots as this, of Jerash on the edge of the empire.

Jerash, like most places in the Middle East, consists of history in layers. The present layer is a very thin one: modern Jerash is merely a small Circassian village annexed to an Ancient Monument controlled by the Antiquities Service: during the long centuries of Arab and Turkish rule it was merely the village, with the ruins disregarded and uncared for beside it. Before the Roman period, it was a Nabataean caravan centre. In the early years of the Empire, it formed one of the prosperous league of cities east of the Jordan, known as the Decapolis. From here, many people came to hear Jesus preach as the fame of his ministry spread. With the decay of Rome, Jerash became a moderate-sized Christian town. The remains of this period, tucked away amidst the Roman ruins, look rather incongruous in their classical and pagan setting. There are several small churches, and one remarkable mosaic floor.

★

The arrangements for our stay in Jordan were in the hands of an amiable but not very intelligent official. The difficulties of communication were enhanced by the fact that he was one of that curious class of people who speak a foreign language better than they understand it. (When in Czechoslovakia next year I was in the care of a similar personage. One morning I asked him which of two plans we had envisaged the day before was to be adopted. He replied with the customary phrase with which he disguised his lack of comprehension: 'It is possible.' 'No, no,' said I, 'you misunderstand me. I wanted to know *which*.' 'Yes, *which*,' he answered; and I gave up.)

Since our bear-leader occupied a position in Jordan somewhat analogous to that of the then Permanent Secretary of the Ministry of Education in

22. *The unique elliptical Forum of Roman Jerash*

Britain, we hit on the device of referring to him as *Sir John Maud* when we wished to relieve our feelings by discussing him in his presence. 'It is a great pity that Sir John Maud doesn't understand the virtue of punctuality' we would say when he kept us waiting three-quarters of an hour, trying to arrange at the last moment what he should have arranged on the previous day; or would discuss the probable effect of Sir John Maud's personality on the progress of education, when our questions on the system in Jordan failed to elicit any comprehensible reply.

I managed to doze in the plane. This was not unnatural, since we had been strenuously on the go ever since 4 a.m. It was also fortunate, since a formal reception, with myself as guest of honour, awaited us in Amman. I found the reception a little dull. I was ascribing the fact to my fatigue when the real reason dawned upon me. It was a strictly Moslem function, which meant no women and no alcohol; and in these circumstances, lemonade, however fresh, and Jordanian civil servants, however distinguished, lacked a certain sparkle.

★

There are some ten places in the world which I have treasured in imagination as goals of pilgrimage, whether or no there seemed any possibility of attaining them – the Hoggar Mountains in mid-Sahara; Bali and the Balinese way of life; Macchu Picchu in the Andes of Peru; the Great Rift Valleys of Africa (which I have managed to see); the east coast of Formosa, ever since Professor Goldschmidt told me that it had sea-cliffs five thousand feet high; Pekin; a really good coral island; Ang Kor and the old temples of India; the great Antarctic ice-barrier with its volcanoes, its penguins, and the strange phenomena of its polar skies; and Petra, longer desired than any of the others.

Back in Europe, a friend commented that, from my description, Petra sounded surrealist. No, said I, not surrealist, for after all it is real. But you might call it *surimaginist*, because no one could just imagine such an extraordinary reality.

I had always wanted to see Petra, ever since I first heard the line about the rose-red city half as old as time. (I always manage to forget the author's name; but there – I have looked it up again, and it is Burgon, and the line comes in his Newdigate Prize Poem, though he stole the phrase 'half as old as time' from Rogers's *Italy*.) Later, I read some account of Petra . . . the entrance gorge, the fabulous landscape, the city of rock-hewn tombs, the place abandoned, deserted, unknown for a thousand years to the West save as a dim legend, rediscovered by Burckhardt at the risk of his life (though he had already been converted to Islam), still visited at the traveller's peril up to a bare half-century or so ago.

And now I was going there. In spite of the fact that my total stay in Jordan was fifty-two hours, the authorities very kindly made a visit possible. *Just* possible! To reach it meant getting up at 4 a.m., travelling 2½ hours by plane, 2½ hours by car, 2½ hours on horseback, and 2½ hours roughish walking, apart from meals and sight-seeing; with an official reception to face when we got back to Amman in the evening. But it was worth it.

A little five-passenger biplane took us down to Ma'an over the edge of the desert that stretched unbroken and interminable to the east. Below us ran the Hejaz railway, constructed in happier times with the aid of contributions from Moslems all over the world to secure better access to Medina and Mecca, but its linking function then destroyed by T. E. Lawrence's raids during World War I. To the west, a few valleys leading down to the Dead Sea, with occasional settlements, and a glimpse of Kerak, the huge castle built by the Crusaders to safeguard their desert flank.

At Ma'an, we went to the military headquarters. I had great difficulty in restraining my Arab companions from proceeding immediately; but luckily common sense prevailed and a much-needed breakfast appeared. Men of the Arab Legion had been sleeping on camp-beds in the courtyard: they were a fine-looking lot, and showed what good training could accomplish with the admirable human material available. If the Middle Eastern countries could arrange to utilize human catalysts like Glubb Pasha in other than military fields, such as public health or education or agriculture, the entire region might acquire a new dynamism. In any case, as a writer in *The Times* has pointed out (12 Feb. 1950), 'in Jordan the Legion is the main factor in the smooth transition from nomadic to settled life'.

Then off by car across horrible country – level desert strewn with black pebbles and stones. After a bit the road began to wind down a valley in the calcareous scarp, revealing little fields in the valley bottom bright with enormous red poppies. So to Ain Musa, Moses' Spring, at the head of the dry torrent of the Wady Musa. There we changed from car to horses – but some of the most miserable specimens I have ever seen, and not even furnished with a rein, only a halter. A little way down the stony track, I saw that one of the Arab members of our party (who prided himself on his idiomatic English) was walking, and asked why. Affably, but with some heat, he replied, 'Because my bally horse is no dam good.'

Before us lay a great purple and brown rampart – the range of sandstone mountains from which Petra – 'the Rock' – takes its name. On the outskirts of Ain Musa were the only spots of green in the huge landscape – terraces with figs and almonds and vegetables contouring the steep slopes. Soon we were in desert again – but now a desert of ivory-coloured sandstone, dissected by the weather into valleys bordered with strange rounded domes and bosses, like human constructions which had begun to melt and lose their sharpness of outline. Then suddenly we found ourselves before the entry of the famous Siq, the astonishing approach to the city (pl. 26, between pp. 128–129). Local tradition has it that the Siq was made by Moses' rod when he struck the rock. Actually it is a gorge or very narrow canyon, cut by water in the red and brown and purple sandstone which makes the inner girdle or bastion of Petra. Every traveller has been struck by it, and with reason, for it is as great a wonder as the dead city itself – no, as the rest of the city, for the Siq is an essential part of Petra.

Here, the landscape of old ivory comes to an end before a barrier of low red-brown cliffs. This barrier is pierced by the torrent-bed – a narrow opening, hard to detect, even though marked by the remains of the works which the men of Petra added to the entrance of the great defensive work provided for them by nature.

The entrance leads round a corner into an exceedingly narrow gorge with vertical sides. As the torrent-bed pursues its course through the mile of sandstone rampart, the gorge deepens rapidly, from a mere 70 or 80 feet at the outset to over 300 feet near its other end. It curves and twists its sinuous way, never more than a dozen yards wide, and sometimes narrowing to five or even four. Here the walls curve a little away from the perpendicular, there form an overhang, according to the caprice of the floods of past ages, which have cut the canyon and polished its smooth sides. Wild figs and oleanders have managed to find root-hold in the shady cleft; and at intervals tributary torrentlets have cut back the upper lip of the gorge, revealing sandstone ridges and peaks in the sunshine far above.

Today the floor is just a torrent-bed, covered with loose stones. But there are remains of the original pavement, composed of large blocks more than $1\frac{1}{2}$ feet square, which converted the Siq from a rough track into a real road, a noble if a strange approach to a great city.

Along the wall, you can see the remains of conduits, which led the waters of Ain Musa into cisterns within the thirsty city. Besides the original open conduit which the Nabataeans cut in the solid stone, there are the remains of the more ambitious system of the later Roman rulers, of pipes let into the rock. Modern travellers have described the alarming floods that sweep through the Siq after the rare but heavy rains: in Nabataean times these were largely diverted from the road and into the city's water-supply, by means of a tunnel of which traces still remain.

It was almost impossible to visualize the traffic that passed through this astonishing place two thousand years ago – caravans of camels, spice-laden, arriving from Arabia or leaving for Damascus and Aleppo; strings of mules; rich men and cavalry soldiers on horseback; the common people and the infantry on foot; the King himself leaving on a campaign; two centuries later, the Roman Governor, messengers from Rome, Roman architects and actors, soldiers and engineers. Could wheeled vehicles ever have passed through the Siq? I do not know.

Of a sudden a new wonder announced itself. Before this moment, the only sunlight had been hundreds of feet above our heads. Now, rounding a bend, we saw the two dark walls framing a vision of sunlit rose, with pilasters and architraves – instead of shadow, sunlight; instead of nature, art.

The Siq debouches into a valley at right angles to its previous course, green with a rich growth of oleanders, and so much broader that it is flooded with sunshine. And precisely opposite the opening, doubtless deliberately, the Nabataeans carved the most beautiful of all their monuments, called in Arabic Khazné Faraòun, Pharaoh's Treasury (pl. 27, between pp. 128-129).

It represents a temple façade, some 90 feet high, sculpted from the rosiest-red of all the rocks of Petra, around the beginning of the Christian epoch. There are the remains of rich carving, both in the round and in relief; the columns across its entrance are matched by pilasters at the side. Between the two halves of the much-stylized broken pediment at the top is a delicious little miniature *tholos*, or circular temple, of extreme elegance. Only four examples of this type of façade are known, none of them from actual buildings: three are rock-cut monuments in Petra, one being the Deir (p. 125), and the fourth is in a wall-painting at Pompeii.

The tholos is surmounted by an urn, which is much damaged, since up to quite recently every Beduin who passed would shoot at it in the hope (mis-guided, for the urn is of course solid) that he could hit some secret spot which, as in a gambling machine in a modern bar, would discharge in a flood the treasure it was firmly believed to contain. In the interior are three chambers cut in the rock, from which a strange and lovely view appears between the rosy pillars. The place is probably the tomb-temple of one of the latest Nabataean Kings.

As we followed the valley down, tombs became more and more numerous: indeed, at one place, the right-hand wall was an almost continuous cemetery. These are mostly small tombs, of the so-called pylon type, representing a single-storeyed small house-front, but with a slight batter and the two sides converging, and a single doorway leading into the funerary chamber. The top is adorned with a battlement motif, sometimes free-standing, but usually in relief only, each battlement having three or four steps. In the later tombs of this kind, this motif is reduced to the two half-battlements at the corners, enlarged and nearly meeting in the centre, so as to give the appearance of a double staircase. This motif seems to be confined to Nabataean tombs, here and at other sites such as Heger in the Hejaz, the southernmost town of the Nabataean kingdom. Most of the rock here is darkish brown-chocolate, or with a tinge of russet.

On the left is the theatre, probably of the 1st century A.D., when Roman influence was invading Arabia Petraea. It too is of course wholly carved out of the rock, and here and there in its back walls are square black holes, where tomb-chambers have been cut through – a surprising juxtaposition: as Professor Libbey says, 'Amusement in a cemetery! A theatre in the midst of sepulchres!'

Eventually the valley broadens out into a relatively level space, rather over a square mile in extent. The exit gorge from this basin drains south, to fall over the rim of the great rift into the Ghor. It is so precipitous as to be impassable to man, and the caravan route to the southward had to climb out over its shoulder. The exit gorge and the Siq are the two canyon ends of a torrent draining westward from the hard limestone scarp by Ain Musa and cutting down through the sandstones. The entry of the Siq marks the transition from the soft ivory sands to the harder red sandstones; conversely, the basin in which Petra lay has been produced by erosion of the somewhat softer strata on the torrent's middle course.

In this basin, along the stream-bed, are the remains of the Roman city, built wholly or mainly after A.D.106, when Arabia Petraea was incorporated into the Empire. Little is standing now save fragments of a temple and a triumphal arch; but study has shown that there were three large markets or caravanserais, a forum and portico, a couple of gymnasia, various shops, and as in other contemporary cities' of the region, a colonnade of pillars along the main road – which was here built as a continuous viaduct over the torrent-bed. So far, no trace has been found of any free-standing constructions from the earlier purely Nabataean period; however, there must certainly have been palaces for the kings, government buildings, and caravanserais for the merchants.

Even in the Roman period, there are no built houses which can be ascribed to the local inhabitants as opposed to their Roman rulers, and some archeologists go so far as to suggest that the bulk of these nomads, when they turned into sedentary exploiters of caravans, were content with that first approximation to a house provided by a cave. At any rate, there are hundreds of artificial caves all over the place, some of which have certainly been lived in; from those shelters we may imagine the Nabataeans looking down with a good deal of resentment on the alien conquerors who had degraded Petra from its metropolitan status in favour of Bosra which they proclaimed the capital of their *Provincia Arabia*.

The city-basin appears at first sight bounded by a continuous rampart of rock, often nearly vertical; but actually, not only does the Wady Musa make its entrance and its exit through the basin-walls, but a number of hidden tributary ravines run down from the heights, and these too, made accessible by staircases cut in the rock, are crowded with caves and tombs and other rock-cut monuments.

The north-eastern part of this rampart, continuing the crowded cemetery I spoke of above, is covered with rock-cut façades, including three or four huge ones of two storeys, and one monster of three, so high that the top storey could not be carved in the cliff's receding lip, and had to be finished in masonry. These large tombs or tomb-temples are mostly russet-brown; but just beside them is a smaller one in a marvellous multi-coloured stone Burgon's phrase, the 'rose-red city', had impressed me so much that I thought all Petra would be pink, or at least russet, and was not in the least prepared for the variety of its colours. Edward Lear records that his cook Giorgio, 'who is prone to culinary similes', said, 'O master, we have come into a world where everything is made of chocolate, ham, curry-powder, and salmon.' Ivory I have already mentioned, and the various shades of red and russet (Dean Stanley speaks particularly of dull crimson, and Kammerer of raspberry); but there is also sepia, and violet, and finally the multi-coloured sandstones (pl. 25, opp. p. 128).

These last have often been deliberately employed by the rock-sculptors to give a particular effect. For instance, the tomb just referred to has been cut back further than usual until its façade appears multi-coloured, but in a brown framework; and in other tombs the multi-coloured stratum has been used for the ceiling. But the effect when they appear in the external land-scape is almost as extraordinary. The celebrated sands of Alum Bay, which one can buy in striped bottlefuls, are not nearly so fine. These at Petra consist of a repeated series of coloured bands, each series usually beginning with ivory, next light bluish-grey, then indigo, and finally a flaming rust-red. The bands are wavy and of unequal width, so that the effect is of a gorgeous if somewhat barbaric piece of watered silk.

A young British officer and his wife whom we had met at Ma'an had luckily told me that El Deir – 'the Monastery' – was among the most extra-ordinary of Petra, and that the rough climb of under an hour needed to reach it would be well repaid. When I broached the subject, our Arab companions, backed by the local guide, said it was much too far and too strenuous, and said we ought all to have a rest and a comfortable lunch by the Roman temple. However, after a babel of discussion, we three from Unesco – two Englishmen and a Mexican – firmly said we would try, taking the guide, a boy, and our lunch. The guide was not at all pleased, and kept on grumbling about our going too fast for his old bones: but when we found that he could give me fifteen years, we didn't worry too much about his bones.

The way led up a steep and narrow ravine, by way of Nabataean staircases cut in the rock. At one place on a narrow shelf under an overhang there were 'baths' – cisterns of some sort – still with water in them, a rare commodity in desert Petra; higher up, in a region of scattered pines, the path came out on to the edge of a precipice from which an astonishing view opened into a deep and narrow canyon, with the little hermitage marking the reputed site of Aaron's Grave on top of Mount Hor in the distance; and, after a climb of 700 feet, finally emerged on to a col. From this the land dropped over a vertical mile to the Ghor beyond, that part of the Great Rift Valley which leads downhill from near the Gulf of Akaba to the Dead Sea in its deep depression. The view of this drop was stupendous, if inhospitable in the

23. Desert life: a baby gazelle found by a young Arab among the rocks of Petra

extreme – bare bones of mountains, ribs carved by subaerial denudation, a landscape all desert and all erosion, down to the rift-bottom and up to the tableland of western Idumaea beyond.

On the hither side of the col was a green sward of grass, with the mountains rising on either side. And on the north was El Deir – apparently a huge two-storey temple of reddish-brown stone, with the same type of façade as the Khazné, but in reality just the sculptured end of the mountain which rose above and beyond it (pl. 28, opp. p. 129).

El Deir is over 140 feet high and thus much bigger than the Khazné, but later in date and not nearly so beautiful. French writers have compared it to the façade of St Sulpice in Paris, and Dean Stanley, with the anti-classical eye of the Gothic revivalist, to 'a London Church of the 18th century, massive, but in poor taste, and with a somewhat debased style of ornament'. This is a little unfair: the Deir lacks elegance, but it has a certain grandeur and in its strange setting is extremely impressive. Its solitary interior chamber is the only one in Petra to contain an altar. Although it was possibly a royal tomb, its main function was probably that of a temple. In any case, public rituals were held in this high suburb, for there are remains of large-scale seating accommodation on the flat sward. And its traditional Arab name of The Monastery may signify that it was once used as a Christian place of worship, either before the Arab conquest or during the brief century when the area was in the hands of the Crusaders.

The grass by the temple was sprinkled with white camomiles and scarlet anemones: visitors in other seasons record a profusion of wild tulips. Here, surprisingly, we heard a Great Tit busily giving his see-saw note in some bushes. It was a long way from the bare coloured mountains to the English woods and gardens that the sound automatically evoked – a reminder of how wide-ranging many bird species can be; the Great Tit are of the widest-ranging of any. Libbey and Hoskins, the Americans who visited Petra in 1905, saw seven fine ibex here: we had no such luck, nor did we see the coneys – the hyraxes, or rockrabbits, those improbable relatives of the elephant – which are said to be common in and around Petra, where the 'stony rocks' of the 104th Psalm abound for them. Their existence in Palestine and Jordan is a reminder of the African origin of much of the Middle Eastern fauna, as the Hyracoidea are a typically African group.

---

24. *A late tomb in the suburbs of Petra, with its crown of four obelisks*

10*

After lunch we made our way up steps and rock slopes to the top of El Deir. It was a shock to come out behind the façade and to be made forcibly aware that it was just a bit of the mountain converted into stupendous stage scenery, designed to adorn the perennial human drama of death. From the top you get a new impression of its size. The vertical drop from the cornice made us feel giddy, and our guides looked very remote as they busied themselves on the sward below: we discovered later that they were engaged in picking camomiles for camomile tea.

Everywhere on its top and back little water-channels had been cut. This artificial gathering of water from the tombs and stairways was widespread. Without it, a city population estimated to have reached 30,000 could not well have existed in the midst of the desert.

When we told our companions of all we had seen and that we had taken only 50 minutes up and 30 down, they were sorry they had not come with us. But they had lost their chance, and it was time to get on our horses again and start back (with many dismountings, in spite of stiff and rather weary limbs, to take photographs).

Outside the Siq, in the ivory-coloured country, we met a young Arab with a gazelle fawn in his arms (pl. 23, opp. p. 124). He had just found it among the rocks, and wanted to know if we would buy it. It was a lovely little creature, but the last thing we wanted to add to our impedimenta. Here too we saw small flocks of brown-and-buff birds about the size of jackdaws. I conjectured that they might be some kind of chough, but they turned out to be Tristram's Grackles, birds of the starling family called after Canon Tristram who wrote the celebrated Victorian *Natural History of the Bible*. Ravens we saw too, and falcons, and sprightly desert chats like black-and-white wheatears, and grey cliff-haunting martins.

In this area, outside the central basin and the city proper, are a few late tombs, one of them, with a crown of obelisks, in a style peculiarly its own (pl. 24, opp. p. 125).

Unfortunately we had no time to see any of the High Places on the tops of the hills. It must suffice to say that *the* High Place, apparently the official centre of the city's religious life, seems to be the best-preserved in the world, and to give a wonderful picture of the religious practices, so violently denounced by the Hebrew prophets, of the Edomites and their Nabataean successors. Blood-sacrifice was practised, and the two great 'obelisks' are reminders that the Semitic peoples of the region originally supposed the gods to inhabit sacred rocks. These were later squared, and eventually developed into the so-called obelisks, which combined the function of god-rocks or god-pillars (*not* idols, for they were not representations of anything) and of altars. Robertson-Smith, the great authority on Semitic religion, includes such rocks under the term 'god-boxes'. Indeed, there is some evidence that Jehovah was originally a god-rock (or rock-imprisoned god) from this very area. In any case, the term *rock*, so often applied to Jehovah (and to other gods) in the Old Testament, was not used in any metaphorical sense, but literally, to mean the piece of rock which was sacred as the dwelling-place of the divinity.

The chief god of the Petrans was Dusares or Dushara, which means *Lord of Seir*, Seir being the name of the region, and roughly equivalent to Edom. In many tombs and temples of Petra there are little niches, containing squared blocks of stone which represent the dwellings of Dushara and other divinities.

* * *

What functions did Petra's strange assemblage of rock-cut monuments serve? Though the experts still disagree, the general consensus is that, though a few may have been dwelling-houses, the great majority were either tombs, or places for celebrating feasts for or with the dead, or both combined. Some of the larger ones were royal tombs, and these may also have served as temples. And a few, such as El Deir, may have been only temples.

Petra is unique in two respects – in its tombs and in its fortifications. Almost all ancient cities had to be made safe against attack. They were fortified with great walls and ramparts, and were often on top of a hill or crag. Petra is unique in lying in a deep hollow, provided by nature with cliffs as ramparts and with the Siq as a defendable entry unrivalled among the defensive works of man.

In many ancient cities, the necropolis, or city of the dead, was as important as the city of the living. So in Palmyra, in Etruscan cities, in the Old Kingdom of Egypt (though there the necropolis was for kings and nobles only), at Ras Shamra, and elsewhere. Petra is unique in having used its natural ramparts as its necropolis, and also in the fact that while the city of the dead has largely survived intact, the city of the living has been crumbled by weather and earthquake to a heap of fallen ruins.

* * *

There remains the problem of Petra's history.

Any account must be given with some diffidence, for our ignorance of its early origins is still abysmal, and can only be dissipated by the excavator's spade; and the experts disagree in their interpretation of what is known.*

The essential fact is that Petra was a caravan city pure and simple, which yet became for a brief period the rich capital of a caravan empire. Because of the extraordinary natural strength of its position, together with a reasonable supply of pure water in a waterless land, it was a key point on the caravan route from Arabia Felix, the land of the Queen of Sheba, to Syria and Egypt. The myrrh and frankincense of the Hadramaut – these above all; but also the ivory, apes, and black slaves (but not peacocks!) of East Africa and Abyssinia; the rose-coloured pearls of the Persian Gulf; the spices and precious woods and other luxuries (including a small proportion of the silk in transit from China) brought in coasting vessels from the Indies, all these were assembled in the Sabaeans' country near Aden. They then started north on camel-back along the west of Arabia, through Mecca, up the east coast of the Gulf of Akaba, and so to Petra. From Petra one important route led westwards to Gaza and thence south again to Egypt, another continued north to Damascus and so either to the Phoenician coast or, if required, to Aleppo and Antioch. On the coast they could be put aboard ship for Greece and Italy and other Mediterranean countries. And of course there were other goods flowing in the reverse direction – Phoenician purple is one example.

Incense was the most valuable or at least the most essential element in the trade. It was available only in the semi-desert areas of southern Arabia and Somaliland, and it was required in large quantities for the religious cere-

* For those desiring to pursue the subject, there is M. A. Murray's *Petra, the Rock City of Edom* (London, 1939); the excellent work of A. Kammerer, *Petra et la Nabatène* (Paris, 1929), with a valuable analysis of the architectural styles; the two volumes of W. Libbey and F. E. Hoskins, *The Jordan Valley and Petra* (New York, 1905); and the monumental works of G. Dalman, *Petra und seine Felsheiligtümer* (Leipzig, 1908) and of R. E. Brünnow and A. von Domaszewski, *Die Provincia Arabia* (1904). Sir A. Kennedy's *Petra, its History and Monuments* (London, 1925) contains some good photographs and maps. Lear's account of his visit (in Angus Davidson's *Edward Lear*, London, 1933) is, as one would expect, fascinating; and Rostovtzeff's *Caravan Cities* is full of general information.

25. *A Nabataean tomb at Petra, carved in multi-coloured sandstone like watered silk*
26. *Where Moses struck the rock? The Siq, the astonishing entry to Petra*

monies of all the nations of antiquity, from Egypt to Rome (Nero is said to have consumed more than a year's supply of incense for the funeral rites of Poppaea). Thus it was the idea of propitiating divinities and adding efficacy to sacred rituals by means of fragrant smells that led to the Arabian caravan trade and determined the rise of Petra. Here is economic determinism in reverse – ideas determining material events, and not vice versa.

The traffic came overland because in early antiquity land, however inhospitable, seemed less dangerous than sea – especially the Red Sea with its rocks and reefs and waterless coast. The caravans were a great source of profit to the communities through which they passed, for there were heavy dues and tolls to pay at each main stage: but in return, the authorities had to do all in their power to protect the caravans, which would otherwise have been pillaged and their personnel massacred by the desert nomads.

Joseph was sold by his brothers to a caravan going south through this area: this route brought Solomon his chief luxuries, as well as the Queen of Sheba herself. In those days the area was populated by the Edomites, although David had brought it, as well as Moab to the north, under the control of Israel ('Moab is my washpot, and over Edom will I cast out my shoe'). A kingdom existed here, under the name of Sela in the country of Seir, but it is not certain that there was an actual city at Petra, and any physical remains from that period are still buried under layers of later cultures.

Somewhere about the time of the Captivity, a new wave of desert Semites began pressing on the region, pushing the Edomites out into Idumaea, which had been left almost empty by Nebuchadnezzar's deportations. These were the Nabataeans; and with them, Petra as we know it began to grow up. Under their rule, Petra was a compulsory stage in the caravan journey. Here the teams of men from the south handed over their goods, to be taken on by new teams to west or north; there must have been huge warehouses for the royal stores and for the bales awaiting distribution, caravanserais, stables, shops, and all the paraphernalia of a port – though a port on the coasts of that land-sea, the desert.

The Nabataeans maintained the independence of their kingdom, in spite of the attempts first by one and then the other of the two powerful empires of Alexander's successors, the Seleucids and the Ptolemies, to subjugate them.

---

27. *The Treasury of Pharaoh at Petra, a vision of sunlit rose between the Siq's dark walls*
28. *El Deir, a piece of the mountain carved into stupendous stage scenery*

Indeed they were able to exploit their intermediate position to such good effect that their wealth and power grew rapidly, until for a few decades in the early 1st century B.C. they actually controlled the entire area from Damascus to the north-western corner of Arabia. The great majority of the rock-cut monuments date from the two rich centuries between 100 B.C. and A.D. 100. During this period, a Hellenistic style was adopted for an increasing number of tombs and temples, with growing Roman tendencies as time went on.

For the power and influence of Rome was increasing. The Jewish revolt of A.D. 67 was a stimulus, and its successful and drastic crushing by Titus an encouragement, to a Roman policy of expansion and firmness in the area; and the result of that policy, so far as the Nabataeans were concerned, was the annexation of their kingdom in A.D. 106, and its incorporation in the *Provincia* of Arabia, with Bosra as its capital, on the road to Damascus.

Early in the imperial period, Rome had attempted a direct control of the incense trade at its source. In 24 B.C. Augustus dispatched an expedition under Aelius Gallus to southern Arabia. He was encouraged to do so by Antas, King of the Nabataeans, who sent his minister Syllaeus to guide the expedition.* According to Strabo, who was a personal friend of Gallus, Syllaeus led them astray, and they turned back after considerable hardships and losses, convinced that the Nabataeans had all along intended to deceive them. This conviction doubtless strengthened the Romans' later decision to gain control of the incense trade by the conquest of Petra itself.

It seems probable that the Romans were able to take advantage of the Roman Peace which they imposed, to divert the main caravan route between Arabia and Damascus somewhat to the east, not turning aside into Petra, as the Nabataeans, much to their own profit, had previously insisted. Furthermore, the Romans consolidated their hold on the west coast of the Red Sea during the 1st century, and then drained off much of the trade between Arabia Felix and Egypt into their own ships. Finally, from about A.D. 130 the northern and eastern caravan route via Palmyra and the Persian Gulf was rapidly developed under Roman impulsion.

The fortunes of Petra went down as those of Palmyra went up; Petran merchants began to move to Bosra and even further afield; fewer and fewer monuments were carved in Petra's rock walls, until by the late 3rd century

---

* In his historical novel *The Eagle and the Sun* (1951) Lord Belhaven has given a lively if somewhat romantic account of the expedition.

it was almost abandoned – to be rediscovered by a small Christian community of hermits who found this desert retreat to their liking. In the 5th century, it had become a small diocese and a place of pilgrimage. One of the larger tomb-temples was converted into a Christian church in the year 447, under Bishop Jason, as an inscription tells us. Of the next few centuries we know nothing. The Crusades saw the erection of small Frankish fortresses in and round Petra. These, with Kerak and Shobek, served to hold a line along the westward edge of the open desert, down to the head of the Gulf of Akaba, thus cutting the Moslems' chief access to the Red Sea. But after Saladin's final victory the region seems to have been wholly abandoned to the occasional visits of the scattered Beduins.

All knowledge of its glorious heyday was lost; the only traditions that persisted were those from the time of Moses: Ain Musa is the spring that Moses caused to gush forth, and Moses is one of the commonest names among the population of Wady Musa; the Khazné and the Roman temple have been ascribed to Pharaoh, and Mount Hor, still a goal of pilgrimage, is crowned with the tomb of Aaron. The holy man who inhabits it must lead one of the loneliest lives in the world.

So Petra remains today, provocative, unique, fantastic. It should be one of the starred exhibits in a world museum of civilization. But for this to happen, it should be properly conserved, fully studied, and made accessible. Comparison of the Khazné today with its condition as shown in the careful drawings of earlier visitors, shows that in less than a century it has suffered serious deterioration from weathering; and clearly all the rock-cut monuments will slowly suffer, unless remedial action is taken.

Scientific excavation has scarcely begun, and would certainly bring to light the earlier stages of Petra's history. A Petra Museum, either in Petra itself or at Ma'an or Amman, is needed to give the visitor the indispensable background to the site, as the Museum at Candia does for Knossos. And finally, easier access, with accommodation in or close to Petra itself, is essential.

For this, Petra should be fitted into some general framework. The Middle East gives a unique picture of the growth of civilization, from its earliest origins up to the present. Ur and Babylon, Nineveh and Persepolis, Isfahan and Shiraz, Baghdad and Ctesiphon, Petra and Palmyra, Baalbek and Byblos, Damascus and Aleppo, Sidon and Tripoli, Jerash and Dura, Ras Shamra and Qalat Seman, fortresses and castles of every period – what a list! And this includes nothing from Egypt or Turkey: if they too are brought in, the wealth of wonders becomes prodigious.

Why do not the countries of the Middle East club together and work out a plan for 'cultural tourism' by which these treasures of civilization could be made readily available for modern pilgrims? Doubtless that would require careful organization, and probably international help from some body such as Unesco: but it could and should be done.

★

In any event, Jordan is so small (its total population is less than half a million) and so poor that it can not expect to develop very far in isolation. If cultural history could provide one focus for combination, physical geography indicates another.

Though the Dead Sea is one of the world's strangest geographical phenomena, yet according to Libbey and Hoskins no one before 1837 realized that it lay below sea-level. In that year the Englishmen Moon and Bebe made an estimation, based on the boiling-point of water, which put its level at −500 feet. Today every schoolboy knows that it is the lowest body of water in existence, with its surface nearly 1300 feet below that of the Mediterranean less than fifty miles away. Its deathly salinity has caused extraordinary stories to gather round it. The legend that no birds can fly over its noxious waters is presumably based on the fact that no birds do normally fly over its waters, since there are no fish for them to catch.

For much of history since the destruction of Sodom and Gomorrah, the Dead Sea has been unfrequented, though ancient historians record boats on it, and the Crusaders in Kerak made quite a good thing out of the navigation dues they levied on Dead Sea shipping. Although so barren, it must be very beautiful with its green waters, its rock rampart of brightly coloured sandstone, and the occasional canyons debouching from the eastern plateau.

But though biologically barren, it is chemically fruitful. The most significant fact about it is not just its excessive saltiness, but the unusual elements that make up that saltiness. It is estimated to contain 2000 million tons of potash and hundreds of millions of tons of bromine, besides astronomical quantities of magnesium.

29. *The stuccoed gateway of an 8th-century Arab château from the desert outside Palmyra*

If we extend our view to take in the Jordan river, the region offers immense resources in the way of hydro-electric power, as well as of irrigation and of semi-tropical agriculture. The Lowdermilk Plan for the Jordan valley has blue-printed the possibilities of the rift. However, to realize these possibilities it would be necessary to treat the rift not as a frontier and a barrier, but as an area of co-operation between Israel and Jordan. Without this, the chemical and physical resources of the Jordan basin will never be adequately exploited. But if once this limited co-operation could be assured, the advantages of more general economic co-operation between these two largely complementary countries would become increasingly obvious.

Alas, there is little visible sign that common sense and economic advantage are prevailing over political suspicion and ideological hostility. The outside observer can only point out how the facts of geography emphasize the benefits of co-operation, and hope that they will eventually dictate constructive action.

---

30. The glorious colonnade of the Great Mosque's courtyard at Damascus

8

DAMASCUS, PORT OF THE DESERT

THE AEROPLANE REVEALS THE cardinal fact that Damascus is a port – not a sea-port but a desert port. From the air, the white city in its green oasis is seen protruding from the mountain slopes into the tawny yellow of the desert. There is no comparable desert port east of the mountains and the coastal plain. For over a thousand years it has been the point of embarkation for the pilgrim caravans to Mecca. With the fading of the overland caravan trade, desert navigation from Damascus diminished, but now, with cars and jeeps and six-wheeled desert buses on the land and planes in the air, it is increasing in importance again.

Another cardinal fact is that Damascus is the oldest continuously inhabited large city in the world. It was a city a thousand years before the time of Abraham, and it has never lapsed into ruin or been reduced to small town or village status. By reason of this continuity of habitation, we are never likely to learn much of its origin and pre-history : they cannot be unearthed while the city's life still throbs above them.

The motor road from Beirut to Damascus takes you down the eastern slope of Anti-Lebanon through the savage and winding gorge of the Barada, whose waters make the existence of Damascus possible. 'Just the place for brigands', remarked one of our party in November. Afterwards, we discovered that earlier in the year the Syrian Finance Minister had been held up by brigands in a very similar situation : apparently they thought he carried the country's finances about with him. The armed guard wisely handed over his revolver, so there was no bloodshed, nor any loss to the treasury.

Either on this route, or perhaps more likely on that from Caesarea across the shoulders of Mount Hermon, St Paul had the vision that brought about his conversion. Breughel has painted this fateful occurrence in one of his most imaginative works; and Edward Lear, with less genius but still with considerable power, has depicted the wild landscape in which it took place.

★

On my first visit in April, I was invited to an open-air lunch the President was giving in the Ghuta. The Ghuta or Garden of Damascus is not a garden in our sense, but a great cultivated oasis – miles of brilliant green fields market gardens, orchards, threaded with water in the irrigation channels. It is as rich an expanse of greenery as one can hope to see, and richer by contrast with the empty desert sands against which it abruptly ends.

Under tall trees, with a meadow and a clear stream beyond, was spread a prodigious length of trestle-tables piled with food. The President was there, in Arab dress – an outsize man towering over most of his compatriots, with oblong face and powerful frame. He was receiving his guests – government officials and business men from the city, and many simple landowners and sheikhs from far and near, a patriarchal assembly. I shall long cherish the scene after the meal – a conjurer in ordinary European morning dress; the bearded Arabs in their traditional clothes, the more rustical among them as openly delighted as children with his time-worn tricks; the big President amiably surveying his subjects.

Large official meals are the rule in Syria. In December, when the Syrian Government invited a number of people from the Unesco Conference to Damascus, the stand-up lunch in the Orient Palace Hotel was heaped in almost incredible profusion on the table – mutton and rice, big shrimps, patties, cakes, and something I have seen nowhere else – 'antelopes' horns' made of pistachios. Unfortunately, punctuality is not the rule: we were kept waiting for what seemed an age before the President arrived. By the time the guests had done, there was no time for the chauffeurs to finish up the ample remains, and the poor fellows had to drive hungry back over the two great ranges to Beirut.

In April, I paid my official respects to the Minister of Education. He was a poet, and a very nice man. But life in his office seemed to flow in rather a muddled way: while I was there he was rarely involved in less than two conversations simultaneously.

Some sort of national celebration was in progress that day; lorry-loads of singing Arabs from remote regions were parading the streets. During my visit to the Minister a decorated float drew up at the door, bearing a big model of a school, a bevy of little girls in white, and chubby little boys dressed as soldiers, with helmets, blue tunics and red trousers. We trooped out, Minister and all, to receive their greetings.

Later, one of the little boys in uniform was making an impassioned speech on the steps of our hotel, loudly applauded as he slashed away with a toy sword – doubtless killing imaginary Jews.

Since 1948, Syria has initiated a sweeping educational programme. Twenty per cent of national revenue is now to be devoted to education, to be raised to twenty-five per cent if possible. Everybody to whom a school diploma was issued during the last ten years must help in the campaign against illiteracy and popular ignorance: in particular all entrants into the civil service, including postmasters and customs officials, must devote three months to teaching. It will be interesting to see what results this unusual method of filling the teaching gap will achieve.

★

Damascus has souks as fine as any city. The largest is the 'Long Market', over a quarter of a mile in length, high and vaulted, with occasional sunrays striking down into its dim coolness. Families of hill people in their bright clothes were wandering through the place enjoying the sights of the great city.

The Long Market emerges into an open street, flanked by a well-preserved Roman arcade. The booths here sell cheap coloured prints of a cheerful crudity, depicting Moslem heroes and legends, or sacred history, or quite modern events; also beautiful brocades with gold or silver thread, copied from ancient Persian and Syrian ones originally made on hand-looms. In the crowded street, men in all kinds of costumes gesticulate and discuss business deals. The sight of this variegated crowd in an Arab market against a Roman background remains in my mind as typical of Damascus.

★

The Museum is excellent. Admirably organized by the French, it is being developed in an enlightened spirit under Syrian direction, to provide windows on to the country's varied cultural past.

---

31. The Arab castle at Palmyra, through the Triumphal Arch of the great colonnade

The most striking single exhibit is the group of subterranean family tombs transported bodily from Palmyra and rebuilt in the basement of the Museum. The visitor descends a steep flight of steps to the original entrance – a stone door with imitation stone knocker, turning on stone pivots – and finds himself surrounded by life-like portrait heads and full-size effigies of men and women of that strange civilization.

Another unique exhibit is the reconstruction of the Jewish synagogue from Dura Europos, that Palmyran outpost on the Euphrates. In this area, in the first centuries of our era, there flourished one of the hybrid civilizations of the Middle Eastern melting-pot, containing Greco-Roman, Anatolian, Parthian, Jewish, and Early Christian elements. Dura Europos was the Pompeii of this culture; but its beautifully preserved remains have only come to light during the past 30 years.*

The Jewish synagogue and its wall-paintings were preserved by a strange accident of fortune. Soon after it was built and decorated, around A.D. 245, the defences of the city had to be strengthened against the Sassanians to the east; and it was filled in and covered by an earth embankment designed to strengthen and heighten the city wall. When the city fell in A.D. 257, the embankment remained undisturbed. For close on seventeen centuries it kept the synagogues' walls from crumbling and their paintings from decay.

The entire interior of the synagogue was covered with frescoes. Only in the 1st century A.D. did the more liberal rabbis try to escape from the rigid interpretation of the injunction in Exodus, against making the likeness of anything, especially anything animated. They took the line that the injunction was really against the worship of any such likeness or idol; and that the representation of scenes from sacred history in the synagogue was not only legitimate, but a valuable adjunct to worship, giving a visual reinforcement to the rabbi's words.

By good fortune, the congregation at Dura adopted this liberal view, and these unique frescoes are the result. The earliest paintings, on the Torah shrine, are a compromise – the figures are all in back view, with mere black blobs for heads; but the later series are frankly representational. Each series seems to have been the gift of some rich member of the congregation.

* See Rostovtzeff's *Dura Europos and its Art* (1938).

---

32. A mosaic townscape in the Great Mosque at Damascus

Some of the prophets are very fine; and the general effect is impressive, though most of the work is just pleasant and rather naïve pictorial story-telling. The restoration and reconstruction in the Museum have been wonderfully executed: the spectator feels himself inside Jewish history, which is doubtless the impression that the painters intended.

Then there is an interesting 3rd-century fresco of a Christian wedding. To my western eyes, it had a slightly Indian flavour about it – I suppose part of the general oriental component of the mixed Dura Europos culture.

Among the Hellenistic and Roman objects I recall a delicious terra-cotta Venus rising from the sea, with robe fanned out to form a sort of niche for her graceful nude body: a Roman bronze in arrogantly bad taste, with real gold necklace and bracelets: a unique silver portrait mask set in a ceremonial helmet; and a Roman lamp in the shape of an elephant, filled with oil through the trunk. And there are some queer Moslem animals that I noted as 'surrealist and Max Ernst-ish'.

Round one of the entrances of the Museum, work was busily proceeding on the reconstruction of the white gateway and gate-towers of the desert château of El Heir. This was a revelation to me: I had no idea that Islam had produced anything like these desert palaces. This particular château was built south-west of Palmyra in A.D. 727 by the last great Ommayad Caliph, Hisham. The gateway is impressive in its combination of strength and lightness; the upper parts of the towers are surprisingly decorated in stucco, with a combination of Sassanian, Byzantine and purely Syrian motives. The Ommayads and their chief nobles, in the close of the 7th and the first third of the 8th century, built themselves a number of these fortified country residences in the desert, where they could avoid the heat and hustle of the city, hunt with cheetah and falcon, and enjoy themselves away from censorious orthodoxy.

The Ommayads were not averse to wine, and were great patrons of the arts, including music, poetry and the dance as well as the visual arts and architecture. It was not until the Abbasids had gained power in 750 that the representation of animate objects, especially the human form, was definitely banned. The Museum at Damascus has many beautiful examples of animate representation, including female figures. One of the desert châteaux boasted extraordinary mural paintings, representing nude dancers as well as the Muses of Philosophy and Poetry.*

---

* Fedden devotes a brilliant chapter of his *Syria* to these desert châteaux: and Hitti has many interesting facts about them in his *History of Syria*.

The Museum provided an excellent introduction to the brief but glorious Ommayad period, when Damascus was the site of a splendid court and the centre of a rich artistic life, as well as the metropolis of an empire larger than Rome's ever was, extending from Spain almost to the borders of China. I was thus better prepared to appreciate the Great Mosque, for this epitomizes the Ommayad Caliphate at the height of its greatness. It is still regarded as the fourth holiest place of Islam.

The mosaics in the great court are the most remarkable single feature of the Mosque (pl. 32, opp. p. 137).* When Caliph Walid in 705 took over the Cathedral of St John from the Christians, with whom it had previously been shared, he resolved to transform it into the world's greatest and most beautiful mosque. To this end, he employed Indian and Persian decorators, and, so it is said, borrowed Greek craftsmen from the Byzantine Emperor. The mosaics certainly show Byzantine influence, though here in the holy confines of the Mosque no animal or human figure has been allowed. Many of them are landscapes and townscapes of great beauty, representing Damascus, with its crowded buildings and bridges and its river bordered with graceful trees, standing out against the golden background. The buildings, piled romantically in a curious pseudo-perspective, reminded me somewhat of the airy creations of Pompeian wall-painting. The landscapes and the more formal designs of trees reveal a rare love of nature, as well as great technical skill.

The Christian basilica was built on the site of a Roman temple dedicated to Jupiter, a temple which rivalled that of Baalbek in splendour. One tower from Roman times is still used as a minaret. Walid expended seven years' revenue on the Mosque; and the interior must originally have been stupendously rich, with its six hundred lamps suspended on golden chains from the roof, its walls covered with mosaics and murals of gold and semi-precious stones. Much of its splendour has been destroyed, by Mongols or by fire, but it is still very handsome, though to a Westerner, accustomed to churches in which the eye is led up to the altar at the east end, it suffers from a lack of orientation. The design is amphisbaenic, with two similar ends instead of a differentiated axis.

In the centre is a shrine where the head of John the Baptist is said to have rested. When I was there, two learned men were sitting in a little enclosure,

* For a fuller account, see K. A. C. Creswell, *Early Muslim Architecture*, and J. Sauvaget, *Les Monuments Historiques de Damas*.

reading enormous folios, and pigeons were happily flying about in the roomy interior.

But the great court is now the real glory of the place (pl. 30, opp. p. 133). Its mosaics I have spoken of. Its arched colonnades are very beautiful, rich yet simple, with a timeless quality that makes one forget to enquire into their date or special stylistic character. The great square minaret, crowned with a steeple a trifle reminiscent of one of Wren's London churches, introduces the element of height into the court's spacious dignity. The bareness of its central expanse is pleasantly broken by two small buildings, one of them a sacred book-store, the other a really lovely 'Treasure House', raised on pillars against thieves, and with no access except by ladder.

Every visitor to Damascus is taken to the El Azem palace. This represents the culmination of 'modern' Arabic domestic architecture, in the early part of the 18th century. It was interesting to see the painted cupboards in which bedding was stored in the daytime, and the protruding fireplaces not unlike our Gothic *cheminées*. The place is certainly very attractive, with its richly painted woodwork on walls and ceilings, its porticoed courtyard gardens with their lemon trees and fountains, and a blackcap in full song. But an Englishman could not help reflecting how much more beautiful the gardens might have been made; the style has sacrificed classical dignity to richness. It is an interesting museum piece, embodying a certain luxurious way of life that was available to a small section of the population in the 18th-century Ottoman Empire.

Near the Great Mosque is the tomb of Saladin. The simple white-domed building which contains his big stone sarcophagus, together with that of one of his companions, I found very moving. Saladin's undoubted greatness lay less in his statesmanship than in his personality. This was strong enough to unite the disrupted Moslem world against the Christians, and to ensure the final collapse of the kingdom of the Franks. It was striking enough to make him a legendary figure – the royal general who was also a saint, the fierce warrior who yet could give his Christian opponents lessons in chivalry and clemency. One of the oddities of history is the fact that, in 1898, Saladin's tomb was repaired by the generosity of Kaiser Wilhelm II.

One of the later mosques I remember for its whiteness against the lucid blue of the Syrian sky. This pattern of luminous white and blue in Islamic cities on the fringe of the desert is an aspect of visual beauty that is lacking in our moister temperate lands.

Still another mosque, of Sultan Selim, has an interior of beautiful proportions as well as a fine dome and minarets. Its big courtyard had been taken over as a temporary quarters for various departments of the new National University. In the section where pilgrims once slept was the university library, crowded with students; near by were the departments of Law and Anatomy, and, most curious of all, a series of dark medieval-looking rooms fitted up as a chemical laboratory, and full of the most chemical smells. When the University moves to its new building, the place may be taken over by the Waqf, that interesting organization which administers the innumerable and sometimes peculiar pious foundations of Islamic countries.

The Syrians are very proud of their new national (and secular) university, as opposed to the foreign (and religious) institutions in the Lebanon (p. 78). Already they have quite a number of women students, of course all unveiled – ten to twenty per cent according to faculty. In spite of efforts to encourage science, law is still much the largest faculty. The Rector told me that all instruction is given in Arabic: this, I gathered, involves some difficulty in coping with technical scientific terms. The medical school and hospital seemed flourishing. In the maternity section, they were experimenting on the psychological effect of colour: each of the private rooms was painted a different colour, and many expectant mothers booked their colour in advance.

★

At the time of my visit Syria was visibly in the throes of transition. There was a trend towards westernization of the educational and economic systems, but this was countered by a nationalism which too often spilled over into xenophobia, by a fairly strong current of Islamic orthodoxy, and by a widespread dislike of all things French which had persisted from the days of the Mandate.

These various forces are superposed on a pattern of social structure unlike anything in Europe, a pattern of different ways of life. There is in the first place the cleavage between the nomad Beduin and the rest of the nation. In addition to that there is the existence of a mosaic of minority groups, differentiated by religion or racial origin or both, which often play different functional roles. The various groups and sections have not acquired any such sense of belonging together, any such body of common ideas and purposes, as exist in any European national state.

To add to its problems, Syria as it existed at the time of my visit was an unnatural unit. It was separated from Lebanon on political grounds of considerable validity, but with serious economic results. Further, the boundary had been arbitrarily drawn to exclude some of Syria's best outlets to the sea. And Turkey has taken over Antioch and the Sanjak of Alexandretta, which provided the chief and most natural gateway to Syria from the north-west.

In Turkey, the possession of the Sanjak is sometimes rationalized by appealing to archeology – is not the area the original home of the Hittites, and are not the Hittites ancestral to the Turks? Unfortunately the answer to both questions is in the negative. But the mere fact that the argument has been put forward demonstrates that pseudo-scientific archeologism could become a dangerous political weapon, just as pseudo-scientific racialism actually did in Nazi Germany.

The major problem before Syria in 1948 was how it could transcend the artificial boundaries, economic and social as well as political, that have been imposed upon it. An apparently simple solution would have been the creation of a Greater Syria, combining Syria, Lebanon, Iraq, and Jordan into a single nation. We all know what has actually happened – Arab nationalism under the influence of Nasser's ambitions has brought into being another artificial and probably impermanent entity, the United Arab Republic, consisting of the two disjoined and dissimilar countries, Syria and Egypt. The problem of minorities still obtrudes itself: the Christians are a majority in Lebanon, and do not relish the prospect of becoming a minority in a larger state. The Maronites and Kurds and so-called Devil Worshippers (in fact, a highly moral if theologically pessimistic sect), the Druzes, Alawis and various relict Christian sects, the Armenians and Jews and other communities, still further complicate the cultural mosaic of the region.

Meanwhile, Damascus is there as a welcome reminder of the continuity of civilized life through the most violent political and religious vicissitudes, and of its essential unity in spite of extremely diverse component elements.

9

PALMYRA, THE CARAVAN EMPIRE

WHEN I WAS IN WARSAW IN the early summer of 1948, it was a delight to find, among the utter devastation of most of the city, that the attractive 18th-century palace called the Summer Bath, in some ways reminiscent of the two Trianons at Versailles, had escaped almost unscathed. By the shores of the lake, I was shown its little open-air theatre, with its rows of stone seats and its busts of the great dramatists. It is, I believe, unique in having its stage on a little island, separated from the audience by a few yards of water. The stage was furnished with a permanent set, which had been somewhat damaged in the war. I asked what was the classical scene that I discerned through the wooden scaffolding: and my guide answered 'it represents the ruins of Palmyra'.

To find Palmyra thus commemorated in Poland is a measure of the interest aroused throughout Europe by the publication of Robert Wood's great book, *The Ruins of Palmyra; otherwise Tadmor in the Desert*, republished in 1817 together with his equally remarkable account of Baalbek. As Wood remarked, these are 'perhaps the two most surprising remains of ancient magnificence which are now left to us'. Wood's detailed descriptions and architectural drawings of Palmyra, with its gigantic temple and scarcely credible colonnades of Corinthian columns, in the midst of an enormous desert, provoked a gasp of astonished admiration from the entire civilized world. And the extraordinary story of Queen Zenobia invested Palmyra with that touch of personal romance which made its appeal irresistible. There was even a time when St Petersburg was called (with singularly little justification!) the Palmyra of the North, and the French admirers of the Empress Catherine compared her to Zenobia.*

Palmyra and Petra, though so extremely different in so many ways, have in common the fact of being great caravan cities: they owed their prosperity, and indeed their very existence as cities, to the ancient trade-routes across the deserts and semi-deserts of the Middle East.

They were both legendary places. But Palmyra emerged from the mystery and semi-oblivion of legend earlier than Petra, which was not re-discovered for the world at large until the early 19th century, long after the features of Palmyra had been made familiar all over Europe. In places like Damascus and Aleppo you could hear much more about the pillared city of the sandy desert than about the rock-hewn city of the savage mountains. Accordingly, in the last decades of the 17th century, English merchants living in Aleppo had already made the journey to Palmyra; it was their reports which fired the imagination of Robert Wood.†

As Fedden records in his *Syria*, the last (1912) edition of *Baedeker* for the area 'informs travellers that the trip out and back takes nine days, and that an armed escort is necessary'. However, in the last 25 years everything has changed, and now the intending visitor to Palmyra can hire a car in Damascus, cross the desert in half a day and put up at an excellent hotel close to some of the noblest ruins. Our transportation problems were still further simplified, for the visit to Palmyra was officially organized for the Unesco Conference by the Lebanese and Syrian Governments, and we flew. We left Beirut aerodrome after an early breakfast, and were back by sunset.

In an hour we had climbed out of the rich coastal strip, with its oranges

---

* There is an excellent illustrated guide to Palmyra by Starcky and Munajjed, published by the Antiquities Service at Damascus, and good accounts in Fedden's *Syria* and Hitti's *History of Syria*, beside superb photographs by Hoyningen-Huene in D. M. Robinson's *Baalbek; Palmyra*.

† There are some (not very inspiring) engravings of Palmyra in Halifax's account of this journey (Phil. Trans. Roy. Soc., vol. 19), and a big picture dated 1693, by Hofsted van Essen, who was one of the party, in the University of Amsterdam; also a drawing now at Upsala, made in 1710 by Cornelius Loos, the architect sent out by Charles XII of Sweden during his refuge in Turkey, to draw ancient monuments in the Middle East. Loos's drawings were not adequately published at the time, and Wood seems not to have known of them: they are described, and some reproduced, by E. Wrangel (Karol. Förb. Aarsbok, 1931).

and grapes and its memories of great forests on the westward slope of the Mountain, passed out of sight of the smiling sea, traversed the still fertile plain of the Bekaa in the Great Rift, and crossed over Anti-Lebanon to find ourselves in the great Arabian desert, with its mantle of arid sands, from which emerged the unclothed ribs of bare low mountains and projecting scarps.

Suddenly, in the midst of this inhuman landscape, which yet was not without its tawny beauty, a series of tower-like structures appeared. They stood in a narrow valley between two ridges, with a track along its centre following the course of the ancient main caravan road from the west. Then, almost before we had grasped that these were the famous tower-tombs of rich Palmyrene families from the dead ancient world, we banked to find ourselves looking right down into the harsh but impressive Turkish castle; this was built about 350 years ago to dominate the oasis, which still had its strategic importance even if the great city had shrunk to a wretched Arab village. And there beyond it was Palmyra itself, once white, now transformed by time to a delicate rosy fawn, with its far-stretching colonnades and its huge main temple.

Robert Wood thus describes his first impressions of the place after passing through the Valley of the Tombs: 'We had scarce passed these venerable monuments, when the hills opening discovered to us, all at once, the greatest quantity of ruins we had ever seen, and beyond them, towards the Euphrates, a flat waste, as far as the eye could reach, without any object which showed either life or motion. It is scarce possible to imagine anything more striking than this view: so great a number of Corinthian pillars, mixed with so little wall or solid building, afforded a most romantic variety of prospect.'

Palmyra arouses the same feelings today, even if we express them in rather different language. The abundance of what is still intact and standing makes an immediate visual appeal that is lacking even in the most interesting fallen ruins or the most complete excavations; the imagination is violently struck by the contrast of the richness of the dead city with the surrounding waste of desert; and the apricot colour of the stone blends with tawny desert sands and clear blue desert sky into a luminous unity of beauty.

The most famous feature of Palmyra is the great colonnade, about twelve yards wide, traversing the city from north-west to north-east, with nearly 150 of its original 375 or more superb Corinthian columns still standing (pl. 33, opp. p. 152). Such colonnaded avenues were general in Greco-Roman Syria. I have written of the one at Jerash; and I remember Sir Leonard

Woolley once saying that T. E. Lawrence had personally discovered traces of over 120 colonnaded towns within a 20-mile radius of Aleppo. But Palmyra's colonnade certainly takes pride of place today. The avenue has not the true Roman straightness, but, after a slight kink marked by a quadruple arch or tetrapylon, makes a sharp bend south towards the great temple. This second deviation was doubtless determined by religious reasons, since the temple was the most important place of the city, and its site must have been sacred from the earliest days when Palmyra was 'Tadmor in the Wilderness': as Rostovtzeff writes, 'the caravan road obeyed the dictates of the deity.' The short stretch from the bend to the temple seems to have served as a Via Sacra: on one side of the sacred way was a sort of stand or exedra, from which the people could watch the religious processions and the caravans at their leisure. On the day of our visit, the only sign of life was a raven perched on one of the columns.

The existence of the sharp bend at the origin of the Sacred Way led to the construction, about A.D. 200, of a remarkable piece of architecture, the so-called Triumphal Arch (pl. 31, opp. p. 136). This consists of a great central arch, flanked and buttressed by two smaller sets of arches; however, its two sides are not parallel, but diverge somewhat to the north. The structure could thus present its two faces almost squarely to the two branches of the colonnade, so as to give the impression of a triumphal structure closing the straight vistas, while yet effectively masking the kink in the city's main thoroughfare, a deviation which must have offended the Palmyrenes' Romanized taste.

A subsidiary road passed through the tetrapylon, more or less at right angles to the main colonnade. The arrangement is clearly an attempt to impose the Roman symmetry, of main axial road or *decumanus* and secondary axis or *cardo*, on an alien and asymmetrical arrangement.

Many of the columns have brackets or consoles projecting from them. These detract somewhat from their beauty, and must have done so still more when they carried their original burden of statues. The statues commemorated benefactors of the city – sometimes military men, but for the most part rich bankers or caravan merchants. They might be commemorated for their services in some official position, or for having organized a successful caravan, or merely for having paid for one of the pillars. One man might have more than one statue; a certain Marcus Ulpius Yarkai (note the combination of Roman with Semitic names), who was one of the most important caravan entrepreneurs about A.D. 160, had ten.

When that extraordinary character, Lady Hester Stanhope, rode (in Beduin attire) to Palmyra in 1813, in defiance of all advice, the desert chieftains gave her a wonderful welcome. The brackets of the pillars were all occupied by Arab dancing-girls; and the most beautiful of all was let down on a rope from the Triumphal Arch to place a crown on Lady Hester's head, while the crowds of welcoming Beduins, including Arab dancers and musicians, shouted applause. The Freedom of the Desert was then formally conferred on her. What a film the scene would have made! Accompanied by her 'much-tired' companion, Mrs Fry (also in Beduin costume), she proceeded to pitch camp in the Temple of Bel for a week.

Just south of the tetrapylon are two sadly ruined constructions, the Agora or main public square, and the great Caravanserai. Next to them is a building in the form of an open-air theatre. Rostovtzeff thinks that, although plays may sometimes have been given in it, its primary purpose was to serve as the centre of the town's civic life, for discussion, for the voting of honours, and as place of official assembly for civic and semi-religious ceremonies.

To the north of the colonnade lay the chief residential area of the city. Some of the private houses here must have been veritable *palazzi*, with splendid rooms and fine colonnades round their central courtyards. Rostovtzeff describes two which were recently excavated as 'even finer and more elaborately ornamented than those of the rich merchants of Delos', which were famous for their magnificence. As with most things in this strange city, many influences were blended in them – Greco-Roman pillars, a ground-plan derived from Mesopotamia, Parthian luxury in the furniture, north-Syrian influences in the sculpture.

There is an impressive jumble of great blocks at the west end of the colonnade. However, it is not the fallen ruins that make Palmyra so memorable, but those that still stand. Among these, the great temple of Bel is the most imposing. It stands in a great courtyard, over 200 yards square, the whole raised on a masonry base, and originally approached by a splendid staircase leading up from the end of the Sacred Way to a formal Propylaea (converted in the 12th century into a military strongpoint by the Arabs). The courtyard was surrounded by covered porticoes, many of whose pillars still survive. Their outer walls are pierced by handsome windows, through which one gets glimpses of the ancient city, the modern village and oasis, and the distant spaces of the desert. In the court are the remains of a sacrificial altar and a lustral basin.

For centuries, Palmyra survived only as a poor Arab village which had taken refuge inside the great court – a site from which the villagers were only dislodged in 1929 by the French *Service des Antiquités*.

The temple proper, or cella, is very strange. It is long and narrow, and not quite symmetrically placed within the court. Its entrance-gateway, of Roman magnificence in size and proportions, is carved with oriental richness. It was surrounded by a peristyle of enormously high slender columns, a row of which still stands. They were originally surmounted with false capitals, Corinthian in style, made of gilded bronze moulded on to a stone core; but the Arabs long ago stripped off the bronze, leaving only the core to reveal the architectural falsehood that had been practised. Their entablature is surmounted by triangular step-battlements, reminiscent of some of the rock-tombs at Petra. If the gilt and bronze of the false capitals gave a touch of oriental luxury to the Greco-Roman style of the building, the battlements added something strangely Semitic.

Yet with all these exotic influences, the peristyle and gateway are clearly something classical and Greco-Roman, while the cella itself is most definitely oriental. Rostovtzeff thinks that it, or a predecessor of the same size and orientation, originally stood in a small Babylonian temple-court, but that when the temple was enlarged to live up to Palmyra's new prosperity, the cella emerged 'from the narrowness and darkness of the courtyard of the Babylonian temple into the brilliant sunlight of Greek temple-architecture, and was surrounded, to its great surprise, by Greek columns'.

Fedden, on the other hand, sees the entire temple as a growth from the primitive Phoenician sanctuaries of the coast, like that at Amrit (p. 159). Presumably, Phoenician as well as Babylonian and Greco-Roman influences were at work at Palmyra. As a curiosity of history, it should be mentioned that the temple was consecrated to Christian use in the 5th and 6th centuries, and in the 12th was converted into a mosque: in this capacity it functioned until 1929, when it became an historical monument.

Wandering round, I came across a paved ramp leading up to the interior of the courtyard through an aperture in the foundations of the great wall. This, it seems, was the access for the animal victims to be sacrificed to Bel and the other gods worshipped in the temple – sheep, oxen, and even camels (but no pigs). The crowd watched the sacrifices and ceremonies from the courtyard: the cella was not for the *profanum vulgus*, but only for the priests of the gods whose habitation it was.

The tombs remain as the final astonishment of Palmyra. In the Damascus Museum, as I have already mentioned, there is a reconstruction of one of the underground mausoleums, a veritable house for the dead. It contains an elaborate system of rooms and passages, here with a niche for offerings, there with rows of funerary busts looking down upon their 20th-century visitors. In my diary at the time I wrote, 'the portrait heads of the dead are very varied, some of the men looking like Gauls with moustaches, others bearded, others clean-shaven; the women very richly dressed, one looking as if at a first night at the Opera. The most important figures are of reclining priests, large and well-liking.' One relief showed a whole array of sculptured people apparently at a funeral banquet, all in flowing robes, and some of the men with the strange sub-cylindrical headgear, like an enlarged and more elaborate fez, which was worn by the Palmyrene priesthood. It was my induction into a new compound civilization, of which my classical education had carefully kept me in ignorance.*

More surprises await the visitor to the tombs in Palmyra itself. As in many other ancient civilizations, the city of the dead was quite separate from the city of the living. At Palmyra, instead of a single necropolis matching the living city on a corresponding site, as in some Etruscan towns, there were three separate ones, of which I have already mentioned the most spectacular.

The multiple nature of Palmyra's culture is again revealed by the existence of three totally distinct types of tombs. One was the temple-tomb, of which the finest specimen closes the west end of the great colonnade – a pillared and pedimented façade, within which was a one-storey tomb, in the form of a temple cella, originally full of paintings and sculptured reliefs.

Then there were the subterranean mausoleums. These are nothing much to look at above-ground, but, as I have already described, they may contain veritable underground palaces, with halls and passages, niches and arched rooms, and a population of stone personages. One was cut out of solid rock to resemble a Hellenistic house, with a central colonnaded peristyle; around this were found 38 fine sarcophagi in rock-cut compartments. Another had a hall nearly 45 feet long, out of which opened two rooms or exedrae, with innumerable busts and sculptures, representing the rank and fashion of early

---

* Malraux, in his *Psychologie de l'Art* (*La Création Artistique*, pp. 17 f.) gives some fine photographs showing the variety and occasional outstanding quality of Palmyrene funerary art, together with an interesting if not wholly convincing discussion of artistic trends during the decline of the Roman Empire.

2nd-century Palmyra – 'a party in a parlour, all silent . . .' Some good examples of painting have survived. One of the most curious was the legend of Achilles revealing himself among the maidens of Scyros; this was used as a symbol of the human soul, here on earth in borrowed raiment, but about to enter a truer and more glorious life!

There must also have been plenty of paintings in the temples and private houses, but in Palmyra these have perished. In Dura Europos, however, many frescoes have been discovered, which give us an idea of what has disappeared in Palmyra. One of these, figured by Rostovtzeff, is a fine work of art, showing tall priests conducting a sacrifice: their ritual vestments, of white robes and conical white hats, give an impressive Magian effect.

The last and most extraordinary type of sepulchre at Palmyra is the tower-tomb, of which there are over 150. These commanding structures, austere yet elegant, may reach 70 feet and four storeys in height, each storey containing mortuary niches or sarcophagi. There may be handsome window-niches halfway up the outer face, sometimes representing the end of a sarcophagus under an arch, which add greatly to the architectural effect. The flat tops seem to have been used as lookout posts.

These strange structures are found in various parts of the Middle Euphrates region, but in full development only at Palmyra. They may owe something to the several-storeyed 'tower-houses' of Persia, and something to influence from Babylon and Egypt. In any case, they must have evolved from tombs in the form of little one-storey houses, which also exist at Palmyra. The intermediate step seems to have been the erection of a steep pyramid of masonry on the top of the tomb, a fashion of which examples can still be seen on the Phoenician coast, as at that strange place Amrit.

Once the scene of formal banquets and family gatherings, their solitude today is broken only by the curiosity of tourists or by the passage of a Beduin shepherd and his flock (pl. 34, opp. p. 153).

There are many other interesting ruins, but I must be content with a bare mention. The god Bel-Shamin, 'the Lord of Heaven', was one of the great rivals of Bel, 'the Lord'; he seems to have been a Phoenician product, while Bel originated in Babylon. His temple is the best-preserved of all the buildings in Palmyra, and, though small, is exceedingly beautiful – 'massive, monumental and richly ornamented', as David Robinson says. It is difficult to visualize this grandly pagan structure converted to use as a Christian church, as it was for a century or so.

Then there are the remains of the military camp built under Diocletian in the late 3rd century; and the great wall and aqueduct built by Justinian in the early 6th – a bulwark of Christianity which proved of no avail a century later against the surge and expansion of Islam; and the wall built under the Ommayads, enclosing a much smaller area; and the sulphur springs that have made Tadmor an oasis from time immemorial (as we passed, Beduin women were washing clothes in their warm, slightly mephitic waters).

Sooner or later, the traveller begins to ask himself what sort of a life the Palmyrene led, and how Palmyra fits into the course of history. Luckily, there are various works in which he can satisfy his curiosity, notably Rostovtzeff's *Caravan Cities.*

Palmyra's greatness was of brief duration. It was already a not unimportant caravan and trade centre during the 1st century B.C.; rose rapidly to riches and power during the next hundred years; became even more rich and powerful up to the time of Zenobia; but, after her defeat in A.D. 272, entered on its irrevocable decline.

In its heyday, with a population of probably over 30,000, it was the most important of all caravan cities – a commercial centre, the hub of a far-flung trading system, a great banking headquarters, and for a time the financial capital of the eastern half of the ancient world. As outposts, it set up commercial agencies – *fondouqs* or trade-counters, something like the offices of 'John Company' in India, or the business establishments of various European countries in modern Shanghai: they comprised warehouses and offices, and of course the private residences of the Palmyrene merchants and clerks, and sometimes their own temples. They seem to have been thoroughly integrated into the general politico-economic system of the Palmyrene state. They operated under 'presidents', who were important personages, ranking with the 'chairmen' (archempori) of the metropolitan commercial companies, and with the synodiarchs or commanders of the caravans.

The main agencies were established to the east, between Babylon and the mouth of the Tigris; but Palmyra also had outposts in Egypt, on the Danube, in Spain, and even in Gaul. There was a large Palmyrene colony in Pozzuoli and one in Rome itself, with temples dedicated to the gods of the desert city over 1500 miles away. Juvenal complained that the Roman way of life was being corrupted by the Orontes flowing into the Tiber. If he had lived in the 2nd century he might have lamented the invasion of Rome's fertile land by the sands of the Syrian desert.

The Palmyrenes got around the world not only as traders and financiers but also as soldiers. The Romans used Palmyrenes extensively in their armies: there are records of Palmyrene soldiers serving as far away as the Roman Wall in Northumberland. Palmyrene mounted archers were famous. The caravans were protected by a body of these, doubtless very similar to the famous light cavalry of the Parthians, who delivered their 'Parthian shots' from horseback as they turned to gallop away. Other members of the armed escort were probably mounted on camels: we know definitely that the Romans organized a regular Camel Corps, of what the French call Méharistes, in these desert regions.

The Palmyrenes do not seem, however, to have gone in for heavy cavalry, such as the Roman *cataphractarii*, which were developed as a counter-measure to the extraordinary *clibanarii* of the Persian armies. A sketch on the walls of a billet in Dura Europos, doubtless drawn by a soldier of the Roman garrison, shows a mounted Persian knight, both rider and horse protected by chain-mail, who looks as if he had stepped out of the Bayeux tapestry on to the banks of the Euphrates.

Politically, this rich city of the desert was organized on a Semitic clan system, but with a few clans monopolizing almost all power and high office. During the second century, political life became largely Romanized, many prominent men became Roman citizens, and added Roman family names, like Ulpius or Aelius, to their Semitic patronymics. But there were many other influences besides Semitic and Roman. All educated men were bi-lingual, but in Aramaean and Greek, not in Aramaean and Latin, though Latin was of course widely understood. For writing Aramaean, they used a special Palmyrene alphabet of their own. Their intellectual life was essentially Greek. Their houses were developments of the old Babylonian pattern, but their furniture, dress and weapons, their jewellery, ornaments and household utensils, were overwhelmingly Parthian in type. Their architecture I have discussed. Their art was woven out of many strands. In many superficial ways it is Greco-Roman, while the preoccupation with detail and pictorial subjects is 'oriental'; some of this oriental element doubtless comes from Persia, but there was also an important late Hittite influence, from Anatolia and Northern Syria.

The long-continued intermingling of cultures in this region is illustrated

33. The great colonnade at Palmyra

by the story of Crassus's head being used as a stage 'prop' by his Parthian conquerors in a performance of the *Bacchae* of Euripides.

Their religion was amazingly syncretic. At its core were the great gods from Babylon. Then there were Semitic Arab gods, like Dushares from Petra; Phoenician gods like Astarte; North-Syrian gods, perhaps originally derived from Anatolia; Parthian (Iranian) gods, though disguised under a Babylonian veneer. Appropriately enough, two of the divinities, Arsu and Azizu, were caravan gods, and are often shown riding or even leading a camel. It seems that, although there was a professional priesthood, prominent citizens could sometimes function as priests on certain religious occasions. Inscribed clay tesserae served as admission tickets for religious ceremonies. The most sought-after were presumably those for the elaborate feasts in honour of the dead, celebrated inside the great tombs and mausoleums.

There remains the question: why was Palmyra so important, but important only for so short a time?

In a world where trade depended so much on overland caravans, the oasis of Tadmor, the future Palmyra, was predestined to some importance by its position. Mesopotamia was the main collecting and distributing centre for the goods of the Orient, while the Phoenician coast performed the same function for the Mediterranean West. Between these key regions three main caravan routes were possible. There was the northern route, cutting east from near Antioch through Aleppo to reach the Euphrates at its great bend (or, as a variant, ranging still further northwards through Apamaea and Edessa to follow down the Tigris); there was the middle route through Emesa (Homs) or Damascus, and then via Palmyra across the desert to Dura Europos and down the Euphrates; and there was the route between Egypt and the south end of the coastal strip, through Petra to the lower Euphrates or Tigris at Babylon or Seleucia (see map, pp. 10–11).

The northern route had the advantage of avoiding the desert; but it was by far the longest. The southern route was the most direct; but it traversed a wide and difficult expanse of desert. The middle route struck across the narrowing north end of the desert where it is only some 250 miles wide: and the oasis of Palmyra cuts this desert journey in half.

Presumably the Palmyra route began to be regularly utilized not long after 2000 B.C. We know that, at the beginning of the first millennium, Solomon

34. The enduring pastoral life: an Arab shepherd and his flock at Palmyra, with an ancient tower-tomb in the background

fortified 'Tadmor in the Wilderness'; quite possibly it was he who first had the sagacity to see the full value of this route, and to organize it for the benefit of his kingdom.

However, the main caravan centres in the region were still the towns on the western fringe of the desert – Damascus, Homs and Hama. They would certainly not have encouraged the growth of Palmyra as anything more than a halting-place, and doubtless retained for themselves the profitable activities of buying and selling, outfitting and financing, as long as possible.

This state of affairs continued through the earlier Hellenistic period, when the rival Seleucids and Ptolemies came to a working arrangement over the valuable caravan trade. The Seleucids concentrated on the routes from Antioch to Mesopotamia, where they founded the great city of Seleucia-on-Tigris, and thence across the Iranian plateau. The Ptolemies took the routes that passed from Western Arabia, northward along either side of the Phoenician coast range, and westward to the mouth of the Nile, thus promoting the rapid growth of Alexandria.

The *tertius gaudens* from this state of affairs was the Nabataean caravan kingdom of Petra, which was able to begin its spectacular rise to power by taking advantage of the increasing weakness of the two great powers to north and south of it.

One by-product of this deserves mention. The Ptolemies, in reaction against the dominance of Petra in their area, began attempts at more direct maritime trade with India and the East. It was in pursuing this trade that, two centuries later, Hipparchus discovered the monsoons, which made the direct voyage across the Indian Ocean a matter of routine. Thus the first awareness of this basic fact of world geography was one of the results of the over-ambitious expansion of Petra, and helped to bring about its decay.

During the 2nd century B.C., the weakness of the Seleucid empire allowed several little independent states, greedy and quarrelsome, to spring up in northern Syria, so that the northern caravan route became more difficult and even unsafe. As a result more traffic took the middle route by way of Palmyra. And Rostovtzeff thinks that this tendency may have been deliberately fostered by the authorities at Petra. Petra was extending its power ever further northward, to include first Bosra and eventually Damascus itself: by taking Palmyra under its wing, the Nabataean kingdom would control its own caravan route all the way from Akaba to Dura on the Euphrates.

Palmyra thus began to grow. But its phase of real wealth and importance came later, and was the outcome of a stalemate between the two new great powers that emerged to dominate the middle-eastern scene -- Parthia and Rome. During late Hellenistic times the power and the ambitions of the Parthians had been steadily growing in the east, while Rome had been extending its conquests from the west, eventually incorporating Petra and its dominions as a Roman province. The two powers thus faced each other across a strip of desert. Parthia was never able to push Rome back to the Mediterranean coast; Rome never succeeded in crushing Parthia.

It was Augustus who first realized the futility of constant war on this frontier. As Rostovtzeff writes, his diplomacy 'enabled Palmyra to become a neutral semi-independent town, wherein the goods of these two officially hostile powers, Parthia and Rome, might be exchanged'. A century later, after Trajan's expensive military interludes, Hadrian renewed Augustus's pacific policy. From his time onwards, the two empires agreed tacitly to live in peace, both profiting by the trade which flowed across the desert through Palmyra.

For this peaceful policy to succeed, Palmyra could not be formally annexed to Rome. It was allowed to develop in nominal independence as a go-between state, although Roman influence and Roman technical skill helped greatly to increase the efficiency and safety of its caravan route.

The 3rd century was one of anarchy and trouble for imperial Rome: it also saw the supersession of the Parthian empire by the more bellicose Sassanians, who twice in twenty years invaded and devastated Syria, the second time reaching Antioch and the sea.

Palmyra took the opportunity provided by the weakness of its Roman protector to build up its own power and independence. However, in the conflict between Rome and Persia, it decided to take the side of Rome, largely no doubt because Rome was distant and the aggressive Persians close at hand. One particular Palmyra clan or family had become virtually all-powerful, and in 238, the head of this family, Septimius Odenathus, had taken the oriental title 'King of Kings', while at the same time he was glorified by the Romans with the title of *Imperator*.

In A.D. 260, Valerian, in revenge for the Sassanian invasions, invaded their empire in his turn. But after crossing the Euphrates, he was defeated, captured, flayed, and his skin stuffed with straw was hung up as a trophy in a Sassanian temple.

Odenathus took the field against the Persians and gave them a sound beating. In return for this, he was declared *Augustus* by the Roman Senate, and treated as co-partner and colleague of the Emperor. And then, in 266, he was murdered. His murder provided the opportunity for Palmyra's final self-defeating burst of rocketing glory, under the legendary Zenobia.

Just as I find it difficult to say Boudicca instead of Boadicea, I shall persist in calling this extraordinary woman Zenobia, although this is but a latinized version of Zainab, which in its turn is the Arabic version of her real name, Bat Zabdai.

Zenobia was Odenathus's widow, and ruled as regent for her son Vaballath. The noted pagan philosopher Longinus, author of the *Treatise on the Sublime* (until quite recently a set book at Oxford), was her Prime Minister, but she took great interest in Christian theology, and earned from the Jews the title of Protectress of Rabbis.

Zenobia was handsome and attractive, capable of great physical endurance, intelligent, and with varied intellectual interests. She personally led the Palmyrene army to conquer Egypt, and in four years extended her dominions from the Nile to the plateaux of Asia Minor. Petra had grown into a caravan kingdom; Palmyra now became, for a few brief years, a caravan empire.

But Zenobia was ambitious; and her ambition caused her downfall, and that of Palmyra with her. Her successes inevitably alarmed Rome: a powerful and truly independent Palmyra would be almost as bad as a powerful and expansionist Persia. Zenobia finally confirmed Rome's fears by her foolish gesture of issuing coins on which her head appeared alone, instead of in company with the emperor's; and Aurelian marched against her.

The rest is familiar – Aurelian's victory in the field; his siege of Palmyra; his offer of generous terms of surrender; Zenobia's deliberately insolent rejection of them; her eleventh-hour capture by the Romans as she jumped into the boat that would have taken her to safety across the Euphrates; her appearance in Aurelian's triumph at Rome, bound with golden chains, walking on foot in front of her own gorgeous chariot. After that, we have the choice of believing that she died broken-hearted in a hunger-strike, or (more probably) lived on for years in a villa near Tivoli.

There is one black mark against her character. After her capture, she put all the blame for her policy on others, in particular assigning to Longinus the responsibility for the insolent reply which had so infuriated Aurelian. Partly as a result of this, Longinus and many others were executed by the Romans.

The description of Aurelian's triumph gives some idea of the fantastic pitch to which the craving for spectacle had pushed such celebrations in 3rd-century Rome. Aurelian's chariot could not be drawn by anything so ordinary as horses, so stags were trained instead. Twenty elephants and nearly a thousand gladiators marched in the procession, accompanied by tigers and some 200 other wild animals, to assure the populace that they would soon have something worth seeing in the amphitheatre.

The defeat of Zenobia is usually considered to mark the beginning of Palmyra's downfall. However, that downfall had been prepared half a century earlier, by the Sassanian conquest of the little independent kingdom at the mouths of the Twin Rivers of Mesopotamia, which had harboured the main trading posts of the Palmyrenes. After this, so long as Palmyra was allied with Rome, and Rome was at war with the Sassanians, one of the main sources of Palmyra's wealth was cut off. Only by imperialist expansion north and south, while living largely on its reserves, could it hope to gain new sources of wealth and power – and this expansion inevitably incurred the hostility of Rome.

After Zenobia, Palmyra ceased to play any major political, financial, or commercial role. It did, however, become a not unimportant garrison town and military centre for one large sector of the vast frontier zone or *limes* which Rome organized between its empire and the East – a zone criss-crossed with paved roads and irrigation works, and dotted with fortified posts, lookouts, and garrisons or colonies of soldier-farmers.

Under the Moslems, Palmyra was for centuries moderately prosperous, though of course thoroughly cut off from the western world. After about 1400 it decayed, presumably in correlation with the decay of the overland caravan trade, to become a mere Beduin village.

*

As I walked along the colonnade towards the great temple-tomb, a covey of swift sandy-grey creatures with pointed tails flew off from among the ruins – *Syrrhaptes*, the sandgrouse. After reading so much about this interesting bird, it was good to see them in the flesh. The sandgrouse, in its adaptation to aridity, has evolved an extraordinary method of supplying its young with water. The adults gather each evening to drink at the nearest oasis, maybe many miles from their nest; after satisfying their own thirst, they wet their breasts thoroughly and fly back to let their young suck the moisture from the damp feathers.

The sandgrouse also provide an avian counterpart of the pulse of human migration. As Brooks* and others have made clear, the human populations living in the semi-arid fringes of the great Asiatic deserts are particularly sensitive to climatic fluctuations. When the climate changes a little for the cooler and wetter, they thrive and multiply; but when it swings towards drought, they suffer and have to move.

The climatic fluctuations responsible for these human movements are quite irregular in their periodicity, and are measured in terms of centuries. The sandgrouse are subject to a regular and short-term cycle. Every eleven years on the average they tend to over-multiply and then migrate, spilling over into countries hundreds and even thousands of miles from their desert homes, sometimes as far as England. Every second spurt of multiplication tends to be more intense, giving a twenty-two-year cycle.

*

Among the dead beauty of the ruins, it was hard to imagine how alive the city once was. Yet here, Chinese silks and Tyrian purple, Arab frankincense and Persian rugs once made life rich and agreeable for the Greeks and Jews, the Roman soldier-administrators, the Beduins turned financiers, the Arabs and the Phoenicians and the Parthians that lived within its walls.

What did they think of the waste of sand in which their city stood? They celebrated banquets in their family tombs: did they ever picnic in the desert – did they ever hunt gazelles? They thronged the colonnade and the public places to see the caravans and the civic celebrations: did the richer citizens ever take their wives for a holiday on the coast, or to see the metropolitan spectacles of Rome?

Palmyra testifies to the power of man to triumph over his environment. And yet, as a great and wealthy city, it was unnatural. But for its convenient position between two rival imperialisms, Damascus and Seleucia-on-Tigris would have sufficed as great commercial centres for the exchange of goods between the eastern and western worlds, and Palmyra would never have become more than a convenient halting-place on the route. The Palmyrenes themselves assuredly never bothered their heads about anything of the sorts but threw themselves into the opportunities provided by the situation, to build something unique in human history, of which the memorial happily remains to be a place of pilgrimage from every country.

* C. E. P. Brooks, *Climate through the Ages,* London, 1949.

10

NORTH SYRIA AND ITS DEAD CITIES

Aᴼᵀᴱᴿ ᵀᴴᴱ ᴮᴱᴵᴿᵁᵀ ᶜᴼᴺᶠᴱᴿᴱᴺᶜᴱ
and its appendages were over, I was a free man. So we hired a car and chauffeur to explore northern Syria and the Antioch region. This chapter is a
record of those ten wintry days.

Passing the familiar landscape of Byblos and Tripoli, we drove northwards
across the Syrian frontier to Amrit, the meagre relic of a Phoenician city.
Here, on a marshy flat towards the coast stands a queer monument called in
Arabic The Tower of Snails – why, nobody knows. A squat cubic building
of enormous stone blocks, it probably served as a mausoleum.

It is strange enough, but not so strange as the two Spindles of Amrit, on
the slopes inland. The Spindles are heavy cylindrical pillars, standing side by
side on low pedestals of stone, but differing curiously in detail. One, topped
with a carved hemisphere, has four crude lions carved on its pedestal; the
other is devoid of carvings, and has a pyramidal top. Nobody seems to know
what the Spindles were for. Possibly they are late and enlarged versions of the
sacred stones inhabited by Semitic deities. They are unlike anything else I have
ever seen or read of, and make a mysterious and slightly sinister impression.

The Amrit temple arouses no sinister feelings. It is a rectangular space cut
back into the low hill above a stream. Thus three of its sides were once live
rock, while the fourth side was enclosed by a wall with an entrance gateway.
Isolated in the centre stands a little stone shrine, with a spring by its side.

In Fedden's *Syria* there is an interesting discussion of this Phoenician type
of sanctuary, with its large enclosure often cut out of the living rock, its

sacred spring for lustration, and its little central shrine. This lay-out spread rapidly through the region, and is seen in magnified form in the Temple of Bel at Palmyra, while the lustral basins at Baalbek are 'the sophisticated descendants of the receptacles which held the waters of the natural spring at Amrit'.

Out to sea we could see the island of Ruad (p. 72), once the Phoenician island-city of Arvad which founded Amrit.

In Tortosa we came to familiar types of construction – the Crusader castle and cathedral; and thence, with the mountain range rising ever higher to the eastward, to the Crusader castle of Baniyas on its tawny spur. I cherish the bill for our lunch at Tortosa: '2 Repa, 1 Bur, Chofer, Çerviç' – which being transliterated is 2 Repas, 1 Bière, Chauffeur, Service.

That evening we reached Latakia, celebrated today for its tobacco, stigmatized by St John the Divine for its lukewarmness. Here we enjoyed the hospitality of an able young Syrian, Gabriel Saadé, and his parents and sister. Saadé's intellectual home, I felt, was Paris, but he was anchored in Latakia by his responsibility for the family tobacco business.

In the large Victorian house, his mother held undisputed sway. She was a splendid and efficient matron who, like many Syrian women, enjoyed smoking a hookah. Every morning she took her hookah and her knitting to the kitchen, where she spent some time keeping an eye on the domestic staff.

One of the interests with which Gabriel Saadé enlived his intellectual isolation was archeology. Since 1929, the French, under Claude Schaeffer, have been making all sorts of interesting discoveries at Ras Shamra, near the coast a few miles to the northwards; and thither, an invaluable guide, Saadé escorted us next morning.

Ras Shamra was the ancient Ugarit. The settlement here goes back to neolithic times; as a city, the place is almost as old as Byblos. Situated about a mile inland from a convenient harbour, it became one of the most important entrepôts of the region, handling much of the trade between Mesopotamia and the eastern Mediterranean. It was at the height of its prosperity about 1500 B.C., and the most famous finds date from this period – the Ras Shamra tablets. They are interesting both for their unique alphabetic script, with cuneiform instead of Phoenician characters (p. 53), and for their content. They are not merely business documents or formal commemorative records; they include ritual prescriptions, religious poems, glossaries and grammars, and exercises for use in a scribes' school. The pupils seem to have been Canaanites, but had to learn Akkadian.

The religious documents are written records of much earlier compositions. Some of the poems are reminiscent of the Hebrew psalms; others are mythological, and some may have served as summary texts for sacred ritual dramas. One of these records the basic neolithic drama of the vegetation god who dies in autumn and is later resurrected – the same compound of myth and magic ritual which gave rise to the Adonis cult.

The excavations* have revealed a central acropolis with the King's palace. The introduction of horses, at first solely for military purposes, led to the building of what have been called the royal stables but were really the cavalry barracks, and then to a considerable re-planning of the city and its roads to permit the passage of chariots. In one place a stretch of the city wall has been uncovered, revealing a formidable stone glacis, perhaps the first ever built, and parent of all later glacis in the history of fortification.

The houses were jumbled together along narrow tortuous streets. Their strangest feature was the incorporation of a resting-place for the family dead. Each house contained in its basement an ancestral tomb: the dead were buried beneath its floor, and the funeral rites celebrated in the little room which served as a mortuary chapel. Its corbelled false vaulting of overlapping horizontal slabs gave a striking arched roof, high and narrow. A runnel in the stone floor served to conduct running water, but for what religious or practical function is unknown. This crowded cohabitation of the living and the dead makes a deep impression.

A large triangular stone with a hole through its apex had been unearthed – apparently an early anchor, serving some Ugaritic ship on its voyages to Cyprus and the Cretan seas.

Ugarit disappeared from history after being sacked by the Philistines and other Peoples of the Sea as they made their way southwards around 1200 B.C. Their destructiveness and power depended largely on their new weapons – weapons of iron instead of bronze. Goliath the Philistine was chiefly formidable as a warrior because his spear had an iron head, though also because of his size, a giant member of a tall northern race. It is somewhat ironical to find that Dagon, the fish-god, long worshipped at Ugarit, should have been taken over by its Philistine destroyers as their chief divinity: it was at a celebration of Dagon that Samson pulled down their temple at Gaza.

Thirty miles to the north, just by the Turkish frontier, the snow-capped peak of Jebel Akra rose thrillingly above the flat expanse of the coastal

* See C. Schaeffer, *Ugaritica,* and R. Dussaud, *Les fouilles de Ras Shamra, etc.*

plain. Jebel Akra is the ancient Mount Casius. Its isolated mass, reared nearly six thousand feet in air, projects into the sea just south of Antioch. It must have been a potent landmark, a mountain naturally predetermined to become a Holy Place. A Holy Place it was, with an important shrine near its summit, to which many potentates, including the first Seleucid King and the Emperors Hadrian and Julian, ascended to render their devotions. The place is still covered, according to the guide-books, with the ashes and charred bones remaining from countless sacrifices, first to the Phoenician High God, then to the Greek Zeus installed in his place.

★

One day we were taken to the Saadés' country place high in the Alawit mountains. After a distant glimpse of the Crusader castle of Sahyun (p. 83), we stopped to see the place where the Saadés' tobacco was flavoured – a windowless stone building about 3000 feet up, in which were burning smoky fires of green wood from an aromatic shrub that grows near by. The fragrance impregnates the leaves from which Tabac Abourika, a special scented tobacco, is made.

The people here were living a primitive peasant life, the women, some of them very beautiful, wearing traditional peasant dress, with handsome bright skirts (pl. 35, opp. p. 200). Snow was lying in patches near the Saadés' villa. Their local major-domo lit a very smoky fire which took off the chill, and started preparing lunch. Meanwhile, a number of men from the village had been assembled, and entertained us with some dances. In the most remarkable of these, the protagonist, a small lithe man with mobile expressive face, danced with a pair of knives in his hands. With these held to his head to represent horns, he danced the part of a savage bull, tossing and charging. Then, changing his role, he arched back, making as if to stab himself, then advanced with threatening grimaces and contortions. In the background, the other men (alas, largely in western costume) acted as chorus, linking arms and executing a rhythmic movement, sideways, forwards, back, and sideways again, all the time chanting a monotonous song.

The Alawit country was a restricted area: we had to obtain official permits to enter it. This was an aftermath of the troubled times of Sulman Murshed. He was an able and unscrupulous man, who lived high up in the Alawit mountains with his thirteen wives. In the middle 1920's he proclaimed himself God, and began to dominate the region with a combination of religion and robbery. He made forcible levies on his neighbour's crops, and was not above organizing highway robbery. Although a self-proclaimed god, he sent some of his children to be educated by the Jesuits in Beirut, paying for this in eggs and fowls and other produce. The French supported him out of opposition to the Syrian nationalists. After Syria became independent in 1945, he was arrested and hanged at Damascus: his son is still in prison.

This story is symptomatic of the Alawit Mountains. They are the home of a backward island of population, with peculiar religious traditions: the task of integrating them with the rest of Syria is a difficult one. The Administrator of the Hafé district had little good to say of the French, except for the roads they constructed for strategic purposes. In education, not only was French the official language of his nation, but children were fined for talking Arabic, even in their recreation periods. 'History' was entirely French history.

Since 1945, a great educational effort has been made, and there are now elementary schools all over the Mountain. In less than four years since Syrian independence, no fewer than 220 had been started, 20 of them for girls, catering for nearly 25,000 children. For secondary education, Alawit children from the Hafé district still had to go to Latakia (some families migrated there while their children were at school), but it was hoped soon to start a secondary school in the Mountain. Instruction is now in Arabic, but all children have to learn either French or English as a second language

*

Next day, after a glimpse of the handsome Roman tetrapylon in the old town, we left for Antioch. The formalities at the Syrian frontier post did not delay us long: but on the Turkish side the language problem appeared insurmountable. Eventually a local inhabitant was found who could provide the missing link in the chain of communication. The frontier officials asked a question of the local inhabitant in Turkish; the local inhabitant translated into bad Arabic for the chauffeur; the chauffeur re-translated it into bad French for us; and our reply went back through the same channels. After an hour or so, we were cleared, only to be halted for another half-hour at the military post outside the village. At neither place did anyone even suggest that we might find the pass over the mountains difficult.

After leaving the military post, we did not see a single house or meet a single person. As the road began to wind higher and higher, with more and more snow on it, as the pine forests became denser and the gorges along whose sides we travelled deeper, we began to have misgivings. Suddenly the car skidded, and began churning helplessly in the deeper snow at the side of the road. We decided to turn; but the chauffeur could not back out of the drift, in spite of our laying brushwood under the wheels. The only thing to do was to seek help; and my wife and I started to walk the eleven miles back to the village.

After an hour or so of this cheerless tramp, we heard a sound – it was the car: the chauffeur had miraculously extricated the car and turned it on the narrow road.

At the frontier, all the formalities had to be solemnly repeated, so that we did not arrive back at Latakia, a little crestfallen, until nearly sunset.

★

Next morning we set off for Aleppo. The road follows the only easy route to the interior which is to be found in the hundred-odd miles between the Homs-Tripoli gap and that north of Antioch.

From the watershed we twisted down through clumps of wild oleander and pallid fields with hedges along their stone terrace-walls to the rift valley. In the valley was a bustling little town with blue-washed houses and graves, and a grand Roman bridge, very long and curiously un-straight, over the brown Orontes. Leaving the rift, with its occasional small volcanic craters and its ugly villages with windowless thatched houses of blackish stone, we climbed on to a bare but fertile upland plain. The villages here looked pleasant, with cubical off-white houses: and then suddenly we had our first sight of that extraordinary phenomenon, a beehive village (pl. 36, opp. p. 201). We stopped to explore the place, and found ourselves surrounded by a crowd of the rather free-and-easy inhabitants.

A smiling, handsome woman showed us over one of the huts. The entire construction is of unburnt mud or clay, the floor slightly raised above the soil outside. The interior was spotlessly clean, with a recess for cooking and attractive decorations in bright tinsel paper on the walls. Though only a few yards in diameter, its high conical roof gave it a sense of space. A curtained opening led into a second 'beehive', which was presumably the bedroom. Some of the other buildings had only one beehive dome, others four.

These beehive dwellings are characteristic of a large region round Aleppo. One can see that they are well-adapted to life on these open uplands: but why are they not to be found in similar areas further east?

An hour later, we were on the outskirts of Aleppo, looking across to the famous citadel rising above the jumble of roofs and protruding minarets. The citadel dominates the city, crowning the protruding hill that nature provided as the obvious focal strongpoint for the place. It contains a mosque erected in the 12th century to commemorate Abraham, who is said to have pastured his flocks on the summit. As a matter of fact, the hill was occupied by a fortress long before Abraham's time.

The entrance gateway, largely the work of Saladin's son at the beginning of the 13th century, must be one of the most imposing pieces of military architecture in the world, jutting out in superb pride over the formidable glacis, once faced with stone, that slopes up to the fortress walls above. The gateway is approached up a great ramp built on an arched substructure. Inside its huge doors, set with horseshoe motives in iron, the solitary passage mounts on its narrow way to the interior of the fortress, traversing no fewer than five sharp elbows and two more massive gates. The gates are surmounted by magic emblems carved in stone, the first by dragons, the second by lions. The second is also flanked by lions, one laughing, the other weeping, as a symbol of human existence.

On one of the immense walls a Wall-creeper, a bird I had only seen before on wild rock faces in the Alps, was jerking up the stony surface, revealing an utterly unexpected patch of rich crimson at each flick of its wings. The sight of a Wall-creeper is always exciting: on this fabulous fortress it was doubly memorable.

The fortress was also a palace: you can still see the remains of the huge barrel-roofed brick vaults, the mosque, the harem, the Turkish baths, and the 15th-century throne-room with its handsome windows.

Sir Leonard Woolley once told me of how he visited Aleppo before the First World War, when it was still part of the Turkish empire. At first he was told that he could not see the citadel, as it contained military stores; but was eventually allowed in, under the supervision of a soldier. He asked if there really were any military stores in the place – 'Oh, yes,' replied the guide; and showed him a sort of cellar full of stone cannon-balls, and a room with piles of bows and arrows in various stages of decay, including some composite bows bound with sinews.

Aleppo was the great trading centre on the least desertic of the routes between east and west, along the northern arc of the Fertile Crescent. It has a more northern, less oriental air than other cities of the region such as Damascus or Baghdad or Cairo. This is partly the effect of physical geography. It is cold in winter (we shivered throughout our stay), and it possesses neither a great river nor a rich oasis to relieve the heats of summer. It has always been the home of prudent merchants, with brief interludes of royal court life. Even after the establishment of the sea routes to India and the Far East, it was so important a trade centre as to attract companies of European merchants.

The architecture is serious and solid. I was greatly struck by the fine masonry of the buildings and the handsome but restrained stone-carving over doors and windows. Aleppo is famous for its Souks and its Khans. The Khans were built primarily as warehouses, but also as caravanserais for merchants and travellers. There are a surprising number of small Khans, and some very handsome large ones. I remember especially Khan El Wasir, built in the 17th century, with a façade of black and yellow stone, and a great entrance arch, across which chains are stretched to prevent the unauthorized entrance of vehicles.

The Souks were largely built in the 13th century, straight and long. The great covered market that they constitute is obviously still the main centre of the city's activity, more so even than in Damascus or Baghdad, in spite of the fact that, with the splitting up of the region into separate nation-states after 1918, the westward and northward flow of trade was seriously impeded.

The Souks were crowded with all sorts and conditions of people – men in abbas, brown, ochre and buff in various stripes, some very farouche with long matted hair, jostling peasant women in cerise and yellow; fat merchants wearing the tarboosh; boys in European clothes ringing the bells of their brand-new bikes to clear a way through the crowd; a madman who kept up an incessant flow of talk; coffee-sellers clinking their cups; a donkey carrying a boy as well as a load of cauliflowers; hawkers of cheap American goods on trays; vendors of sweetmeats and cakes; boys selling unleavened bread by weight; money-changers; a family of Beduins from the desert.

Exposed for sale were carpets, cotton in bales, silks (largely artificial), gold and silver filigree, saddles for horses, some of them very splendid, bicycle-saddles, some made of sheepskin, others of some synthetic material, and a surprising number of revolver holsters. The strangest objects were camel carcases for eating, the hump of fat decoratively cut into radiating strips to look like a monstrous white fleshy flower.

An elderly guardian unlocked the door of a staircase and took us up to the roof of the Souks. This was a very queer place – a grass-grown expanse of stone, with occasional iron-barred holes to give light and air to the market below. In the spring, it is enlivened with hen-coops and with sheep and goats put out to graze; when we saw it, it was deserted save for fierce dogs chained up at intervals to guard against nocturnal robbers. It was hardly credible that below our feet were the corridors with their crowd of busy buyers and sellers.

Just outside the market was the street of the blacksmiths. Some of the men were making large nails individually, by hand – a depressing degradation of human skill and energy – while others were turning out triumphs of skilled workmanship. Here was exemplified the dilemma of the machine age – how to keep alive beauty and the satisfactions of individual craftsmanship side by side with mass-produced utility and convenience.

At the excellent little photographic shop where we went to buy picture postcards, the proprietor told us that many views of Aleppo were banned for military reasons; and the agreeable card of the crowded Souks which he sold us could not be sent through the post because it was supposed to be derogatory to Syrian dignity.

Then there was the Halawiye Mosque, originally the Christian Cathedral founded by the Empress Helena herself, and still showing some Byzantine capitals of the exquisitely romantic wind-blown acanthus pattern; and the 13th-century Mosque of Paradise, a very beautiful Moslem building with some gaunt half-starved cattle browsing in the graveyard, figs and vines in its court, and ruined mosques and mausoleums all around – the remains of the medieval Court quarter.

The Museum had an interesting collection from Ugarit, and a number of local votive clay figurines of strange bird-headed female divinities. The most striking exhibit was a pair of late second-millennium Hittite statues, from the interior, a hideous over-life-size black basalt god and goddess, crude-featured and frightening; there seemed no appeal from the doom in their staring black and white eyes. The Syro-Hittite work was much finer – people had better taste on the coast.

Our guide was a young Armenian who had learnt fluent English and French at the American College, just outside the city. This we later visited at the invitation of its energetic American President, Dr Alford Carleton.

The American College, with its annexed High School and Elementary Schools, is an excellent example of the good work done for education in the Middle East by western religious bodies. One great achievement of the place was the friendly mixing of students differing in religion, language, and social status – Moslems, Christians and Armenians in about equal numbers, with a sprinkling of Jews. Young Syrians evince great interest in engineering, and courses in this are provided by the American College, as well as by a Syrian Engineering College in Aleppo. Dr Carleton was hoping to start a special rural course for the sons of leading landowners: this might teach them to ask for scientific advice, and to understand something of their social obligations. Agriculture hereabouts is run on very feudal lines: many of the peasants are share-croppers who receive only one-third of their crops.

A curious zoological fact from this area was recently (March 13, 1951) reported by Dr Hindle to a meeting of the Zoological Society of London. The golden hamster is a handsome semi-desert rodent which has been added to the list of domesticated species in the last twenty years. It is now extensively used as a laboratory animal for physiological and medical research, and also as a pet. The tens of thousands of hamsters in our laboratories and pet-stores are descended from a single female which, with her twelve young, was captured near Aleppo in 1930. According to Dr Hindle, the only other wild specimen to be scientifically recorded was the type specimen of the species, exhibited at another meeting of the Zoological Society in 1839.

A single couple, a rodent Adam and Eve, have thus produced the entire race of domesticated hamsters, incidentally illustrating how isolated islands might derive their small mammal population from the accidental transport of a single pregnant female, and also demonstrating that inbreeding need not necessarily be harmful.

The north Syrian region has many other points of zoological interest. Sir Leonard Woolley once told me that the grandfather of a trusted overseer of his had killed a lion. 'Where had he gone to do that?' I asked. To which he replied that he had gone nowhere; he had killed the lion in his home region, the tribal area of the Damalkas on the right bank of the Upper Euphrates.

Here and there in the foothill region of northern Syria, lions survived well into the second half of the nineteenth century.* If a man wished to acquire

* Bodenheimer, in his *Animal Life in Palestine*, states that they still existed in 1935 in the jungles of the Upper Euphrates.

fame and fortune (and also if he was strong and somewhat foolhardy!), he would announce that he would challenge a lion to single combat on a certain date.

On the appointed day he would set out, followed by a large crowd of spectators (for it is not every day that one can see a fight between a man and the king of beasts) to the wady where the lion was in the habit of lying up. The challenger advanced up the wady, followed at an increasingly respectful distance by the gallery of spectators. In a loud voice, he proclaimed his challenge to the lion, urging him to come out and fight if he was not to be considered a coward. Public insults were shouted at the beast; and if this did not suffice, heaped on the heads of his mother, grandmother and other female relatives.

If the lion was a clever lion, he would creep round in hiding, so as to leap on the bombastic disturber of his peace from behind; and this would be the end of that foolhardy fellow. But most lions are far from clever, and the animal would generally come angrily out of his lair straight towards the challenger.

The challenger was bound by certain traditional rules. He was allowed no weapon save a single sword. He was, however, allowed to swathe his left arm and hand defensively. This he did by wrapping them in enormous quantities of black goat's-hair yarn (the stuff of which the black Beduin tents are woven).

The lion advanced, and eventually sprang. This part of the business I do not fully understand, for I should have thought that a man could not normally avoid being knocked down by a lion springing to the attack. However, the lion-killer's grandson assured Woolley that the man – in this case his grandfather – thrust his left arm forward, full into the lion's open mouth. Lions, as they bite, automatically bring up their great fore-paws to help them hold and injure the prey. But here both fangs and claws spent their force in the entangling wool. This was the moment which the man must seize. While mouth and fore legs were thus occupied, he must manage with one stroke of his sword to hamstring the lion's left hind-leg. It is then only a matter of skill and agility to keep out of range of the jaws while stabbing the creature to death.

I say 'only'; but obviously the skill and agility required were very considerable, and the man might still be mauled. However, the overseer's grandfather killed his lion safely. He thenceforward had the appellation of

Lion-killer added to his name, and never had to do any more work, as lion-killers were entertained at the public expense for the rest of their lives.

I must say that this survival impressed me. In early historic times, only three or four thousand years ago, lions must still have been quite abundant in the entire region across from India through Persia and Syria and Asia Minor into Greece. There were still plenty of them left in the Syrian-Palestinian region at the time of the Crusades. And wherever wild lions existed, the lion-killer inevitably became a hero. Hercules' greatest feat of strength and bravery was killing a lion with his bare hands. So was Samson's when he came to Timnath and the 'young lion roared against him' and Samson 'rent him as he would have rent a kid'. Even if these particular feats were mythical, they crystallized the legend of the heroic lion-killer. And when Saul told David that a boy like him stood no chance against Goliath, David took his stand upon the fact that he had killed a lion, which (allied with a bear) had taken a lamb out of the flock he was herding.

In historical times, Assyrian Kings are often represented in single combat with lions: Tiglath-Pileser boasts on one of his monuments that he had killed 120 lions on foot and 800 from his chariot! Here, again, one would like to know whether they really fought the animals in single combat, or whether, as I suspect, the hunt was elaborately organized so that they could have the glory of killing a lion without too much of the risk: there are bas-reliefs showing lions being let out of cages, apparently to serve as royal quarry.

Small wonder that in those lion-infested countries the lion should become the symbol of strength and glorious but savage power. The famous Lion Gate at Mycene embodies this symbol: and of course, the Hittite Kings had lions everywhere in their palaces.

In Ankara, the traffic policemen at the most important road-junctions do their work from a little pedestal flanked by two obviously Hittite lions – part of the effort to give modern Turkey an ancient tradition (pl. 17, opp. p. 108). I said to a Turkish acquaintance how good an idea it seemed to me to produce casts of these historic objects for this purpose. But he was indignant: 'Casts,' he said. 'What d'you take us for? They're not casts, they're genuine antiques!' And so they were.

It was natural for the lion to become the symbol of power in countries where it was an actual embodiment of the very real power of wild nature with which man had to struggle. It was also natural for the symbol to spread later to other lands and other regions, where no lions had ever existed; it would be extremely interesting to trace the steps of this extension, but that is a matter for the specialist. I suppose that the symbolization of kingly power by the lion was reinforced by the medieval bestiaries, which conferred the title of King of Beasts upon the lion. Be that as it may, all the lions which play a symbolic part in the Western world are descended from the real lions of the Mediterranean and Middle East, not from those of India or Black Africa; and the lion which Woolley's overseer's grandfather challenged and killed in the time of Queen Victoria certainly shared a common ancestry with those that floated on her Royal Standard, as well as with the Lion that confronts the Unicorn in the Royal Arms and in Lewis Carroll's poem, and with other lions of other royal houses of Europe.

But my greatest zoological surprise was to discover that elephants existed on the Euphrates in considerable numbers throughout most of antiquity. They lived on its north bank where it bends eastwards after emerging from the mountains. For a long time, a minor king in the region of Antioch exploited their ivory. In the New Kingdom of Egypt, Amenenhep, general of Thothmes III, while on his Syrian campaign, took part in an elephant drive here in which 120 animals were killed or taken. Ashurnasipal II captured some for his Zoo, and Tiglath-Pileser III brought back four live elephants and ten pairs of tusks. The species was probably wiped out in the Euphrates region about this time.

While on this subject, perhaps a word on Hannibal's elephants is in order. Sir William Gowers, in his interesting studies of the animals of classical antiquity, seems to have established that the elephants used by the Carthaginians were African elephants, but of a forest subspecies considerably smaller, and presumably more easily tamed, than the typical bush elephants of Central East Africa today, and in fact smaller than the quite distinct Indian species.*

In Carthaginian times, this smaller subspecies flourished in the forested hinterland of the North African coast (Hanno saw some on the Atlantic coast of the Atlas) and it was from here that Hannibal drew his living tanks. The elephants on the Euphrates seem to have been an outlying group of the Indian species: but they had been exterminated long before Hannibal was born.

Zoologically speaking, the history of the world since our own species, *Homo sapiens*, first appeared on the scene, is one of the progressive reduction and extermination of all the larger forms of life. If we are surprised at the late

* See *African Affairs*, July 1948, p. 173.

survivals of large animals in the Middle East, it is because we have grown so used to their extermination in our own countries.* If we took the trouble to remember that in Britain wolves and beavers survived until a few centuries ago, that the wild bull or aurochs was common in Europe at the beginning of our era, that well under 15,000 years ago European bison ranged abundantly to the Pyrenees, and that less than a hundred years ago, its American brother-species roamed in tens of millions over the Great Plains to the Rockies; if we recalled the fate of the Dodo and the Great Auk, the Quagga and Steller's Sea-Cow – in fact, if we began to reflect at all on the subject, we should not be surprised at the survivals, but horrified at the extinctions.

Let me give a few more examples of the process in the Middle East and North Africa. Sir William Gowers has made it clear that the rhinoceroses brought to Rome for imperial shows were not the (relatively) common African species of today, which is impossibly bad-tempered, but the more manageable White Rhinoceros with his superb horn up to five feet in length. In Imperial times, White Rhinos must have existed over most of Africa; today, they are reduced to two small remnants in the heart of the continent.

For northern Syria, we have the evidence of Xenophon, who was a great devotee of hunting. During their march towards Babylon, from near Thapsacus, on the left bank of the Euphrates, the Greeks marched eastwards for five days through a level steppe rich in aromatic plants. 'Wild asses were very common, and there were many ostriches; also there were bustards and gazelles.' The wild asses ran much faster than the horses, and could only be caught by stationing horsemen in relays. Their flesh was excellent, very like venison, only more tender. 'No one succeeded in catching an ostrich.' There are no longer any wild asses or ostriches in the region, and bustards and gazelles are being rapidly reduced in numbers owing to the combination of cars and modern firearms.

The wild bulls, hunted by the ancient monarchs in the Lebanon and elsewhere in the region, have disappeared entirely; in the Arabian desert, camels are no longer there to be hunted as they were till the late 19th century; the many species of antelope of ancient Egypt have dwindled to next to nothing; bears exist now only in a few wild haunts, though Layard only a century ago found them 'too abundant' in some of the mountains above Mosul, together with plenty of ibex.

* See Ritchie's admirable *Influence of Man upon Animal Life in Scotland.*

But why continue the sad catalogue? The wild life of the region is on the way out, and will be reduced to scattered and miserable remnants unless something is done.* I do not suggest that man is not justified in killing off the larger beasts of prey, or in appropriating fertile plains from the hordes of large ungulates that once dominated them. But I do suggest that he should consider his responsibilities in the matter. It is a grave responsibility to wipe a living species off the face of the earth – something that can never be replaced. Even from a selfish human point of view, it is wrong. I have seen big game wild in East Africa, and can testify to the extraordinary stimulus of the spectacle. There are many people for whom wild nature affords unique satisfactions of enjoyment and wonder; and where possible, wild nature should include not only wild scenery, however grand, but also wild life. Wild life is one of our world's resources, and needs conservation as much as other resources.

The formation of the International Union for the Preservation of Nature, under Unesco's auspices, is a step in the right direction. I hope that conservation may be implemented in the Middle East before the region has lost more of the species it might conserve. It is unlikely that wild asses and ostriches will once more abound along the Euphrates: the governments of the Middle East might be persuaded to think in terms of conserving what they still possess – creatures like ibex in the Arabian mountains, gazelles, bears, leopards, and the hosts of migratory birds, large and small.

*

One of my chief reasons for visiting Aleppo had been to see Qalat Seman and others of the 'dead towns' remaining from the early Christian period in the region. Unfortunately, if not off the road altogether, they are all on side-roads, and side-roads in northern Syria are impassable in muddy weather such as befell us: so we had the tantalizing experience of having to leave without seeing anything of this unique civilization. A little money spent on providing easier access to the monuments of past ages would be a profitable investment for Middle Eastern countries, as well as a contribution to world culture.

* F. S. Bodenheimer, the eminent zoologist at Jerusalem, in his book *Animal Life in Palestine* (London, 1935), gives a detailed picture of the position for the whole region, and makes suggestions for proper wild-life conservation and the setting up of nature reserves.

However, the picture I was able to build up in my mind, though at second hand, was so vivid that I feel impelled to set something of it down.*

The rolling stony hills which the traveller sees to the west of Aleppo, now sparsely populated and poorly cultivated, were once the scene of a prosperous civilization, lasting from the 4th to the 7th century. Over a hundred dead towns, with an enormous number of wine and olive presses, attest the past fertility of the region.

The primary reason for the collapse of this civilization seems to have been deforestation: the forests were cut down to make room for fields and vineyards and olive-groves, to provide timber for the multitude of buildings, and for fuel. The resultant soil-erosion was hastened by the switch-over to cereals introduced by the conquering Arabs in the 7th century. The Arabs were also hostile to the Christian culture of the region, and were not concerned to keep up the elaborate standards of agriculture that had grown up there. The disorders of the Crusades and the misrule of the Turks completed the tale.

The dead towns are often well preserved. They are almost all unfortified, the product of a settled peace: like the unwalled Cretan cities, they could not well survive in the disorder of war. They had developed a distinctive but essentially classical architecture of fine stone masonry. Some of the ecclesiastical buildings, with their well-proportioned simplicity and their rows of severe round-arched windows, look curiously post-renaissance; others have rich decoration, including lovely wind-blown acanthus columns.

If the architectural style of the region was classical, its life certainly was not. Qalat Seman, the largest and most important of the dead towns, grew up round the reputation of St Simeon, that man of excessive holiness. The extraordinary facts of his life are attested by his biographer, who knew him well as a personal friend. He joined a monastery at the age of sixteen, but was eventually expelled because his exaggerated ascetic practices were too much for the brethren. Nothing daunted, he became a solitary hermit, and then, in A.D. 423, took up his position on top of a ten-foot pillar. The height of his pillars grew with the growth of his ascetic ambitions; and he spent the last

* There is an admirable brief account in Fedden's *Syria*, and many details in Dussaud, Deschamps and Seyrig, *La Syrie antique et mediévale illustrée* (Paris), and Mattern's *Les Villes Mortes de Haute Syrie* (Beirut). The incredible history of St Simeon can be read in the *Dictionary of Christian Biography*. Some day I hope to find time to read Delahaye's large work on the general subject of pillar-sitting, *Les Stylites*.

thirty years of his life on the summit of a fifty-foot column. To prevent his falling off, an iron collar round his neck was fastened to the stone by a chain, and a low railing was built round the edge of his tiny platform; this was so small that though he could sit or kneel on it, he could not lie down. A ladder permitted the monks to bring him his exceedingly meagre daily rations, and twice weekly to administer the Eucharist. At least once a day he preached to the crowds below, and prostrated himself in prayer over a thousand times. We found how cold Aleppo could be: what winter was like to the unsheltered saint on his high perch in the hills, I shudder to imagine.

Not content with these self-inflicted austerities, with the conversions of which he was the instrument, the exhortations he administered to his daily audiences, and the answers he vouchsafed to individual suppliants, he did not hesitate to make pronouncements on numerous points of religious policy, and to volunteer advice to the Emperor and the ecclesiastical authorities. As might be expected, he was extremely orthodox, and favoured a rigorous treatment of Jews and heretics.

In the atmosphere of early Christianity, this fantastically ascetic way of life soon gained him a prodigious reputation for sanctity; and from the beginning of his pillar-sitting career, pilgrims began to arrive at Qalat Seman. Within twenty years, the crowds had become enormous: people came from the furthest parts of the Christian world, even from remote Britain, in the hope of miraculous cures or the expectation of acquiring religious merit. Among them were many women, but the saint allowed none of these, not even his own mother, to enter the circle of stones round the base of his pillar.

Soon after his death the authorities decided to capitalize his reputation, and began the building of the existing great church, which took about fifty years to complete. This must be a very extraordinary edifice. It is unique in its construction, being centred on the saint's pillar instead of on an altar. It consists of four basilicas radiating out like the arms of a cross from a large octagonal open space containing the pillar. Only one of the four basilicas was used as a church; the others served as a religious foyer in which the pilgrims could stroll. I should have said the male pilgrims: the female sex was debarred from entry, and had to be content with distant glimpses of the pillar through the doorways. Fedden states that it was the largest Christian building to be erected before the great cathedrals of the 10th and 11th centuries: certainly it must have been the finest monument of Christian architecture before Santa Sophia.

A monastery, with its own little basilica, was built adjoining the main church, and in the valley below there grew up a large pilgrim town, in which can still be seen the remains of numerous hostels and hotels, some of them running to three storeys, as well as public baths, churches, convents and private houses. It was a fifth-century Lourdes, which preserved its Christian prosperity until overwhelmed by the Moslem flood.

*

Lucian devotes most of his travel-book, *The Syrian Goddess*, to an account of the sacred city Hierapolis. Hierapolis lies about twice as far away from Aleppo as the shrine of St Simeon. It is a pity that Lucian's ghost could not have come back to earth three centuries later to see Qalat Seman: the pilgrim swarms and the commercialized sanctity of the place would have appealed to all his instincts, though the complete replacement of the old by a new religion would have set him a number of puzzles.

A pity also that Carchemish, only a score of miles beyond Hierapolis, had crumbled into ruins and oblivion centuries earlier, for that too would have been a fit subject for his pen, with its luxury, and the great temple that seems to have been the prototype for Solomon's. For indeed this small area saw the growth of three of the great shrines of the ancient world.

At Hierapolis, the temple was the principal source of the city's wealth – 'as I can vouch', says Lucian. 'For much money comes to them from Arabia, and from the Phoenicians, and the Babylonians; the Cilicians, too, and the Assyrians contribute. . . . Nowhere else among mankind are there so many festivals and sacred assemblies.' In the main temple, Lucian saw 'many tokens' that Dionysus was its actual founder – barbaric raiment, Indian precious stones, and elephants' tusks brought by Dionysus from the Ethiopians.

What interests us here is to find that the pillar-sitting habit was not invented by St Simeon, but had ancient pagan roots in the region. Lucian tells us that at the main entrance of the main temple, dedicated to Atargatis, there stood two pillars, 180 feet high, on top of one of which a man spends an entire week twice every year. He calls them 'the phalli which Dionysus erected'; and there would seem to be no reason for rejecting this categorical description of their appearance. It is reasonable to conclude that the twin entrance pillars found in the temples of so many early cults, as at Mycene, Paphos, the temple of the Tyrian Hercules, and Solomon's temple itself, had originally some phallic significance. On the other hand, there is doubtless a 'double determination' at work, the pillar representing not only a phallus, but also that primary symbol of vegetative fertility, the tree.

At Hierapolis, the man climbed the pillar by means of a chain: as Lucian says, 'those who have not seen the process but have seen men climbing palms in Arabia or Egypt, or any other place, will understand what I mean. . . . When he has climbed to the top, he lets down another chain, pulls up anything he needs, such as wood, clothes, and vessels; he ties these together like a nest, and sits on them. Many visitors bring him gold and silver, and some bring brass. Each visitor leaves his offerings and departs, after giving his name. A man standing by shouts the name up; and he on hearing the name, says a prayer for each donor: between prayers, he shakes a brass instrument which produces a loud grating noise. He never sleeps.'

Lucian traces a connection between the man's climbing the phallic pillar and the local custom of putting 'manikins of wood' on all phalli erected in honour of Dionysus. Be that as it may, it is clear that sacred pillar-sitting was traditional in the area.

Religious pillar-sitting continued in the Near East for a long time, dying out only in the 16th century. Curiously enough, it never caught on in Western Christendom: in fact, as Fedden tells us, a Gaulish stylite was forced to descend from his eminence by episcopal injunction, and his pillar solemnly destroyed. Modern pole-sitting is a purely secular stunt, and is mercifully confined to the United States.

★

Our return journey took us southward along the western edge of the rolling plain, dreary under mist and low cloud. The level expanse of the plain was broken by many small hills, some looking like small isolated volcanoes, others like buttes remaining from a denuded tableland. In point of fact, they were all *tells*, mounds produced by millennia of human settlement, and proofs that the plain as well as the hills had once been much more densely populated.

One large tell had a beehive village on its flank. This, the guidebook told us, was one of the relatively few mounds to have been properly excavated. It contained, among other things, an important settlement from about 2000 B.C., a terrace built by Thuthmosis IV in the 15th century B.C. during the period of Egyptian rule over Syria, and the remains of four superimposed Iron Age towns, the latest from the 6th century B.C.

The turning for Apamaea reminded us of the wealth of remains still awaiting excavation. Apamaea rose to importance in Seleucid times, and was noted for its military establishment, including barracks for a regiment of 600 war elephants, and for its schools of pagan philosophy. Once a city of over 120,000 inhabitants, it is now a mere village.

However, we had no time to visit it, and pursued our southward way over the edge of the plain between two fine hills, the Horns of Hama, and down into the rift valley, with the city of Hama on the northward-flowing Orontes. Hama must rival Damascus as one of the oldest continuously inhabited cities; today it is one of the most uncompromisingly Moslem towns of the Syrian region, its style and way of life relatively untouched by western influences. Certainly western ideas of comfort for travellers are absent. The hotel looked most unappetizing; but the railway buffet, the only other eating place in the town, proved worse, and we returned to the hotel for an expensive lunch of omelette and beer. One of the few signs of modernity in the place was a handsome young policeman, who kindly attached himself to us as our guide. With his blue eyes and fair hair, he looked remarkably like a Swiss man of my acquaintance; he had served with the British in the Egyptian campaign, and had been at Tobruk.

My chief memory of Hama is of the norias, the enormous water-wheels, immensely larger than any to be seen in Europe, which laboriously scoop water out of the Orontes to distribute it through overhead conduits to the gardens and orchards and market-gardens for which the city is famous. The norias may be described as machines constructed in a premechanical age. The sound of their wooden groaning never ceases, and makes a background accompaniment to all life in Hama. They are absurdly inefficient: I watched one at work, and estimated that well over half the water it picked up spilled back into the river before reaching the irrigation pipes. But they are imposing and almost magnificent in their giant grotesqueness; and it will be a sad day when they are replaced by efficient modern apparatus.

Our policeman guide of course took us to see the Azem palace. This, now used as a school, was built by the same Pasha El Azem who built the famous palace in Damascus (p. 140). It is a little heavier than its namesake, but has some fine features, notably the fenestrated stone carving over the windows; and its position overlooking the river is superb.

The Keylani House too is a product of Turkish-Arabic culture, but was added to in several periods instead of having been built all in one piece.

Perhaps for that reason, and also because it is still used as a private house, it gives a more intimate impression of an oriental way of life. It belonged to our policeman's uncle, whom he addressed as *effendi*. The somewhat poor-looking windowless exterior concealed a series of surprisingly rich and lovely rooms. We drank coffee in a room with beautiful inlaid mother-of-pearl furniture, some good china, and two pictures on the walls, one of Istanbul in early steamboat days, the other of a pretty pussy-cat from some western Christmas supplement of fifty years back. Another room had little stone alcoves between panels of painted stucco, and a fountain supplied with rather silty water by a neighbouring noria. The balcony was built out over the river, and one could see the yellow turbid water through the cracks in its floor.

Reluctantly forgoing a further sight of the old town and its markets, and with a cordial farewell to our guide, we set off for Homs. On the road is Restan, a big village perched above the Orontes where it flows in an all-but-gorge among rocky hills, actuating a solitary noria. The houses, grim cubes of black basalt blocks, gave a hellish look to the place; but the women, drawing water in their bright blue and red dresses, looked gay enough.

After passing the last of the beehive settlements, we reached Homs, only to find the hotel impossibly uninviting. Two more hours in gathering darkness over a pot-holed road brought us to Tripoli, and a friendly welcome from the hotel we had stayed in ten days earlier.

II

BAGHDAD AND THE TWIN RIVERS

Arriving by air from the west,
it is exciting to see the two great rivers after the expanse of desert. They are
the Twin Rivers which enclose the river-land, Mesopotamia.

Baghdad is situated just where the Twin Rivers are closest, on the narrow
waist of Mesopotamia in the strict sense: a natural location for a great city.
From the air, you see it sprawling flat on the level plain, with the Tigris
flowing through its midst in a gently curving sweep. Down at ground-level,
the breadth of the yellow muddy stream is impressive, and so is the flatness
of the land: the buildings fade away into insignificance along the perspective of the river, and the very extension of their low lines along the
flat banks makes one realize the size of the metropolis.

Hot, dusty, flat, with buildings mostly of ugly-coloured brick, Baghdad
has little charm. However, it can hardly help itself. Lower Mesopotamia is a
country of mud brought down by the great rivers and accumulated to form
land, land without a stone or a pebble over thousands of square miles. The
natural building materials are bricks made out of the sticky soil. Originally
they were simply sun-dried, but later an increasing proportion of kiln-baked
brick was used. While this reduces the tendency of the works of man to
deliquesce or crumble back into mud or the dust of dry mud, it does not
improve the colour of the buildings. In Baghdad, mud has been transformed
into a metropolis, and the city betrays its material origin by its appearance.

Of course, embellishments are possible. The most striking building in the
area is the so-called Golden or Gilded Mosque of Khazimein, just outside the

city proper. It has a truly fabulous gorgeousness. Indeed, it is a demonstration of the marvel of gold. The real preciousness of that noble metal resides in its brilliance and purity of colour, and the fact that it does not tarnish. It is this that fascinated the early metal-working peoples; even the civilized Incas prized it and utilized it not as a medium of exchange but solely for its beauty and for something sacred in its qualities. What a pity that we cannot enjoy it in the same way. Instead, we melt it into dull lumps of solid metal, and store them out of sight in super-safes underground. If we could only agree on some other standard of economic value, we could liberate this precious material from its senseless servitude to finance and use it in the service of beauty and human enjoyment, as has been done at Khazimein. Its two main domes, the balconies and soaring tops of the four chief minarets, the minor pepper-pot minarets around the domes – are all covered with gold, and glisten joyfully against the blue of the sky (pl. 41, opp. p. 220).

To see them properly, the visitor is taken up on to a roof-top opposite the mosque. As it is a Shia shrine, infidels are not allowed inside the mosque or its court. I was able just to look into the courtyard and even to photograph the rich decoration of mother-of-pearl and gilt on the entrance to the mosque proper; but when I put my foot too near the threshold of the gateway, the crowd at once became hostile.

The mosque is one of the chief holy places of the Shia Moslems, and there is a great demand to be buried in its vicinity. You are still quite likely to meet donkeys and camels approaching Khazimein with coffins on their backs. Sometimes the dead man has travelled from a distant region, and the corpse may reach Khazimein decayed or shrivelled; but it will rest in special sanctity. Furthermore, the tombs of two Saints, martyred over 1000 years ago, attract huge numbers of pilgrims, recalling the organized pilgrimages of the Middle Ages to Canterbury or Compostella.

Pilgrimage, indeed, seems to be almost a natural habit of man. To Mecca, to Rome for the Holy Year, to Lenin's Tomb in Moscow, the pilgrimages continue to flow and many tourists are really pilgrims in secular guise. Meanwhile, for many centuries the habit of pilgrimage has helped the interchange of ideas and the spread of information (and rumour) throughout the Moslem world, and has contributed a great deal to its cohesiveness.

Some of the houses round the Mosque have strange and beautiful wood-carving in their doors and balconies. Wood is another material by which brick construction can be embellished; but here it has to be imported. No trees save palms grow naturally in all this area, from Baghdad to the Gulf. In ancient times the people relied largely on the driftwood carried down the rivers. Cargoes were also carried down the Euphrates in wooden boats, and the boats then broken up for the sake of their timbers. They could not in any case have made the voyage upstream, so that their double use as vehicles and as merchandise was an ingenious stroke of business.

In one house we saw the subterranean rooms in which the inhabitants live for most of the summer, retreating underground to get away from the heat. When we in England complain of our chilly summers, we should remember that excess of heat can be worse than its lack. We read that shade temperatures at the site of ancient cities like Ur reach 130° and even 140° F. (when metal and even sand in the sun will inflict serious burns) and we wonder how existence could have been carried on, and still more how civilized life could have developed, in such surroundings. However, in antiquity all the lower Mesopotamian cities were either on rivers or in the midst of a network of irrigation canals, and surrounded with green cultivated fields. The evaporation from the irrigation water and the transpiration from the crops would have somewhat reduced the heat.

The ancient Mesopotamians too had their subterranean cool rooms, and reduced the temperature elsewhere by wet screens of reeds and other methods of utilizing the cooling power of evaporation. Even so, summer must have been a dreadful season. It still is an ordeal in the whole region, right up to the mountains in the north. T. E. Lawrence, when he was still an archeologist, brought his overseer to spend the summer in England. At the close of his visit, the man said 'What a fortunate country you have – winter all the year round.'

*

The Souks or covered Bazaars of Baghdad are famous, and rightly so. They seem more extensive and spacious than those of Damascus or Istanbul. The adjacent Street of the Coppersmiths is perhaps even more impressive. There, after walking down a few steps from street level, you can see craftsmen actually at work, and arrays of their gleaming products, like the big brass trays on which the visitor to Arab tents finds a mound of rice and mutton awaiting his fingers. And the clangour and the cool but dusty dimness give the place an unforgettable quality. My wife once witnessed five sturdy men, bared to the waist, beating out a copper plate with long-handled hammers. The five hammers came down time after time on the same spot in rapid rhythmic sequence. She could hardly tear herself away from the spectacle, which has remained one of her most vivid memories.

I liked the tailors in the Bazaar, sitting cross-legged in the proper fashion for tailors, on raised platforms beside the thronged alleys, stitching and talking busily, equally prepared to make a European or an Oriental suit of clothes. Quantities of cheap mass-produced Western goods are for sale as well as the products of local handicraft, and standards of taste must be in process of debasement; but at least the East is holding its own against the West, and, given a little encouragement, the local spirit may survive and blossom in new forms.

★

The most impressive evidence of what can be done with mud bricks is provided by the Arch of Ctesiphon.

On hearing that I wanted to see Ctesiphon, that famous ruin, my able and friendly guide, Mr Akrawi of the Education Department, arranged to take me there before breakfast – the only way in which I could squeeze it into my schedule. In this country everything that breaks the flatness of the horizon looms up in a surprising way across the plain: Ctesiphon was no exception. As we drew near, a strange silhouette resolved itself into the tragic remains of a great building, the palace of the Sassanian kings, who wrested power from the Parthians in A.D. 226, and ruled over a revived Persian Empire for more than four centuries. Ctesiphon was their capital, and once a great city, but every one of its brick buildings save this has disintegrated and disappeared. And all that is left of the great palace is a stark façade of wall to the south, with an enormous barrel vault on its right hand. This latter, the so-called Arch of Ctesiphon, is really the remains of the central hall of the palace. It was once flanked by two great rectangular wings. The north wing has wholly fallen, and of the southern wing only the eastern wall still stands: its great curtain of brick is adorned with rows of blank arches recessed between pilasters. This gives a very satisfying design even now: it must have looked unimaginably glorious when, if we may believe tradition, it was covered with gold and silver and other precious decorations. Something of its present-day beauty may be seen from the photograph on the dust-wrapper of this book.

The vault of the hall is one of the most impressive architectural constructions that I know. Its span is well over eighty feet, and its curve hangs over empty nothingness in an uncanny way. In section, instead of the semicircle of the ordinary barrel vault, it is a pointed ovoid, which gives a soaring effect. The great dome of Santa Sophia may be more satisfying, but this takes the spectator's breath. His wonder is increased when he learns that it was constructed over empty space, without the support of any temporary wooden centring. This, according to Choisy in his *Art de Bâtir chez les Byzantins*, was done by a method peculiar to Mesopotamia, especially adapted to building with thin bricks of uniform size; the bricks of the vault were stepped inwards with a backward slant against the vertical end wall, which thus served to hold up the incomplete vaulting during its construction. It is frightening to think of the workmen perched on an unfinished arch of brick, curving inward over space a hundred feet above the ground.

The building seems always to have been open to the east. The open exterior vault backed by a main wall is a familiar feature of Moslem architecture, under the name of iwan: it looks as if the idea was a pre-Moslem one, and was utilized to provide halls as well as decorative porch-like structures.

A chronicler asserts that, when the Arabs captured Ctesiphon in A.D. 637, among the loot from the Great Hall was a carpet measuring 105 by 90 feet, woven to represent a garden: the ground was gold, the paths of silver thread, the meadows green with emeralds, the streams white with pearls, the fruit and flowers bright with other precious stones. It has been suggested that the east end of the hall had a similar carpet as a portière – a gorgeous thought.

Even this one relic is dwindling with the years: earlier travellers found the hall much more nearly complete, and some of the north wing still standing. Isaiah prophesied that owls would dwell in the ruins of Babylon. Here at Ctesiphon, birds were nesting in Chosroes' palace, but birds much more beautiful than owls. As I approached the great arch, I saw quite large birds flashing in and out of holes and cracks in the brick, very lovely with soft greenish-blue head and breast and belly and rich chestnut back, and in flight rendered conspicuous by a brilliant patch of turquoise on the wings. The effect was rather like a jay, but much richer and more brilliant.

They were Rollers, a new and valued addition to my list of birds. The roller is only a mere straggler to Britain, and I had thought of it as a southern species, from Mediterranean latitudes. Later, on visiting Sweden, I discovered that it can tolerate continental summers much further north than those with an Atlantic climate, so that it penetrates to Sweden and the Baltic States.

Chosroes is the great name that I associated with Ctesiphon: indeed the local appellation of the ruin is Takhti Khesra, the Throne of Chosroes.

Chosroes has even entered into Christian iconography. In the great hall where he once sat, I thought of that master work of Piero della Francesca, the frescoes in Arezzo dealing with the story of the True Cross. There is depicted the great scene of battle in 627 between Chosroes and the Emperor Heraclius. One of Chosroes' generals had carried away the Holy Cross from conquered Jerusalem thirteen years earlier, and the legend was that Chosroes had had it built into the seat of his throne. In the frescoes, Chosroes' son is killed by an arrow in the throat, while Chosroes himself is taken prisoner, and later put to death by beheading.

Actually, when I looked up the details, I found that both Piero and I were wrong: Chosroes escaped, to be murdered next year in another of his palaces. I was also wrong in imagining that the Chosroes of the fresco was the Chosroes who raised Ctesiphon to the height of its magnificence. The great Chosroes, styled the Blessed, reigned in the sixth century, and was the grandfather of Piero's Chosroes. He was the great-hearted enemy of Justinian and Belisarius. One of his strange actions was to carry off the population of Antioch, and with them to found a new city, 'Chosroe-Antioch', not far from Ctesiphon; and one of the facts of his reign was the emergence of the Turks on to the stage of recorded history, as his opponents in an important campaign. To my further confusion, I find that modern historians have dropped the name Chosroes altogether, and call the builder of Ctesiphon *Anushirwan*.

The Sassanians had resuscitated the Persian empire after five centuries of subjugation, first to Alexander and the Seleucids, and then to the invading Parthians from the region east of the Caspian. The silk trade from China helped to bring wealth to their court: it is curious to think of Chinese merchants gazing at Chosroes' palace on the banks of the Tigris. In Chosroes' reign, Persian medicine flourished greatly; Nestorian Christians brought to Persia the scientific and philosophical works of ancient Greece; translation were made of these, of Jewish literature, including the Psalms, of Buddhist philosophy, of Hindu tales and romances; and the introduction of chess from the east marked the first step towards its later triumphal march through Europe.

Sassanian Persia did not give rise to great discoveries in science, or to great innovations in thought or art: it was valuable in world history as a melting-pot for diverse influences and a reservoir and agency of transmission for classical culture through the Dark Ages of the West, as well as an upholder of large-scale international trade, an essential link between the Far East and Europe.

The barbaric quality which still clung round its civilization may be gauged from the fantastic luxury and ritual of the court. The king, we are told, was never visible to the common people, and only a handful of the nobility and a few favourites had access to his person: foreign envoys and visitors, however important, had to be content with paying their respects to a golden statue.

On the way back we crossed a tributary of the Tigris. The tributary (I have forgotten its name) was considerably broader than any river in Britain; and the stretch of water where it debouched into the Tigris looked almost like the sea. The water was calm and tranquil, its flow scarcely perceptible. Palm-trees grew along the banks, and women in black dresses came up from the water-side with pitchers on their heads just as in the pictures of Bible times that I remembered from my schooldays.

A rattling overhead drew my attention: it was a kingfisher – one of the larger species, not unlike the common belted kingfisher of North America. I am fond of this type of kingfisher, although they have none of the magic brilliance of the small species, like our own bird with its flash of jewelled blue or the even tinier malachite kingfisher of Central Africa: I like their funny big heads and beaks, and their cheerful noisiness. And I thought back to my journey in East Africa twenty years ago, when I first realized that the very word *Kingfisher* is a misnomer when applied to the group as a whole, since the original Alcedinidae were inhabitants of dry woodland and savannah, and first developed the 'fishing' habit on land, by plunging from a branch after insects in the tall grass.

Further along the main road I had a real ornithological treat: the bee-eaters were on migration. Groups of them were all about the place, mostly perched on the telegraph wires like notes on music-paper, but a number sitting quietly on the side of the highway. Now and again, one or a few would take to the wing, hawk round a little for insects, and return to rest.

On my way to Jerash, I had already become acquainted with this bird, perhaps the most elegantly beautiful of living creatures. It is bright with many colours, but neither gaudy nor bizarre, beautifully tailored, without the extraneous attractions of special crests or plumes. The tail is striking, but not exaggerated, longish, with the central feathers protruding to form a point. The wings are slender and pointed, the flight even more elegant (I cannot avoid the word) than a swallow's; the long, slightly decurved black bill is the final triumphal touch in the design.

So ended my visit to Ctesiphon; a few minutes later I was back in Baghdad, where the sun, instead of lending brilliance to the scene, served only to accentuate the mud-brown quality of everything.

★

Like so many cities in the Near East, Baghdad did not just grow after the fashion of London or Paris, but was founded deliberately. There have been many new dynasties in the region, and a new dynasty often demanded a new capital. This was the case with Baghdad. The Ommayad Caliphs had moved the capital of the Moslem world from the inconvenient Mesopotamian site of Kufah to Damascus, where they ruled for some ninety glorious years. But when they were conquered and their race almost exterminated by the first Abbasid ruler, Safar the Bloodthirsty, in A.D. 750, a new capital was clearly needed. Damascus was still full of friends and supporters of the Ommayads; it lay too far to the west, exposed to trouble from the Christian world, and with the desert making too much of a barrier between it and the thriving area of Iran and Mesopotamia; above all, it was an inland city, while the times demanded sea-borne trade and communications.

Safar died before getting round to choosing a new site; but his successor, the great Mansur, took the task very seriously, and for seven years made journeys through the area to find the ideal spot. Eventually his choice fell on Baghdad – a tiny village in his day, though it seems to have been something of a town in the times of Nebuchadnezzar. In 762 he began to build. A hundred thousand workmen were employed, and in four years his new city was finished.

He built on a new plan. His city was circular, nearly a mile and a half in diameter, with three lines of walls and four gates, and the palace in an empty space in the centre. Another unique feature was his employment of huge bricks, weighing up to 100 or even 200 pounds apiece. For its adornment many other cities were stripped. As the population grew, the city spread outside the circular walls.

It was here that Harun al Rashid held his brilliant court at the close of the 8th century, and raised the Abbasid dynasty to its highest pitch. His fame was great, and he, as ruler of the East, exchanged gifts with Charlemagne as ruler of the West: one of his gifts was an elephant – perhaps the very animal immortalized in stone in the porch of Bâle Cathedral. In the *Arabian Nights*, he became a legendary figure on the world's stage. The legend, however, seems to be very different from the reality. Thus we learn that in all probability he never took his famous walks in disguise through Baghdad. He was, on the other hand, a stickler for religious observances, and prostrated himself in prayer a hundred times each day. The *Encyclopaedia Britannica* ends its account on this note of disillusion: 'His Arabic biographers are unanimous in describing him as noble and generous, but there is little doubt that he was in fact a man of little force of character, suspicious, untrustworthy and on occasion cruel.'

There is, however, no doubt of his excessive riches and the fantastic luxury of his court. As Hitti records in his *History of the Arabs*, his wife had nothing but gold and jewelled vessels at her table, and Harun spent 3 million dinars on her pilgrimage to Mecca. This he could well afford, as the confiscation of the Barmecides' estates brought him 36 million dinars in coin, not to mention lands and furniture.

Sad to say, there is not a trace to be seen today of Mansur's Round City, and most of the buildings of Baghdad's glorious age, from the 8th to the 13th century, have disappeared. This is due primarily to the Mongols. The entire civilization of Iranian Mesopotamia received a deadly blow at the hands of Genghiz Khan and his successors. Here in Baghdad it was the very heart of Islam that suffered.

Twenty-five years after Genghiz' death, Hulagu, younger brother of the legendary Kubla Khan, was dispatched to Persia with orders to crush the strange and dangerous sect of the Assassins, and also the Caliphate, which was still centred on Baghdad. It took him four years to wipe out the Assassins: two years later in 1257 he marched against the Caliph, the last of the now decadent Abbasids, and a weak and pleasure-loving character. Besieged and assaulted in Baghdad, the Caliph was deluded into surrendering himself; but Hulagu was no respecter of promises, and had him beaten to death in a sack. The city was taken and was given over to massacre and looting for a week. According to one account, nearly a million people were slaughtered, often to the accompaniment of frightful torture and mutilation. This must be an exaggeration, but certainly a very small proportion of the inhabitants escaped with their lives. After being thoroughly looted, the palaces and mosques were burnt; and in the flames many other buildings were destroyed.

Moslem civilization and culture was at a high level in the 13th century. With the sack of Baghdad it received a setback from which it never fully recovered. Only the fact that Hulagu's army was later defeated by the Mamelukes saved Egypt, the last independent stronghold of Moslem culture, from being blasted and overrun.

Baghdad has also suffered many physical disasters, at the hands of the Tigris. The rivers of Lower Mesopotamia, like the Po and the Mississippi, have built up their banks well above the level of the plain. Now and again these natural levees, though artificially strengthened, break under the impact of a flood rolling down from the northern mountains; and then the city may be badly inundated. The worst disaster of all was the combined flood and pestilence of 1831. The plague broke out in March, and raged for over two months; the death-rate rose to five thousand a day – a daily three per cent of the entire population. When the flood began to rise in April, there were no able-bodied men left to keep the levees in good order, and eventually the waters burst in and flooded half the city. Thousands of houses had their foundations undermined and fell down. When at last the waters retreated, they revealed a field of ruins covered deep in mud, with starving dogs digging out the human corpses from it. Nearly three-quarters of the population had died.

Seton Lloyd, in his *Foundations of the Dust*, gives a vivid account of the disaster and the state of almost incredible poverty and squalor into which the city was plunged; the squalid Baghdad which the English traveller Buckingham had described three years before was not beautiful or rich; but it was at least populous and bustling. Seton Lloyd compares the disaster with those which befell Nineveh or Pompeii, though with the vital difference that the stricken city revived from the blow.

All of Lower Mesopotamia is sadly fallen from its past estate. It is not merely that Baghdad has lost its glory, or that the plain is dotted with the sites of vanished cities: the basis of its life has been smashed. All over the area you may see the remains of irrigation works and drainage channels, either dry or blocked. A great part of a once fruitful land has reverted to infertility, even to desert. To keep the irrigation system working demands peaceful prosperity and efficient organization: what was left of it finally fell to bits under the centuries of Turkish oppression, inefficiency and maladministration. However, what man has done once he can do again; and these melancholy remains also hold out a hope of revival for the future, though new methods of agriculture may be indicated.

Even on my hasty trip to Ctesiphon I had glimpses of the extent of the Mesopotamian flood-plain. But when I looked at the map, Ctesiphon appeared as hardly more than a suburb of Baghdad. The flat of the alluvium begins near Samara, over fifty miles upstream. Its length to the sea is nearly 400 miles, and it is often well over 100 miles wide. It contains the sites of a large number of ruined towns and cities, as well as the great lagoons and marshlands where the Marsh Arabs live a sort of web-footed existence.

According to most historians and archeologists, this area of potentially rich and fertile land only came into existence during the geologically short span of six or seven thousand years. On this view, in about 4000 B.C. the shore of the Persian Gulf extended well to the north of Baghdad; by the third millennium the silt had pushed the sea back to the neighbourhood of Ur; and the further eighty miles of soil to the present shore-line have been deposited since that time. The neolithic inhabitants of the northern uplands, pushing downwards towards the sea, saw the process of land-building in operation – sea becoming converted into freshwater marsh, islands and promontories of soil emerging from the waters, vegetation clothing the islands. They were already confirmed agriculturists, and saw how the fertility of the area could be utilized with the aid of drainage and irrigation. Irrigation was needed because there is no regular inundation, as in the Nile, timed to coincide with the needs of agriculture; drainage was needed to prevent the persistence of marsh and swamp. And so the process of colonization was supposed to have occurred parallel with that of land-formation.

This has now been put in doubt by the geologists. Lees and Falcon, in the *Geographical Journal* (1952, *118*, 24), find no evidence that the head of the Gulf has appreciably altered its position during the six-thousand-year period from when man was first emerging into civilization, though there may have been slight advances and retreats. Geologically, the area is still, it seems, in process of subsidence. It is a tectonic trough or geosyncline, lying between the two firm masses of central Persia and Arabia. These have been very gradually approaching each other, so that the trough has suffered a slow compression. This has led to its deepening, while on its eastern side, the strata have been upfolded into anticlines, producing the great mountain ranges along the margin of Persia. This combined trough-deepening and mountain-building movement has been going on for tens of millions of years: it had its climax in the Pliocene period, and is now much less violent. According to this view, it was millions of years ago that the plain from Samara to the sea was first

formed by deposition of silt; and since then continued deposition has maintained its surface-level while the bottom of the trough has been slowly
lowered by recurrent spasms of compression. The total depth of sediment
deposited by the rivers – not only the two great rivers from the north but also
the Karun from the east, which helps to build a bar across the seaward margin
of the marshy area – must thus be very great.

The process of depression of our flood-plain area was not a steady one, but
episodic; an extra squeeze resulted in a period of (relatively) rapid submer-
gence. Near the coast, some of the elaborate irrigation works of previous
centuries are now actually submerged under the waters of the Gulf.

The two views can perhaps be partially reconciled. The melting of the
great ice-sheets at the end of the last glacial period raised the ocean level by
close on 300 feet. This would have enlarged the Gulf and brought its head far
inland, so that silting would have a heavy new task before land could once
more emerge. The drowning of the upper end of the Gulf might well have
still persisted into the early Neolithic, so that the earliest agriculturists to
reach the region might have witnessed, not the first formation of the flood-
plain, but its re-emergence from the waters.

It is most improbable that the rise in sea-level was the origin of the Flood
legend. Woolley's explanation seems more likely. He found that at Ur,
during its first or El Ubaid period, a bank of silt eleven feet thick had been
deposited against its walls, with the ruined remains of houses below it. The
silt was clean, without any man-made objects or trace of human occupation.
This bed of silt could only have been laid down as the result of a flood bigger
than any other in Mesopotamian history, submerging all the flood-plain
area occupied by man under perhaps twenty feet of water. The larger towns
were centred on artificial hills, and so may have largely escaped actual destruction; but it must have been a momentous disaster for the budding
Sumerian civilization.

In any event, in the flood-plain area no purely neolithic cultures have been
unearthed comparable to those in the foothills to the north and north-east.
Nor do we find remains of the succeeding Tell Halaf culture from near Mosul,
dating from about 4500 B.C. This was chalcolithic, using copper as material
for rare and sacred objects; but it was still essentially neolithic in that people
still used stone for everyday purposes, and lived not in towns but small
peasant villages. In spite of this, it had reached a high level of technical and
artistic skill: its pots in the Iraq Museum are astonishingly elaborate and

beautiful. It has even been suggested that they were the products of a specialized industry.

Only after this phase was the flood-plain invaded, for here the El Ubaid culture stratum always rests on virgin soil. Society must have reached a certain level of organization before man felt able to undertake the works of irrigation and drainage needed to exploit the fertility of the flood-plain. Once he had made the venture, the new environment dictated a considerably higher level of organization, and soon led to the development of true cities. Settled life was born of agriculture in the foothills: civilization was born of organized irrigation and drainage in the flood-plains.

★

But I must extricate myself from the clutches of the past and return to the present. My last day in Iraq was devoted to two visits. The first was to the very up-to-date Agricultural Station outside the city. The Director's garden was a place of charming greenery, full of interesting flowers. And the Station demonstrated how fertile the land could become with scientific methods of irrigation and cultivation. The trouble is how to secure the general application of such methods. The pressure of population is not nearly so acute as in Egypt, and perhaps for that reason, there has been less urgency in coming to grips with the basic problem underlying so much of Iraq's troubles – the system of land ownership, half-tribal and half-feudal, whereby Sheikhs may own huge estates, up to fifty or even a hundred square miles in area, on which the peasants are kept at work as agricultural labourers, usually on very low standards of living.

My second visit was to one of these land-owning Sheikhs, and gave me the opportunity of taking part in a traditional Arab meal. I had read about the huge brass platters, a yard across, heaped high with mountains of rice and meat, from which the guests help themselves with their bare hands; but now I found for myself how agreeable this method of eating can be. The monumental pile of victuals introduces a lordly air of abundance, and in taking food from it with one's fingers one has the sense of partaking in a patriarchal ritual.

My host was a handsome middle-aged man, well-read and cultivated (pl. 37, opp. p. 201). He gave the curious impression of belonging to two incompatible worlds at one and the same time – the tribal world of Arabian life, with its Beduins and deserts, and the cosmopolitan western world of smart international hotels. He could have slipped into place in a Paris salon or the lounge of the Savoy as easily as he could have slipped out of his Arab clothes into a smart lounge suit. In Iraq he performed a useful function in giving western visitors the glimpse of eastern life for which they all crave.

The other chief guest was very decidedly not a man of two worlds. He was the Iraqi Minister of Education, a rather formidable figure wedded to traditional Moslem ideas. However, the western world persisted in breaking in: western science and engineering had to be given their place in Iraqi education; and Unesco must have been a disturbing irruption. He expressed the hope that Unesco never served alcohol, even at its receptions in Paris. I had to admit that it did, which saddened him. However, Iraq continued its loyal support of Unesco.

Some of the local guests arrived in their own cars. I particularly remember one energetic young man, who fifty years ago would have bounded into the saddle of an Arab barb held by a retainer, tinkering with his jeep before triumphantly roaring off across the desert in traditional Arab dress.

It is relatively easy for technical elements of one culture to become incorporated in another, like the motor-car in the life of the Beduin. What is much harder is for two sharply distinct social systems and worlds of thought to become integrated in a new and larger whole.

Today the world will no longer work as a system of separate units. The West as much as the East has to adjust itself to this new situation, in which integrative ideas, like that of partnership in a joint adventure of civilization, are needed. But will they prevail against the disintegrative forces of one-sided exploitation, nationalist competition and ideological intolerance? That is the sort of question that Iraq forces on its visitors: only events can give the answer.

12

THE BIRTH OF CIVILIZATION

THE IRAQ MUSEUM IS ONE OF the notable sights of Baghdad. I was only able to tear myself away from it by reminding myself of all my other engagements before my inexorable schedule took me to the airfield and Teheran. Its rather overcrowded rooms had become for me the spacious corridors of time. In them, for three exciting hours, I walked in history.

The Museum, and the entire Antiquities Department, was the creation of the British as Mandatory Power after the First World War. They had the good sense to obtain the services of Gertrude Bell as Oriental Secretary to the High Commissioner; and to her was assigned the duty of creating an Antiquities Service. Gertrude Bell combined a remarkable knowledge of the past of the Middle East with a deep capacity for understanding the people who lived in its present. In *Amurath to Amurath*, written in 1911, she described not only the historical and archeological results of a long and arduous journey of exploration, but also the sense of change that was then beginning to stir in the Arab world, the demand for that new and mysterious something men called liberty. Today, largely as a result of her work, a free Iraq has become proud of its past.

★

The first objects, chronologically speaking, to attract my attention were the earliest sickles. I had never read of sickles made merely of baked clay: but here they were, rather moving in their obvious blunt inefficiency. Then there were sickles whose cutting edge consisted of small flint teeth mounted in wood or bone. In some of the earliest, the teeth were mounted on rib-bones. But jaw-bones were soon preferred owing to their advantage of being curved; and from them to a full sickle shape in wood or clay was a natural step soon taken. In Mesopotamia, the teeth were cemented into place with bitumen. Flint teeth are a most ingenious device for improving the sharpness and durability of the reaping edge; but they were, of course, super-seded as soon as metal became cheap and common enough.

The curved sickle persisted through all changes of material as man's reaping implement for seven thousand years or so, until it was superseded within living memory by the reaping machine – a drastic revolution in agricultural technique.

Bitumen is a valuable Mesopotamian raw material. Noah used it to pitch his ark, and it is still used to waterproof the guffahs, those extraordinary giant coracles (enlarged and waterproof baskets, as Gertrude Bell calls them) that spin round and round as they ferry people and even horses across the Tigris. And it was used as mortar in the more important buildings before true binding mortar was invented. This is what the 9th chapter of Genesis means when it says that the builders of the Tower of Babel had 'slime' for mortar. Herodotus, who visited Hit, says that bitumen from here was used in building the walls of Babylon: and Ur's modern name was 'the mound of pitch', from the bitumen used as mortar in the ancient city.

Hit, on the Euphrates, has been the chief source of bitumen for five thou-sand years and more. Gertrude Bell gives a vivid description of the liquid pitch welling out of the ground and solidifying into asphalt pavement. The pitch-burners broke this up and melted it over fires of the same substance, fires from which columns of acrid smoke rose into the desert air. The product was loaded in baskets on to donkeys. In the excavations at Ur, in strata near the time of the great flood, a load of bitumen was found with basket-marks still on it; and analysis of the traces of earth on it showed that it had come from Hit, doubtless on donkey-back.

Bitumen is usually used to mean all solid and semi-solid varieties of natur-ally occurring hydrocarbons, like asphalt. It is to oil (petroleum) what oil is to natural gas. In Iraq, as in most cases, it occurs close to large supplies of oil; it seems rather ironical that the greatest single source of wealth in the country was never utilized until the present century. However, this is not really so surprising. It would have been difficult for the ancient Sumerians to find a use for petroleum, and it needed a technological age to exploit the precious liquid usefully, or to extract it efficiently. Do not let us forget that coal was similarly neglected through the greater part of history: even in England coal was not seriously mined until the 16th century.

But to return to the Museum; here the visitor can see with his own eyes the amazing progress that went on during the latter half of the fourth millennium, the so-called protoliterate phase, during which writing was being developed and towns were growing into cities. The continuity of the change was broken (though its advance may have been stimulated) by the irruption of a new people, the bearers of the Jemdet Nasr culture, probably from the east by way of the sea-coast. Eventually their rule seems to have been overthrown by a revolutionary upheaval, which led directly to the beginning of the dynastic period: their latest buildings show signs of having been destroyed by fire, and their decorated pottery suddenly disappears. This revolution introduced the use of curious bun-shaped bricks, flat below and curved above. Woolley suggests that the choice of this unpractical shape was inspired by hatred of the alien Jemdet Nasr rule: the revolutionaries wanted to be different, in their bricks as in everything else.

The Uruk invasion which replaced the Jemdet Nasr people seems to have come in from the north, bringing new arts and new ideas. One of their first introductions was the potter's wheel. An actual heavy clay wheel, some three feet across, with a hole for the peg with which it was spun, is evidence of this notable change, one of the earliest mechanizations of an industrial process. It seems to have been preceded by the so-called 'slow-wheel', which could be slowly turned by hand, but not continuously spun.

The Uruk people brought with them the tradition of building in stone, and continued to use some stone in the flood-plain, in spite of the difficulty and expense of transporting it to that stoneless area. They also brought with them the tradition of worshipping on high places. There being no high places in southern Mesopotamia, they were forced to build great mounds of earth – the ziggurats: there seems no doubt that a ziggurat is an artificial sacred mountain. As technique improved and population increased, the ziggurat grew from a smallish mound to a huge terraced structure, planted with trees to recall its mountain origin, and in its latest manifestations high enough to give rise to the legend of the Tower of Babel.

During these crucial five hundred years, architecture made great strides. The reed huts of earlier ages gave place to houses of mud-brick, while monumental structures, both of brick and stone, appeared, but the form of the monumental buildings continued to recall their humble origin. The original reed hut was made of reed-mats attached to strong upright reed-bundles planted in the ground: as a result their walls had the appearance of a series of panels recessed between protruding columns. This panel-and-buttress effect was retained throughout Sumerian history, though much modified in appearance by the use of bricks instead of reeds. The original doorways were supported by palm logs. In later buildings such log columns were encrusted with mother-of-pearl in bitumen, or brick columns were used, but encrusted with clay studs to simulate the bases of the fronds on a palm-trunk.

Some exciting exhibits illustrate the step-by-step development of a written language, from crude pictographs to an elaborate system of conventionalized signs. There is also what is claimed as the first true portrait known – a very beautiful life-size head in white marble (or was it alabaster?) from late pre-dynastic times, before 3000 B.C. But much of the pre-dynastic sculpture is crude or heavy. Very early we are introduced to the big-nosed, rather thick-set Sumerian type, and to the characteristic kilts and robes of sheepskin with the fleece still on them.

★

The greatest treasures of the Iraq Museum are those excavated by Woolley from the royal graves or death-pits at Ur. They have been described and figured over and over again, but I must testify to the extraordinary impression made by the originals.

The amplest discoveries are dated as from the 29th century B.C., about the time of the first pyramids in Egypt: the death-pits were filled with the bodies of soldiers, women attendants and courtiers, even chariots with oxen or asses harnessed to them, and an abundance of precious objects. In all, sixteen royal burials have been unearthed, together with nearly a thousand non-royal graves.

Let me quote Woolley: in one case, 'the floor of the death-pit was covered with bodies all in ordered rows: 6 men on the entrance side, and 68 women in court dress, red coats with beaded cuffs and shell-ring belts, head-dresses of gold or silver, great lunate earrings and multiple necklaces of blue and gold. Among them was one girl who was not wearing her silver hair-ribbon – it was in her pocket, tightly coiled up, as if she had been late for the funeral [her own!] and had not had time to put it on. There were four harpists with their lyres, and by them in an open space lay a copper cauldron: it was difficult not to connect this with the little drinking-vessel found by every one of the 74 bodies in the pit.' It seems that after the death and burial of the king or queen, a retinue of attendants bearing a collection of rich and precious objects descended a ramp into the pit, lay down, and drank a narcotic to ensure a peaceful death: all the bodies lie peacefully, with no sign of struggle. The bodies were then covered with earth; a ritual feast was held on the new floor, and a few more victims sacrificed and buried. This process was repeated two or three times until the pit was entirely filled up.

Some authorities think that this amazing ritual was associated, not with the burial of temporal rulers, but with the sacrifice of a sacred 'corn-king' and 'spring-queen', a fertility rite, springing from the same source as those of Adonis and Osiris, in which a mystic marriage symbolizing the earth's fruitfulness culminated in the killing of the bride and bridegroom. Or perhaps the ancient fertility rite had been combined with a more modern ceremonial of royal burial. Rituals ensuring that a dead personage shall take his possessions with him to the other world, and not return to vex the living, are amazingly persistent. In January 1953, *The Times* recorded that not sixty miles from London, a gipsy 'queen' had died: her crockery was ritually smashed, her caravan was burnt, and her two horses solemnly shot. Mr Partridge took up the tale and told how he, as a district officer in Southern Nigeria in 1902, witnessed the funeral ceremonies of the King of Igara. Nine oxen were killed to escort the king's spirit; but for Mr Partridge's intervention, nine slaves would have been impaled on spears, and all the king's wives and eunuchs would have been buried alive in the royal grave. It seems clear that the ceremonies at Ur in the third millennium B.C., and in England and Nigeria nearly 5000 years later, are all descendants of the same primeval neolithic rite.

In any case we have at Ur an extraordinary survival of neolithic human sacrifice into an elaborate civilization. For elaborate it was, even at that early date, as you can see in the richness and beauty of its products. There is in the museum a superb helmet from a non-royal grave, beaten out of a single sheet of gold into the form of a wig, with the hair shown in relief. There is a large eight-stringed instrument from one of the royal death-pits, half-way between a harp and a lyre, decorated with gold, silver, shell, and lapis lazuli, and with a golden bull's head, complete with golden false beard, projecting from the sounding-box: the false beard was an emblem of divinity for the sacred bull, just as it was for the sacred Egyptian pharaohs. There are the wreaths and necklaces of the queen and her attendants, with their touchingly naturalistic leaves of gold sprouting from chains of lapis and gold and red stone beads. There are the fantastic 'rams caught in a thicket' – in reality heraldic he-goats, with fleeces of shell and lapis, and face and limbs covered with gold foil, standing erect with their forelegs tied by silver chains to a golden-flowered shrub. There are gold and stone vessels of exquisite shape, richly scabbarded and hilted copper daggers, and elaborate boards, complete with their pieces, for some game whose rules we do not know.

Then there is in the museum the earliest-known article of iron – a dagger from the 27th century; and, of course, a vast number of seals; and the unique collection of clay documents and letters, some of them with clay envelopes for the address.

★

The later history of the region too could be illustrated from the exhibits in the Iraq Museum: but it can best be pursued in books.

As in Egypt, the region was eventually consolidated into a single political entity. But this was never achieved in the first five-hundred-year heyday of pure Sumerian civilization, when the cities of the flood-plain were engaged in a constant struggle for the power that more land and better water-supply would ensure.

The first unification of the region was effected about 2500 B.C. by an alien ruler, Sargon I. He was King of Akkad, the area to the north of Sumer which had been settled by invading Semites, of a quite different ethnic type from the Sumerians.

Akkadian dominance lasted only a few centuries. After this, Ur stepped into the lead, and its kings became the rulers of the mixed kingdom comprising both Akkad and the Sumerian flood-plain. It was then, a little before 2000 B.C., that Ur reached its greatest size and magnificence, symbolized by a new and enormous ziggurat. This, crowned with the temple of the moon-god, and equipped with a vast army of priests and scribes, a staff of sacred prostitutes, and elaborate schools, must have rivalled any of the contemporary monuments of Egypt.

Mesopotamian power was destined to fall increasingly into Semite hands. By the beginning of the second millennium, power had become centred at Babylon, with the cities of the flood-plain in a subordinate position:

Hammurabi is the great figure of this period, rightly famous as the first great codifier of law.

It was during Babylonian dominance that Abraham lived in 'Ur of the Chaldees' and undertook his journey to Palestine. Sir Leonard Woolley, in his *Abraham*, has given us an interesting study of the Abraham legend and its basis of probable fact.

By Hammurabi's time, as can be seen in the museum, early Mesopotamian art had already passed its highest point, and the first Babylonian empire soon fell into decay under the onslaught of Hittite and Kassite invaders. The irruptions of new peoples and the rivalries of new empires, like Hurri and Mitanni, spread confusion through the region. Out of the confusion there crystallized, around 1400 B.C., a new organization of power in northern Mesopotamia – the kingdom of Assyria.

I was unable to see the ruins of the Assyrian cities with my own eyes; but I consoled myself by reading Layard's *Nineveh*, which brought home the excitement of his archeological discoveries. Meanwhile the Assyrian sculptures in the Iraq Museum, though Layard's collection in London far surpasses them in abundance, were sufficient exponents of the sinister quality of this new empire. Although some of the later reliefs include splendid and even beautiful portrayals of wild animals, the general effect of Assyrian art is antipathetic. There is something hateful about the monstrous composite figures of gigantic lions and bulls with wings and human heads, the kings with their crimped beards and stiff gestures, the monotonous succession of scenes of battle, booty, and brutal treatment.

Indeed the Assyrian empire was in many respects the most frightful power in recorded history. It is true that some of the Assyrian kings introduced remarkable technical improvements, such as a military road-system, or Sennacherib's thirty-mile aqueduct to supply water to Nineveh; that administration and business organization reached a new pitch of efficiency with the introduction of a postal system and the use of silver for currency; that the royal libraries of the later empire were the largest yet amassed in the world's history; that architectural technique (though not architectural taste or beauty) reached new heights in the royal palaces of Sargon and Sennacherib. But the emphasis was always on the military machine. New weapons, new siege techniques, new military formations – it was in these above all that the

35. A handsome Alawit woman at the Saadés' tobacco-curing establishment in the mountains

36. *That extraordinary phenomenon, a beehive village, near Aleppo*

37. *In the desert near Baghdad: myself with my Sheikh host on my right and the very orthodox Minis of Education on my·left*

Assyrians excelled; and their power was essentially predatory, only maintained by force and fear and only supported by the flow of booty and tribute.

It has been suggested that the cruelties depicted on Assyrian reliefs were merely propaganda to encourage a submissive spirit in Assyria's enemies. But even if this proved to be true, the Assyrians were, in fact, monstrously destructive and horribly cruel, and their final fall under the assault of the Medes and the Chaldeans was the occasion for universal relief and exultation throughout the ancient world.

Their policy of military conquest left them with no friends among other nations; while the need for a huge standing army led to the deterioration of their economics and the decay of their agriculture. The Assyrian Empire, in fact, was a self-defeating organization, demonstrating the impossibility of building a continuing civilization on a policy of militaristic conquest.

The rootlessness of Assyrian culture and the completeness of its collapse is revealed in Xenophon's *Anabasis*. On the Ten Thousand's northward march, they saw the enormous mounds and ruins that marked the sites of Nineveh and other Assyrian cities. Xenophon records the astonishment of the Greeks at the spectacle of those huge cities lying desolate and uninhabited; but, though only just over 200 years had elapsed since the fall of Assyria, he not only knew nothing of their real history, but was unable to discover anything by his enquiries on the spot. It is as if all knowledge of the Prussia of Frederick the Great had perished out of twentieth-century Europe.

By contrast, the Chaldean or second Babylonian Empire that rose with Assyria's fall was humane and civilized, even if Nebuchadnezzar did carry the Jews away into captivity. But in spite of its magnificence, which so impressed Herodotus, and its vast ziggurat which passed into legend as the Tower of Babel, and its remarkable progress in astronomy, the Chaldean civilization tended to look back towards the glories of the past of the region rather than forwards to the possibilities of the future, and was destined to a speedy fall before the onslaught of the Medes and Persians.

The later objects in the museum are no longer distinctively Mesopotamian, but represent imperial cultures, of larger geographical extent – Parthian, Iranian, Abbasid, Turkish. It is only in the last few decades that, as the very existence of the Iraq Museum demonstrates, the land of the Twin Rivers has again become a political unit in its own right.

New techniques reveal new worlds. As a boy, I experienced in my own person the shock of fascinated surprise with which I entered the new world of minuteness and invisible life revealed by the microscope. New techniques have since extended its boundaries, until we are glimpsing the chemical units of life, while our 17th-century ancestors had not even dreamt of an amoeba or a spermatozoon.

The telescope revealed the world of stars and galaxies, quite unimagined by pre-telescopic ages, and each increase in its power has opened up new and ever more surprising features.

In biology, when Darwin wrote the *Origin of Species*, less than a century ago, not one single fossil series illustrating evolution was known. Today, techniques of stratigraphic geology and organized fossil-collecting have revealed the world of past evolution in all its surprising manifestations, and pushed its time-boundaries hundreds of millions of years into the past.

The very idea of a world of history was alien to primitive man, and the first conscious exploration of it was taken by the classical Athenians. Its techniques have developed enormously in the last hundred years, until we now are beginning to obtain a reasonably comprehensive picture of the world of world history.

The latest world to be revealed is that of prehistory, and the revelation has been effected by archeology. The chief instrument of archeology has always been the spade, but it is its new technique which has revealed the extent and variety of man's history before History – the technique of organized expeditions, careful stratigraphical excavation, preservation and record of every kind of object, skilled reconstruction, correlation of the results into a general scheme of dating.

Baalbek and Palmyra bear witness to the earliest phase of archeology, the phase when curiosity about antiquity sent men searching for its ruined marvels, and its chief instruments were the writer's pen and the draughtsman's pencil in a record of what they saw on the spot.

In the Iraq Museum I had seen so many cuneiform writings together with their translations – commercial transactions, religious myths, commemorative inscriptions, accounts of everyday life five thousand years ago – that I had taken the comprehensibility of the language for granted. One day, however, when I was discussing the origin of writing with an archeologist, I asked him whether there had been any sort of Rosetta Stone, any multilingual inscription which had given the key to cuneiform. Yes, he said, there were multilingual inscriptions, but they were not like the Rosetta Stone, because all the languages were unknown: and yet Rawlinson broke the secret. He whetted my appetite to find out more about the story: and a very extraordinary story it is.

Rawlinson was a cavalry subaltern in India, a handsome young man of great physical energy, but also great intellectual energy and wide interests. In 1833, while on a military mission to Persia, he had seen Persepolis and had been fascinated by it. In 1835 he was made military adviser at Kermanshah, on the western margin of Persia; and at Kermanshah he heard of the Rock of Behistun, 22 miles to the east. Here on a precipitous rock-face, 400 feet up, are great sculptured panels with inscriptions on them, all in cuneiform lettering, but in three different languages. He discovered that this gigantic surface, some 1200 square feet in area, had been carefully prepared beforehand, and bad patches of stone replaced by new pieces carefully fixed in place.

Rawlinson himself scrambled up to take copies and squeezes of some of the inscriptions, but others he could only reach with the help of ropes and ladders. Even so, one was so inaccessible that he had to enlist a 'wild Kurdish boy', who by dint of daring rock-climbing and with the aid of a rope-cradle and some wooden pegs, managed to secure squeezes of the third language – ten years after Rawlinson had published his key to the transcription of the first and easiest inscription.

I may anticipate a little by mentioning that these latest squeezes turned out to be in the Babylonian language, and in the 1880's were badly nibbled by mice in the British Museum in Bloomsbury! – though luckily only after they had been deciphered and published.

Rawlinson started on the one which used the fewest signs, and was therefore presumably alphabetic instead of syllabic (it was in point of fact ancient Persian). He found two phrases over the heads of two royal personages, each consisting of four apparent words, three of them the same in both inscriptions, but one of these three in a different position in the two cases – thus: A, B, C, D; and then E, B, C, A.* Rawlinson concluded that B was a title, that C meant 'son of', and that A, D, and E were names; he further adopted the working hypothesis that the two personages were the two most famous kings of the country, Darius and Xerxes. The working hypothesis

* Actually there were complications concerning the genitive case, etc.; I have merely tried to illustrate the principle.

worked. The two phrases were 'Darius the King, son of Hystaspes' and 'Xerxes the King, son of Darius'. With this he had enough letters to identify a number of other names; and, since these names all had their Greek equivalents, he was able to establish a cuneiform alphabet. The secret was broken; in 1837, two years after he had first begun the exploration of the Rock, he was able to publish a translation of two whole paragraphs of this inscription.

Later on, with the aid of scholars at home, the secrets of the more difficult syllabic languages were also solved; they turned out to be Elamite and Babylonian. The learned men of the day were somewhat suspicious of the claims of Rawlinson and his two chief helpers. Eventually they agreed to a test: the three men were shut up separately with copies of a newly-discovered cuneiform inscription – and all three produced identical transcriptions.

This slightly critical attitude of British scholars was nothing compared with the behaviour of their German colleagues on the same subject. Towards the close of the century it was discovered that, at Göttingen in 1802, a youngish German called Grotefeld had broken the secret of the alphabetic cuneiform by methods almost identical with those that Rawlinson worked out for himself 35 years later. But his paper on the subject was refused publication by the Göttingen Academy of Sciences, on account of the jealousy of those in academic authority. German science thus lost the priority which a German scientist had actually earned.

The history of archeology turns out to be almost as fascinating as archeology itself. But I can only refer my readers to books like Seton Lloyd's *Foundations in the Dust*, and Ceram's *Gods, Graves and Scholars*, in the assurance that they will find them both enjoyable and illuminating.

★

In Mesopotamia, and later in Egypt, I was brought face to face with what is perhaps the most remarkable phenomenon in history – the first origin of civilization. The Indus Valley civilization was probably an offshoot of the same movement of man's cultural evolution, while the birth of Chinese civilization was certainly later.

The term civilization is perhaps incapable of precise definition. I use it here in its primary sense, to mean a way of life characterized by cities; this in turn involves a considerable division of labour, the storage of surplus resources, large units with a complex social and religious organization, monumental architecture, and some system of record. Regarded as a process, civilization is the type of social organization which permits or promotes the growth of organized knowledge and of specialized skills, the accumulation of wealth, the development of written language and codified law, and the growth of government and administrative services.

The origin of civilization demanded two radical changes in human life – the agricultural and the urban revolutions, as they are generally called: the first was an indispensable precursor, though it did not inevitably or universally generate the second. In Middle Eastern prehistory the two revolutions appear as two steps in a continuous process – man's creation of an artificial environment for himself. The first striking fact about this dual revolution is how late it began, and the second is how small a fraction of human time it occupied. Man, in the broad sense of a non-simian hominid, had existed for at least half a million years as food-gatherer and hunter before the first beginnings of agriculture; but the total time needed for the entire dual revolution was well under three thousand years, from about 6000 B.C. to the later part of the fourth millennium. Though the process of change must have eluded the great majority of those who lived through it, even during its more rapid or urban phase, it was truly a revolution.

In the three or four millennia of the Mesolithic period when the fourth ice-sheet began its definitive retreat, man was subject to various changes of climate and environment. The storm-tracks shifted; the forests spread over what had been tundra; areas of parkland and grassland became steppes and eventually deserts; the original Magdalenian culture with its remarkable artistic achievements died out with the big game on which it had subsisted, though in Spain and North Africa (and doubtless elsewhere), organized hunting societies were still very successful.

About 6000 B.C., the Boreal phase of post-glacial climate gave place to the warmer so-called Atlantic phase. Though we still are not sure of its detailed effect on our particular belt of the Middle East, it seems that it favoured the growth of wild cereals in the region's northern hills.

It still remains obscure just why the agricultural revolution began. Was it due to the scarcity of game forcing the utilization of other sources of food? Was it the result of a new level of technological skill, in making flint-tooth sickles to reap the cereals, or in providing pots to hold the grain? Was it a matter of pure discovery? We may conjecture that climatic change was the stimulus; the existence of wild cereal grasses in certain areas was the opportunity; and a certain level of cultural skill was the necessary prerequisite.

Gordon Childe, in *Man Makes Himself* and his later book, *What Happened in History*, has given a brilliant résumé of the double revolution (though sometimes his interpretation of the facts seems a little coloured by Marxist principles), and I cannot do better than refer my readers to him for details. As showing how rapidly the subject is moving, however, I must mention that since he wrote, an actual transition from a primarily hunting to a primarily agricultural life has been found. Near the Caspian Gates, in northern Persia, Professor Coon of Philadelphia found a cave-site in which a continuous succession can be traced from what is virtually a Magdalenian hunting culture to one where the people made pottery and supplemented their flesh diet with a little grain. Then the cave was abandoned, and the next layer of history was in a small village in the open near by; the agricultural revolution had begun: man had started to make settlements in the midst of his crops. Still more recently, Miss Kenyon found at Jericho a settlement dependent on agriculture, but lacking pottery. Whether this represents the stage in man's progress before pottery had been invented, or whether the inhabitants preferred receptacles of some other material like leather, we do not know. Finally it was discovered some time ago that the Natufians of the Mount Carmel region, not so far from Jericho, though still in the mesolithic phase as judged by their stone implements, were using flints set in bone as sickles. But whether the grasses which they reaped were wild or cultivated we do not know.

A new approach to the problem is now being followed by some archeological institutions, such as the Oriental Institute of Chicago. Instead of concentrating on such conspicuous sites as *tells*, or mounds resulting from long-continued settlement, where the lowest layers of occupation can only be reached by elaborate and expensive excavation through the remains of later cultures, search is now being made for small sites, more briefly occupied, which earlier students would have neglected. As a result, one of the most ancient villages in the world has already been discovered near Mosul.

Thus though there is general agreement that the beginning of this crucial phase in man's evolution is to be dated around 6000 B.C., and that its scene was somewhere in the foothills of the mountains that sweep round from Palestine to Persia, there is no certainty yet of the precise area or mode of its origin.

Meanwhile it is clear that the new techniques spread rapidly. Perhaps the spread began as a series of waves of the cultural transmission of **successive** improvements – reaping, cultivation, pottery, and the like – but certainly this was soon supplemented by movements of actual people. For the very success of the agricultural revolution necessitated its physical expansion. Agriculture led to a rapid increase in population, so that there was a constant pressure to take up new land. For some two thousand years, different variants of neolithic culture were on the move, crisscrossing the original agricultural area of the Middle Eastern foothills, spreading soon into Egypt along the borders between the Nile and the desert, extending gradually into new habitats west and north and east, developing a multiplicity of pattern in relation to local needs.

It was an economy of small villages, rarely comprising more than two or three hundred persons, sometimes moving their site with the exigencies of shifting cultivation. In many sites, one culture is often replaced abruptly by another, indicating conquest and replacement by a new invading type. During all this time, each community was practically self-sufficient, at any rate in respect of the necessities of life.

By the time neolithic peoples had begun this relatively rapid spread over suitable areas of the Middle East, they seem to have possessed the following characters. Neolithic man (and woman) had domesticated a number of animals; had developed cultivated strains of wheat and barley; built granaries to store grain during the winter; could spin and weave; had some form of fermented liquor to drink; he had implements such as grindstones and polished stone implements for hoeing; and pretty certainly had a religion concerned largely with magic ritual for inducing and maintaining fertility.

The ritual marriage was enacted to symbolize the generative activity of nature. With the passage of time, the male partner developed into a 'corn-king', the sacred personification of the crops; their fertility was bound up with his vigour, their dormancy ritualized in his death, their spring germination symbolized through his replacement by a vigorous young successor. From the annually sacrificed corn-king to the periodically slaughtered priest-king was one further step, and from this to the permanent king, combining magical functions with those of social leadership, was yet another. Meanwhile the forces of nature were often personified as gods, to be worshipped or propitiated or magically compelled in their turn.

Some such general conclusions seem inevitable on the basis of survivals in present-day barbaric societies, and of what is known of the religions of the earliest civilizations that grew out of neolithic society. Carleton Coon in his book *Caravan* gives a brief account of the Guanches of the Canary Islands, whose late neolithic culture survived until the 15th century. There were a number of tribal units, each with its own king and its own god. The noblemen owned the flocks, but would not demean themselves by using their hands for anything useful. There were holy rocks and caves, and oracles, and god-temples, and 'high places' where sacrifices were offered, and 'nunneries' of holy women, and rain-making rituals, and a cult of the dead; but many details needed for a full evaluation of their religious and social system are unfortunately lacking.

During the nearly two millennia of neolithic economy, various innovations and improvements of technique were introduced. New and better strains of cereals were developed, animals more fully domesticated. The 'slow wheel' and then the true potter's wheel were invented; somewhat later, the idea spread and the wheel came into use for traction also. Elaborate kilns not only gave better firing for pots, but were prerequisites for the full development of metallurgy, since with their aid the high temperatures which they made available could be used for casting and heat-forging became possible.

The primary advantage of metal over stone is that a broken or damaged metal implement can be repaired, while a stone tool cannot. Secondary advantages are that it can be cast and drawn into a much greater variety of shapes, and that one metal can be alloyed with another: but the discovery of this last property was not made until late, and was one of the factors underlying the urban revolution. The use of bricks for building, of boats for river transport, and of primitive seals for denoting ownership and for preventing theft, were three other late innovations of agricultural man. Finally, some neolithic village communities must have begun to improve their crop-yields by irrigation.

Gordon Childe considers that 'metallurgy, the wheel, the ox-cart, the pack-ass and the sailing ship' were the chief foundations of civilization. Certainly metallurgy played an important part. The metal-worker was a specialist, and his esoteric craft made him relatively independent of social discipline and of locality. Furthermore, once there was a demand for metal tools, the original self-sufficiency of the local community was upset: trade had become necessary for its existence.

Meanwhile population pressure was forcing men to cast their eyes on the hitherto uninvaded swamp-lands of Lower Mesopotamia. If they could be exploited, they would give unexampled yields, with a larger and more permanent grain surplus, and support larger communities. But to exploit them, drainage and irrigation works of a new level of complexity had to be organized; and the effort was reflected in a more elaborate social organization, with rights and duties carefully allotted. The fact that neither metal nor stone was to be found in the region made trade indispensable, and the need for greater yields per man-hour of labour soon encouraged the use of the primitive plough.

Thus the invasion and occupation of the Mesopotamian flood-plain seems to have been a crucial incident in a self-reinforcing process, in which greater technological and organizational efficiency not only permitted but demanded higher yields, and the need for higher yields demanded greater efficiency.

In consequence the size of settlements increased, monumental buildings were erected, and the individual symbolism of personal seals was supplemented by the socially-shared symbolism of a system of writing. Cities came into being, and with them civilization. The higher level of organization both permitted and promoted the organization of ideas. The ideas behind magic and sacred ritual became formulated by the priests as primitive theological doctrine, although little attempt was usually made to ensure coherence or consistency; the need for land measurement and for a calendar led to primitive mathematics and astronomy, although their foundations were neither fully rational nor fully scientific. Frankfort and his colleagues have dealt with this stage in the development of thought in a book with the illuminating title *Before Philosophy* (originally published as *The Intellectual Adventure of Ancient Man*).

Each Mesopotamian city was regarded as the property of a particular god, and the god's temple served as collective farm, community storehouse and trade centre, as well as a centre of worship. On the fringes of this planned economy, free enterprise played quite an important part, especially through the merchants to whom external trade was entrusted.

This radical change from illiterate village settlement to organized city with written records and impressive civic centre (as we should call it today) took place in the space of a few centuries. Its initiation was made possible by previous inventions: it was rendered inevitable by economic and population pressure: and once initiated it proceeded with almost explosive speed, until it had achieved a new form of human organization. The change, it seems, could have been initiated only in the flood-plain; but once accomplished, the new type of organization could be successfully utilized in other environments, and it spread rapidly.*

Less is known of events in Egypt. On analogy with Mesopotamia, we may suppose that large organized communities were first developed in the Delta, and only spread southwards into the Nile Valley proper when the new type of organization had been perfected. But virtually nothing is yet known of the Delta's early prehistory. Nor do we know if its colonization was a wholly independent event, a case of parallel and perhaps simultaneous development, or whether, as is perhaps more probable, the Mesopotamian experiment was the earlier, and its success stimulated a similar undertaking in the Delta.

It seems assured, however, that the later progress of the urban revolution in Egypt received stimuli from Mesopotamia, and that without those stimuli its formative course would have been different. Frankfort† sums up the evidence on this point. The most important introductions, besides certain pervasive motives in art, seem to have been the cylinder-seal; the employment of an advanced method of building in brick, which made possible the construction of monumental mastabas, and so paved the way for the pyramids; and the introduction of written language. Frankfort further points out that in the proto-literate phase of Mesopotamia we can trace all stages in the evolution of a complicated script, involving stylized pictograms and ideograms, phonetic symbols, and determinatives; but that in Egypt such a script appears full-fledged at the beginning of the First Dynasty. It looks as If the *idea* of an elaborate written language had been brought across from the Twin Rivers, but was then expressed in a different set of signs – perhaps because of the difference between the writing materials of the two countries, stone and papyrus on the one hand and clay tablets on the other.

There is further an important difference in the pattern of the two emerging civilizations. The general process was similar in both; but the two regions differed in the emphasis laid on different facets of life and different features of organization.

* This seems the most probable course of the process, though it is fair to say that some prehistorians believe that the original transition from village to walled town took place in upper Mesopotamia, or in Palestine: Miss Kenyon has shown that late neolithic Jericho was walled – the earliest walled town yet discovered. However, the full development of city organization certainly needed the stimulus of the fertile but difficult flood-plain.

† *The Birth of Civilization in the Near East*, London, 1951.

In Mesopotamia the emphasis was on the civic unit; it led to the development of city-states, each owned by one or other of the high gods, and administered for him by human ministers. In Egypt, the emphasis was more on the sacred priest-king, as centralized source of power, both civil and religious. The result was that in Mesopotamia the focus of development was the city, in Egypt the kingdom. The urban centres of Egypt, as Frankfort says, 'were no more than market towns for the countryside', with the exception of the capital which served as the seat of government for the whole country. And even the capital was constantly being changed, and old capitals might become mere townships of priests administering the mortuary lands of a dead king. The unification of Mesopotamia did not take place until after 2500 B.C., and even then the older cities continued to maintain a considerable degree of importance as active centres of social life. In Egypt, royal centralism was at intervals threatened by the rise of independent power among the great nobles and provincial governors, but the idea of a single sacred monarchy was strong enough to persist, with merely temporary interruptions, for nearly three thousand years.

A striking consequence of this difference in basic political theory is seen in the domain of foreign trade. In Mesopotamia foreign trade was carried on by private merchants. As a result, an elaborate financial system was evolved; merchants were provided with letters of credit (of course in the form of clay tablets), which enabled them to carry on business on a higher level than that of barter, even in the absence of coined money. Indeed the lack of coinage, which was not invented until about 700 B.C., was in some ways a blessing. It was more convenient for the travelling merchant to have an assured credit system than to lug around great sacks of coin which were a temptation to robbers. Coinage, when it eventually came in the first millennium, was of benefit especially to the small man, enabling him to satisfy his individual needs more flexibly.

The different quality of the two civilizations, even in their initial stages, is also shown by the new ways in which the cultural introductions from Mesopotamia were employed in Egypt. The markedly Mesopotamian style of some of the earliest dynastic works of art, like Narmer-Mane's palette, was soon modified into something wholly Egyptian; the specialized brick construction derived from early Sumerian temples was employed for royal tombs; the new system of writing not merely adopted an Egyptian form, but for a considerable period was employed for different purposes – for monumental record as against trade and practical administration. Meanwhile, the Mesopotamian priests developed astronomy and mathematics to a considerably higher level than their more conservative and less socially-minded Egyptian colleagues.

In general, Sumerian civilization seems to have centred on the propitiation of incalculable powers alien to man, that of Egypt on the ideas of enduring stability and persistence in ordered recurrence, of a community of interest between the human and divine realms. This helps to explain the self-centred nature of Egyptian culture, its conservatism, and the concentration of effort and thought on providing for the persistence of life in the after-world.

But I must not wander too far onwards in history. I want to stress that here in this phase of Middle Eastern history is something of extraordinary significance – the emergence of higher novelty in evolution. It is true that we should like to know more about the details of the process. But whatever new knowledge we acquire, however much the details of the picture are altered, the salient fact remains. Here in the Middle East, civilization was generated for the first time; and its genesis was an evolutionary advance, a truly progressive event. Civilized communities are in some real sense *higher* than uncivilized or precivilized ones.

It is worth emphasizing the point in this time of disillusion and disorganization, when the idea of progress has fallen into disrepute. It is also important to re-define progress in the light of historical and evolutionary fact, instead of on the basis of *a priori* ideas or mere wish-fulfilment. Progress is neither automatic, nor universal, nor inevitable, as some of the more optimistic Victorians assumed; but today we are in danger of throwing out the baby with the 19th-century bath-water of these assumptions.

The outstanding result of the attainment of civilization is that new possibilities can be realized both by human communities and human individuals. The new level of organization permits a greater control of nature, and at the same time a greater independence of nature, through the creation of a more stable artificial environment. New modes of gaining, organizing and accumulating knowledge appear, new possibilities of wealth and splendour, new methods of collective and personal expression. Individuals can participate in a wider range of experience, can feel part of a larger whole, can have access to more varied satisfactions, can develop their faculties to a greater extent. More concretely, the attainment of civilization led speedily to the realization of many new social possibilities such as written language, monumental architecture, organized religion, organized trade and commerce, the beginnings of science, more specialized technology, new art-forms.

There is of course a reverse side to the picture. New types of organization bring new problems and new difficulties, their development is sometimes self-frustrating, or reveals inherent contradictions which then bring about disharmony. Efficiency of organization may be applied to destructive purposes such as war. While the possibilities for fruition and self-development are increased for some individuals or classes, they may be decreased for others. Even for favoured individuals, the very variety of possible experience and action may mean greater difficulties of integration.

The new possibilities may thus be of evil as well as of good, may be destructive as well as constructive. But this does not abolish the positive fact that civilization did open up new and desirable possibilities to the human species, so that the upper level of achievement was in fact raised. It merely points the moral that possibilities are never fully realized, and that regression is possible as well as progress.

However, I must not run off into general disquisitions on the philosophy of progress. I would merely reiterate that here in Mesopotamia and Egypt we are privileged to see an event which is certainly to be called progressive, and makes nonsense of all non-evolutionary philosophies of history.

13

PERSIA AND ITS BLUE MOSQUES

To the outsider, Teheran seems
rather an unfortunate spot for a capital city. It lies in desert country,
and has little history to fall back on. It was promoted to its present status in
1788 largely because it was then so inaccessible to the Russian menace to the
northward. Its main advantage seems to be its position close to the Elburz
mountains, from which water can be obtained, and in which the well-to-do
can find relief from the summer dust and heat of the city. Here, though still
within the main Iranian basin, it is in convenient proximity to the well-
watered areas round the southern end of the Caspian, where an important
part of Persia's population lives.

The Elburz is a grand range. Much as the Rockies tower suddenly out of
the great plains in Colorado, it rises like a wall out of the undulating Iranian
plateau. The range is striking enough when seen from the ground, but
its huge straightness is best brought out from the air. From up aloft, when we
flew to Isfahan, we could see well over a hundred miles of this rocky rampart,
with snow peaks all along it, extending to the horizon in both directions. To
the north-east rose the highest peak in Eurasia west of India – the solitary
volcanic cone of Demavend projected by volcanic forces to a height three
or four thousand feet above that attained by the upfolded rocks of the
main range.

We were lodged in a hotel in a fashionable resort some ten miles out of the
city, where a torrent emerges from a cleft in the mountains. Through lovely
oriental plane-trees (slenderer than our western species) we could see from

our windows the snow on a great whaleback of a mountain, called 'Behind the Castle', towering above the gorge. Behind the hotel I found a few wild tulips, little yellow ones, contrasting agreeably with the artificial monsters of our western gardens. The place was full of luxurious villas, with a *nouveau riche* odour. One had on its flat roof four female sphinxes with powerful electric lights bulging out of their metal heads – a veritable triumph of bad taste.

A drive along the foot of the range gave us our first full realization of the country's desert nature. Bare low hills rose out of the plain to the south: right above us towered enormous mountain buttresses, equally bare. As we looked, a horde of sheep descended their tawny slopes on the way to some village below (pl. 42, opp. p. 221). What the sheep could find to eat was a mystery: those barren brown shoulders looked too barren even for goats.

There was a certain amount of greenery, and luxuriant greenery at that; but it all depended on irrigation. Much of the irrigation in Persia is effected by means of fogaras or qanats, the underground conduits I have already described in Syria (p. 29). There are said to be over 50,000 of these water-supply systems in the country, some of them still functioning after 2000 years and more. They may be thirty miles in length, and some of the shafts are up to 1000 feet deep. The queer rows of circular shaft-openings are a feature of the Persian landscape as seen from the air.*

One day I was taken right up into the mountains, up the valley of the Karaj river to the west of Teheran. The scenery is very grim – cliffs of almost vertical strata; bare rocky shoulders; screes and stony slopes below the edge of the snow. There is nothing like the pine-forests and rich lowland meadows of Swiss valleys. As in parts of Wyoming, you have to go high to escape from the desert. The British Ambassador told me of his fishing camp, up in a high valley where the Persian Army has a horse-breeding establishment. That sounded agreeable enough; but to reach it, he had to climb to nearly 11,000 feet – two good hours by car, and four more on horseback.

In the Karaj valley there were two or three villages – clusters of houses crowded together on rocky knobs, with a few fields, and some poplars for fuel. But for the most part the gorge was too steep and rocky for agriculture. Bridges were very primitive. At one place, where the foaming Karaj divided round a rock, a precarious crossing was provided by two single logs with a primitive hand-rail, one of them reaching up to the central rock

* Anthony Smith's *Blind White Fish in Persia* (1953) gives an entertaining account of them.

at a steep angle. High up in the valley was a small hotel, where people from Teheran came for summer holidays. I suppose the coolness was a relief; but the bare harsh scenery would have depressed me badly.

Time prevented us even from reaching the watershed. I would have dearly liked to see something of the northern slopes: they must present an extraordinary contrast to the arid south, with their heavy vegetation culminating in subtropical luxuriance below sea-level on the Caspian shore. On the slopes there are still large patches of dense jungle country frequented by leopards, and even occasional tigers – the westernmost outpost of the species. Freya Stark has given some account of the area in her book *The Valleys of the Assassins*.

The Caspian is the largest body of water in the world without outlet to the ocean. The geological story of the formation of its basin, with the lifting of the Elburz barrier to the south, is a fascinating one, but too complex for me to summarize here. According to one Persian professor, the imperceptibly slow sinking of its surface level has been accelerated in the last few decades by the Russians taking increasing amounts of water for irrigation from the Volga and other rivers that feed it.

The Caspian contains the world's greatest stock of sturgeon, belonging to several species. (I saw a specimen of the giant species in 1945 in the Museum of Zoology at Leningrad – an enormous creature, getting on for 20 feet in length.) I was told that the best caviar comes from the sturgeon off the Persian shore, though why this should be so I cannot understand.

Anyhow, there was, at the time of which I write, a joint Iran-Soviet company which exploited the sturgeon and other fisheries of the Persian part of the Caspian; and my Persian friends asserted that Persia had the worst of the bargain. The annual production of Caspian caviar is over 100 tons, and of fish over 5000 tons. Under the agreement, Persia got 10 per cent of this, in addition to some cash income. When the agreement fell due for revision in February 1953 it was interesting to see that Persia made the same kind of stand with the Russians over sturgeon that she made with the British over oil and refused to renew the agreement. However, a new agreement on more favourable terms has now been ratified.

On our way back, we stopped at the Government Agricultural Experiment Station, situated in the green and fertile strip irrigated by water from

---

38. The great Mosque at Isfahan, seen through the slender wooden pillars of the balcony of the royal pavilion, the Ala Kapi

39. One of Shah Abbas's great bridges at Isfahan

40. One of the half-Persian, half-European portraits by ' the Dutchman' in Shah Abbas's palace at Isfahan

the Karaj as it emerges from the mountains. It seemed to be efficiently run, and the staff were competent and keen. But it is difficult to see how this sort of effort can accomplish much until the social system is reformed. The poverty-stricken rural population who do all the hard work on the land must be given better incentives before agricultural productivity can be appreciably raised.

The contrast between rich and poor was visible everywhere, in the cities as well as on the land. It was almost as horrifying as in Egypt, and I got the same feeling of corruption and sweated labour lurking in the background. Narcotics too were playing a sinister role in both countries, though in Persia the chief narcotic is opium.* Since my visit a begining has been made in both countries to improve matters.

Various observers have noted the cynical attitude of many Persian business men, who think in terms of deals with quick and high returns, and discount all talk of disinterested public service as hypocrisy. It is only fair to say that I personally met nobody of this type: the men with whom I had dealings were devoted to the cause of education and science, efficiency and good administration. But whether this educated professional minority can exert much effect against the forces of cynical business, rich landlordism, nationalist politics, xenophobia, and religious fanaticism, is a very open question. Since my visit the politicians have plunged the country into what I have heard described as a sea of troubled oil, and it is becoming more and more difficult to pay the members of existing public services, let alone launch the new schemes of development and social welfare that are so desperately needed.

My chief contact while in Persia was Dr Hekmat, a big burly man with a considerable resemblance to Ernest Bevin, a resemblance which I did not expect to find in a Persian. He showed me over the University of Teheran, for whose incorporation in 1934 he as Minister of Education had been largely responsible. The Medical School, started a century or so ago by the French, was admirably equipped. Its students make all the vaccines and bacteriological cultures needed by the Teheran Hospital – an interesting idea; but I wondered whether it might not interfere with their general training.

The recently established 'Technical Faculty', or as we should say, School of Engineering, was also well provided for, but the Faculty of Pure Science was badly housed and poorly equipped. The authorities were hoping to

* J. Seymour, in his book *The Hard Way to India*, gives some vivid impressions of daily life in post-war Teheran, and also of the remote mountain villages of the Elburz.

rehouse and modernize it, but perhaps the financial crisis arising out of the oil troubles has prevented this.

Meanwhile thoughtful people were worried over the exceedingly rapid growth of the University (and the even more rapid growth of the capital to which the growth of the University has contributed), and the Government had just started a second university in Tabriz. The University was set up on a purely secular basis; but there is a religious reaction against Reza Shah's vigorously secularist policies, and orthodox Islam is growing more powerful again. I was told one entertaining story of Reza Shah's methods. In his attempt to discourage the bad aspects of religious life, he decreed that turbans and certain robes should be worn only by two classes of people – by holy men of the highest grade of holiness, and by the despised corpse-washers. His argument was that everyone would recognize a genuine holy man as holy, so that impostors who had no real right to the title would at once be taken for corpse-washers.

I also visited the Conservatoire of Music, which seems to be largely the work of one man – Paniz Mahmoud, who was trained as a composer in Brussels. He had assembled an excellent small orchestra and choir, and was busily noting down folk-songs. But he seemed dissatisfied with the powers that be. He could not get credits to maintain his orchestra properly or a proper recording apparatus for folk-music, and there was no money to finish the huge new opera house where he hoped one day to officiate.

Indeed, even in 1948, lack of money was a major obstacle in the way of all improvement. Everyone agreed that schools and teachers, clinics and doctors were urgently needed. Only about a quarter of the children of school age went to school, in spite of a compulsory education law. Over most of the country there was no medical service, and patients only came to Teheran if their illnesses were far advanced. Yet nobody could even suggest what to do and how to do it. Since then the Seven Year Plan has come into operation (1956), and things are looking a little better.

There was no Academy of Fine Art, but I was shown an institution of *Arts et Métiers* which at least produced very lovely brocades. The shops were full of boxes and the like decorated with miniatures in the traditional Persian style – on the whole a very successful exploitation of the past. When I was in Isfahan I was taken to see a celebrated miniaturist – up two flights of rickety stairs to a small room, open on one side, where he, a rather scrubby and unshaven old man, was busily painting away with three or four pupils.

One of the stock stories about Teheran is that *British Embassy* means drinking water. This is more or less true. Teheran houses have no piped water-supply – water is turned on at fixed hours into the special gutters that run down the side of the chief streets. The mixture of water, dust, refuse, and slops is all that is free. If you want something purer, you have to buy it (at quite a low rate) from perambulating water-carts and water-carriers. And the chief source of this more potable supply is the conduit installed by British foresight in the Embassy grounds.

One morning we saw the fabulous Crown Jewels. The visitor has the feeling of being inside a much-magnified safe: and indeed that is just what the jewels' strong-room is, with its walls and door of massive steel, its combination locks, and its guards. I must confess that objects such as swords with hilt and scabbard entirely encrusted with precious stones, though interesting as quintessential examples of 'conspicuous waste', give me no aesthetic pleasure. There was nothing in the place with the rare combination of great beauty with great expensiveness, like the little bowl I remembered seeing in Buckingham Palace, presented I think by Akbar – plain gold, with ribs of great emeralds between areas of gold. However, I admit to a pleasing childish thrill at the sight of bowls and dishes full of loose pearls, rubies, and diamonds, and badly wanted to plunge my hand casually into the mass of precious stones. Our guide said that the best diamonds and emeralds came from mines in India that are now exhausted, so that there is no other collection of jewels to rival it.

Since then, as I read in my *Times* for March 15th, 1950, a new strong-room has been made by Chubb's. I was fascinated by the account of the door – ten tons in weight and twenty inches deep, with two key-locks, one time-lock, and one combination-lock capable of 100,000,000 combinations. It was pleasant to think of this product of Wolverhampton skill housing the legendary collection of jewels in Teheran.

Teheran is not very exciting as a city, either architecturally or historically. There are occasional tendencies to copy Persepolis and other glories of the Achaemenian past, but such neo-Achaemenian buildings are even less successful than our imitation Gothic. One day, passing a very large building in this bogus style, 'Qu'est-ce que c'est que ça?' I queried (French is the general language of diplomatic converse). 'Ça, c'est la Police, Monsieur – ou plutôt la Persé-police.' I enjoyed the pun: but the sight of the imitation was no consolation for missing the original. I had to choose between Persepolis and

Isfahan, and chose Isfahan. For one thing, it was alive, and I was getting sur-
feited with ruins; for another it would be my only chance of seeing the unique
blue mosques of Persia.

I had to be content with the account of Persepolis written by Dr Godard,
from which I learnt some surprising facts. The Apadana, or Great Hall of
Darius and Xerxes, was of hypostyle construction, with its roof supported by
pillars. But, unlike the ancient Egyptians, the Achaemenids had discovered
how to give spaciousness to this type of building. Its roof was over half an
acre in extent, yet was supported by only 36 pillars. The architects achieved
this by importing enormous beams of cedar all the way from the Lebanon,
capable of bridging the gaps of nearly 30 feet between pillar and pillar – gaps
far wider than could ever be spanned by stone.

The riches of Persepolis must have been staggering. Alexander is said to
have employed 20,000 mules and 5000 camels to transport the treasures of
the place to Ecbatana. The final burning of the Persian national shrine seems
to have been a deliberate act of revenge on Alexander's part, a revenge on
Persia for the invasion of Greece.

★

We were flown to Isfahan in an oldish Anson bomber, now part of the
Iranian air force. The desert unrolled below us – first some salt-lakes, then a
belt of sand-dunes, then a dark stony plain with scattered green oases. In this
we saw a little anticlinal dome-system that might have served as a diagram-
matic model in a giant's museum – a Weald in miniature with central elongated whaleback ridge and two concentric inward-facing elliptical scarps
with flat troughs between, but all in gaunt rock without a trace of vegetation.

Then we flew over a wicked-looking range of mountains – bare purple-
brown slopes of sand and scree with jagged naked rock ridges, brown and
black – into a sandy arid basin with the formidable Zagros mountains
beyond, a few of them snow-capped. In this basin lies Isfahan, by a river
whose green borders stand out against the barren brown all around. There
are plans to irrigate the surrounding area: let us hope they will be put into
practice, not merely left on paper.

Isfahan is a wonderful sight from the air; but we had only time just to
notice the shining blue bubbles of its domes and the slender brick minarets,

41. *The golden domes and minarets of Khazimein*

protruding from the welter of its whitey-brown roofs, before we were across the river and down on the aerodrome. There our attention was diverted to a strange building standing all by itself in the countryside – the Pilgrimage Tomb, pentagonal in plan, with a conical ten-sided tower.

On our way in to the pleasant old-fashioned cool hotel we had a sight of the main street – a very fine double thoroughfare, with a conduit of flowing water on either side, and a double (or was it quadruple?) avenue of trees. I innocently asked whether it was a piece of modern town-planning: but no, it was one of the remarkable creations of Shah Abbas I – 'the Great' – at the turn of the 16th and 17th centuries. There is a legend that the reports of it which reached France from western merchants and ambassadors inspired the plan of the Avenue des Champs Elysées in a later century.

Isfahan as it exists today is largely the creation of Shah Abbas. It is a fabulous city, the embodiment of the dreams of a monarch reared on traditions of fairy-tale splendour. The centre of the city's plan is the Maidan, the great square where polo was played, troops reviewed, and all kinds of festivities celebrated. At one end is the amazing blue Great Mosque, the Masjed-i-Shah (pl. 43, opp. p. 228) with its dome and minarets and iwans a blaze of coloured tiles. The main colour is gleaming blue, inset with golden panels and multi-coloured geometrical and floral designs and inscriptions in giant lettering.

The method which ensures this brilliance is that of tile-mosaic – a jigsaw of separate pieces of tiles, previously fired and colour-glazed and then cut into the required shapes. The jigsaw was fitted together and mounted on plaster panels, which were then set in place on the walls or dome. The effect under the bright desert sun is staggering. I can think of no other architecture which has employed glazed tiles to this extent, or so fully exploited the glory of blue. A later and cheaper method was to paint the pattern in colour-glaze on to large rectangular tiles, which were later fired; but this does not give so brilliant a colour. Shah Abbas was in a hurry to finish his mosque, so employed this method for the interior.

Some of the great iwans have their recesses arched over with so-called stalactite decoration. This complex system of tiny arches arranged in tiers is a characteristic feature of Islamic architecture, but I found it too elaborate and fussy for my taste, taking away from the bold effect of the main lines of the

42. Sheep descending the barren brown shoulders of the Elburz

building. In the central courtyard, a formal pool mirrors the blue dome and minarets in its cool surface.

In the middle of one side of the Maidan stands the smaller mosque of Sheikh Lutfallah, built by Shah Abbas as a private chapel for himself and his family. Its proportions are exquisitely symmetrical, and its dome is covered with the most delicate tile-mosaic. But it did not assault my eyes or my emotions so compellingly as its larger contemporary.

Almost exactly opposite stands the Ala Kapi or 'Sublime Porte', a royal pavilion at the edge of the palace gardens. Here Shah Abbas liked to receive foreign emissaries and watch the spectacles in the Maidan. I was particularly struck by the slender hexagonal wooden pillars supporting the flat-roofed balcony. So I imagined Chinese or Tibetan architects might have built in some period of severe and delicate taste. This same far-eastern flavour is repeated in the verandah of the main palace behind; but here the pillars are taller and give an even more soaring effect. Standing on the balcony of the Ala Kapi, you can see the swelling blue dome of the Great Mosque through the uncompromising slender straightness of the wooden columns (pl. 38, opp. p. 216). The contrast brings home the remarkable achievement of Persian architecture, in having developed two such diverse styles (yet both excellent) in one and the same period.

The Ala Kapi is full of small rooms and alcoves, bright with tiles, painted stucco, mirrors, and other ornaments. In one, the decoration consisted of a pattern of flask-shaped holes cut in a plaster screen, giving a most amusing effect. Elsewhere the painted stucco panels had the air of silvery black brocade. Originally the balcony had a jasper fountain spouting in the centre, the water forced up by a pump driven by oxen on ground level.

The main palace, the famed Cehel Sutun, tucked away in its great garden, and flanked with ornamental pools, is very fine. It is called the Palace of the Forty Pillars. Actually, there are only twenty; but you can see their twenty reflections in the pool – and anyhow 'forty' can be taken to mean 'a great many'! The most curious objects in the Palace are some of the fresco portraits, which are half-Persian and half-European in style, as well as in the dress portrayed. They are presumably the work of John the Dutchman, whom the Shah had hired from Holland to be his court painter.

Shah Abbas was a great believer in keeping up international relations. He obtained the services of western technical experts (as we should now call them) not only in painting, but in the technical arts both of peace and war.

Only after an Englishman had reorganized the Shah's army and introduced the use of western artillery was he able to challenge and defeat the Turks. He had his own ambassadors, some of them Europeans, in European courts; and he welcomed the ambassadors of western nations in Isfahan. Various of those European emissaries (notably Chardin) have left us invaluable accounts of 17th-century Isfahan. We learn of the rigid etiquette of the court; of the cruelty of the Shah (he blinded several of the princes of the blood royal to keep them from the possibility of rebellion), but also of his generosity; and of his architects' constructive genius.

He laid out three wholly new quarters of his capital, one of them the Armenian quarter, where the Armenian Christians could live in safety and worship in their own way without interference. The one proviso that the Shah insisted on was *no bells* – their sound would have been too provocative to Moslem ears. The cathedral built by the Armenians is very curious, with its exterior designed to look like a mosque – perhaps a form of protective mimicry. The interior is entirely covered with rather bad Christian frescoes of the early 18th century, an odd stylistic mixture of inferior late Italian and traditional Persian, the cherubs and angels with simpering sweet baby faces. In the nave are the most horrifying scenes of martyrdom I have ever seen: I prefer not to recall the details.

The three bridges over the broad shallow river are very interesting (pl. 39, opp. p. 217). I particularly liked the legend about the most elaborate one. Shah Abbas, so the story goes, told his architect that the bridge must fulfil many functions beyond that of carrying traffic. It was to provide repose: so in each pier there had to be a stair leading down to a rest-room with couches. There was to be space for wedding-parties (the bridge is still used for such festive celebrations); and a retreat for a holy man; and rooms where singers and dancers and jugglers could entertain travellers. Furthermore, the Shah insisted that even in summer, men's ears should be charmed by the sound of running water; so the architect made a special channel to collect every trickle of dry-season water into a sufficient stream. And when the bridge was finished the Shah visited it disguised in every capacity to satisfy himself that his instructions had been carried out. Only then was the architect paid.

A hundred years later, the style of architecture had changed a great deal. The Madrasa Mader-i-Shah, built by Shah Sultan Husain's mother in the early 18th century as a residential college for theological students, is a triumph of delicacy, surprisingly combining lightness with classical form.

The students' rooms, of which the young Shah reserved one set for his own use, arranged in two storeys round a polygonal courtyard, have large open-fronted alcoves picked out in delicate tracery; and the subdued colour-scheme is a long way from the Great Mosque's blue magnificence.

The great blue mosque is certainly the most spectacular thing in Isfahan; but the earlier Masjid-i-Jami is more austerely beautiful. Before Shah Abbas' ambitious new constructions, this was the city's main mosque, built from the 9th to the 12th century. Its subterranean arcades of pointed arches have the distinction of early Gothic – but Gothic with a difference: they make use of brickwork instead of stone, and they are of an extreme simplicity of form. They are also a reminder that the East invented the pointed arch long before the West. I later saw even more striking examples of Islamic pointed arches in the 9th-century mosque of Ibn Tulun in Cairo, and they make their earliest appearance in the 8th century.* Just how the idea of the pointed arch travelled to the west, to become the primary distinctive feature of Gothic architecture, seems unknown; but in any event it was one of the numerous inventions and discoveries first made in the Middle East.

The two brick domes of the Masjid-i-Jami are of great interest. In the larger, the wonderful transition from square base to round dome, effected by the squinches; the great Kufic inscription seeming to bind the base of the dome together like the chain round St Peter's; the solidity and simplicity of the brown brick; the fine proportions; and the sense of space in spite of relatively small size – all combine to give a rare feeling of architectural nobility.

This was my only sight of the extraordinary brick architecture of Persia. Later, in the plates of Arthur Upham Pope's monumental work on Persian art, I was able to learn something more of its originality and strange grandeur.

The minarets of Isfahan are a further example of this brick architecture. They shoot up above the houses to a height of 200 or 250 feet, looking like a cross between a factory chimney and a magnified and elongated telescope, with a touch of phallic symbolism obtruding itself – a most curious architectural form.

Our return was enlivened first, on the way to the airport, by the sight of a hoodie crow on a window-sill, inspecting the room within – a thing no hoodie crow would dream of doing in Britain; and then, in the air, by a

* See e.g. M. S. Briggs's chapter on Islamic Architecture in *The Legacy of Islam*, Oxford University Press.

frightening thunderstorm which decided the pilot to make a hundred-and-fifty-mile detour round the wicked-looking mountain range.

*

So long as overland movement and trade predominated, Persia was of the greatest importance as a cross-roads area between the East – India and China – and the West, and between the Indian Ocean and the northern land mass. But I have neither the space nor the competence to discuss the importance. All I can do is to mention two or three points in its history which struck me personally.

One was the disproportionately large role played by Persians in the intellectual and cultural life of Islam in its conquering prime. Thus their influence on the cultural efflorescence of Baghdad under the Abbasids was immense. In some ways, their role can be compared with that of the Greeks in the heyday of the Roman Empire.

Another was a query. How is it possible for Toynbee, in his *Study of History*, to regard the Achaemenian empire of Cyrus and his successors as the 'Universal State' of the Syriac civilization? To me it appears as something *sui generis*, the first true empire in history, consolidating many diverse races, peoples, and religions within a single administrative framework, and radically different from the Assyrian and Babylonian and Sumerian states that preceded it in the western part of the same general area. And why does Toynbee classify the earliest Arab Caliphates, of Damascus and Baghdad, as a sort of reincarnation of the Syriac Universal State, and separate them from all the later manifestations of the Moslem world? Perhaps this is no mystery to professional historians; but the simple-minded outsider finds it difficult not to see them as part of the continuous development of Islamic civilization, without significant relation to the Persia of Darius and Xerxes.

The third point concerns an alien intrusive force – the Mongols. After repeatedly hearing of the ruin that had befallen this or that city at Mongol hands, I came to realize that the Mongols were the greatest agency of destruction in all history. During nearly two hundred years before the beginning of the 15th century, Genghiz Khan, Hulagu and Tamerlane (Timur Lang) between them blasted the rich civilization of Iran and its extensions in what are now Iraq and Afghanistan. George Sarton, in his monumental *Introduction to the History of Science*, writes: 'Though this book is primarily devoted to creators, spiritual creators, not to destroyers, Timur destroyed on such a fantastic scale that we must speak of him, even as we spoke of his greatest predecessors, Alexander the Great and Chingiz Khan, and of the Black Death. . . . The eastern Islamic World never recovered from his destructiveness. . . . His appearance is a definite cut in the history of every country that he "visited" (like the plague); we must speak of it as it was before Timur, and after Timur.'

There was also a constructive side to the Mongols – we have only to think of the empire that Genghiz Khan established, of Kubla Khan, or of Tamerlane's court at Samarkand. But the pyramids of skulls, the literal extermination of entire city populations, the destruction of the irrigation system of Mesopotamia – these, and the memory of unexampled horror and cruelty, are what the Mongol conquerors left behind them in the Iranian lands. There was, of course, a later revival of Persian culture and learning – for instance, under Shah Abbas; but we can only guess at the heights to which they might have risen if the Mongols had never passed across the land.

The Mongols also illustrate the influence of individuals and of accidents on the course of history. Without doubt there would in any case have been some overflow of the Mongols from their Asiatic steppes into more fertile and richer countries. But equally without doubt the expansion would not have been so forcible, so rapid, or so extensive if it had not been for the ruthless genius of Genghiz Khan. That at least is the impression left on me by reading books such as Harold Lamb's *Genghis Khan* (1928). His special capacities for leadership and organization were needed to weld his nomads into a disciplined imperial army and convert a tribal chieftainship into an empire. The improbable combination of genes in Genghiz Khan's chromosomes influenced the fate of nations.

A little later, the accident of the death of Genghiz Khan's son Ogotay in all probability saved Western Europe. The conquering Mongol armies had reached Poland and Hungary, and were still advancing without much effective resistance, when the news of Ogotay's death reached them, and the generals decided to make the long journey home to make sure of their position under his successor. Had they not done so, Germany and France would almost certainly have been overrun and devastated, and not only Russia but most of Europe would have remained for over a century under Mongol domination.

14

ON THE BANKS OF THE NILE

The END OF MY FIRST VISIT TO Cairo was spent recovering from an intestinal upset: the notes with the writing of which I occupied some of my enforced idleness will give something of the reactions produced by a first contact with Egypt.

'Cairo: What a noisy, bustling, cosmopolitan, vicious, gay, mixed place! Posters of Rita Hayworth and of Egyptian film actresses jostle each other. "Sphinx Tea" on a café by the Pyramids. In the wine list were Crû des Ptolémées, a decent second-rate white wine grown near Alexandria; Aphrodite, Apollon demi-sec, and Osiris dry.

'Shepheard's Hotel (since burnt to the ground in the riots of 1952) is a vast place, cosmopolitan, a little gaudy and blowsy, but pleasant. In one's bedroom the third bell summons "Native Valet". The waiters go about in tarbooshes and long robes and coloured embroidered jackets. The fat ones (and there are a fair number) look either like eunuchs or like horrible executioners whom one expects to out with a scimitar. Other waiters are pure aboriginal Egyptian—slight, brown, dolichocephalic, with slightly aquiline nose.

'Last night at the Lebanese Legation I sat between two very likeable people – Nimr Pasha and Taha Hussein. The former was born in 1855 (!) and lost his job at the American University at Beirut in the late '70's for having written approvingly about evolution, on which he corresponded with T. H. Huxley. He is an Academician and still goes to speak at meetings of the Academy, in spite of his ninety-two years. He said that he *had* to come out in the evening to see me. He had been feeling rotten, depressed by events in general; but reading about Unesco had given him hope.

'Long ago he edited an Arabic review which was for a time the chief contact of Egypt with the advanced and scientific thought of the West. Taha Hussein told me that it was his *only* contact, until he started learning French in his middle twenties (now he has a charming French wife). Hussein went blind as a child of four—not until he was seven did he realize he was essentially different from others. I must read his autobiography. (Later: I have now read the book, and very interesting and moving it is.)

'A jumble of impressions remain in my mind from the last few days. The vast Nile in the middle of its green ribbon of fertile land: I remember seeing it nearly twenty years ago at its origin—a little river tumbling over the Victoria Falls at Jinja. The forests of date-palms, all their tops pointing one way when the wind blew strong; they live only about forty years. . . . All the world and his wife (or wives) and family, often very large, proceeding out of the city in donkey carts for the Coptic New Year – celebrated much as was the New Year in Dynastic times. . . . A party of young lads singing and drum-beating by the Pyramids; a guide in Egyptian dress with a tall cardboard conical hat with paper feather-tassels. . . .

'The site of Memphis stretches far – nothing but mounds of mud. No one would think that here stood one of the greatest cities of the ancient world, the first capital of united Egypt. As a city it lasted, but with an increasing number of its buildings in ruins, until the Moslem conquest. Then it was abandoned and despoiled when the conquerors transferred their capital to Cairo. Legend asserts that the capital had to be on the east of the river, because the Emir said there must be no water between it and Mecca: strange passion of a desert-lover! The ruins were still described as stupendous by an Arab historian over 500 years later.

'The huge Colossus of Rameses II, horizontal in its ugly shed with stairway to reach a viewing gallery, is very enormous and rather imposing. It is a pity it and the lesser one in the open are too broken to sit or stand upright. Apparently the saltpetre rots all stone exposed to the soil.

'(Later: The first name of Rameses II was *Wesirmatra* or *Usimatre*, which suffered the somewhat surprising corruption to *Ozymandias* at the hands of the Greeks. This is not the particular colossus whose "vast and trunkless

---

43 One of the blue mosques of Isfahan : the Madrasa Mader-i-Shah

legs", standing solitary in the desert of the antique land, prompted Shelley to his immortal sonnet. But Rameses was prolific of enormous colossi of himself, and the famous words

> My name is Ozymandias King of Kings:
> Look on my works, ye mighty, and despair

are perfectly in the spirit of Rameses' self-glorifying inscriptions.)

'Near by is a recent and unique discovery – the place where the sacred bulls of Memphis (Apis) were prepared for mummification – two huge alabaster slabs, one nicely arranged for drainage of the blood and body-fluids; there is a relief of a lion-headed bed on the side, the lion to keep away evil spirits while one is unprotected in sleep (pl. 46, opp. p. 232). Later in the day we saw the catacomb of the sacred Apis bulls: forty of their monstrously vast stone sarcophagi are there in the Serapeum, each in its private side-hall off the main passage. If only there had been sacred god-hippos or god-elephants the coffins would have been even huger! It is one thing to read about zoölatry, another and very different thing to see its results in practice. I hadn't realized how the old animal-worship had not only lasted on among the common people but was part and parcel of the elaborate ritual of the official "high" religion.* No wonder Herodotus was horrified at the Egyptians' beast-gods.

'Nor did I know how much of the religion was sacred acting – ritual plays or dances which were supposed somehow to compel Nature: the animal-headed creatures so often seen in reliefs and paintings were priests with animal masks, who performed strange dance ceremonies. The whole religious system was such mumbo-jumbo, and so elaborate and expensive! – so largely based on pitifully simple bits of propitiatory magic or of power-complexes or wish-fulfilments, but dressed up in granite blocks and white limestone facings, and equipped with huge priesthoods and bequests.

'And then there was all the business of building up a pantheon – the little "local", "one-city" gods coming together, sometimes becoming identified with others, sometimes entering into partnership with them – in triads,

* Margaret Murray has some interesting facts about Apis. The divine bull was closely connected with Osiris. Like the early priest-kings, he was not allowed to die a natural death, for fertility was tied up with his vigour. He was killed, and parts of him probably consumed at a ritual feast, before the rest was mummified and ceremonially buried with divine honours.

44. *The massive hypertrophy of Egyptian architecture: columns at Karnak.*

enneads and the rest. All very nice as supernatural insurance – the more gods the better, for then the more different divine forces you could placate and have on your side. But it became more and more expensive, keeping them all up in due style.

'Here are seen, as it were magnified hundreds of diameters by being made part of the official religion of a rich, powerful and well-organized country, the material projections of all sorts of primitive psychological tendencies and forces.'

★

So much for my meditations on Memphis.

I was anxious to see a little of Cairo on my own without benefit of guides and free from the tyranny of a time-table and of sights that I must be made to see. So, one morning before breakfast, I got up early and started wandering round the streets and up side-alleys, taking occasional photographs of the crowds, of a camel swinging along under an old wall, or of a corner where old and new styles were mingled.

I very nearly got no breakfast at all, for suddenly a man, after some obviously hostile remarks, went off and came back with a policeman, who, in spite of the barriers of language, soon managed to convey that I was under arrest. At the police station, I was told that taking photographs in the streets of Cairo without a special permit was illegal, and I would have to stay in charge. With some difficulty, I persuaded the officer to let me telephone to the Under-Secretary for Education, who was also the Egyptian representative on the Executive Board of Unesco, and my official bear-leader during my visit to Egypt. He was, I think, slightly amused at my predicament: said he had never heard of the regulation about photography; wondered why on earth I should have wanted to go off on my own; and eventually, with a few words to the officer, secured my release.

There was about the incident a flavour of that xenophobia which later grew so rapidly and culminated in the Cairo riots in 1952. And this was, I am sure, reinforced by a sense of inferiority and a desire to prevent foreigners from seeing too much of the appalling cleavage between rich and poor.

Appalling it certainly is. That morning I had turned off into an alley, and after twenty yards or so found myself in a little court which combined the worst horrors of the slums of Dickens's London with those of the insanitary and fly-ridden Orient. Dozens of families must have lived in the high narrow court. Untidy men and women peered furtively out of doors or windows. The place was dilapidated and dirty in the extreme. A few unwashed and ragged children, with flies round their eyes, sat among the cans and other debris on the slimy unpaved floor, in the middle of which a pool of filthy mud had accumulated. The stench was overpowering and filled the court.

I believe that one can or could see even worse slums than this in India. Certainly I had never seen anything so bad. Yet it was but a few steps from a broad shopping and business street, not in the same class as Bond Street or Fifth Avenue, but reasonably clean and efficient, part of the equipment of a modern city.

But this striking contrast was only one aspect of a general cleavage. There was just as great a contrast between the average life of the fellahin and that of the wealthy landlords and business men who live luxuriously in Cairo and Alexandria, or of the tax-dodging corrupt politicians whom General Neguib was then purging from public life. I felt the same sort of cleavage in Mexico, but here in Egypt it was still starker, Disraeli's two nations still more distinct. The Common Man simply does not exist.

A minority of thoughtful Egyptians were concerned about this really dreadful situation, and a certain amount was being done to remedy it. Here again I cannot do better than quote from my notes on the schemes I was shown en route to the Nile Barrage at the base of the Delta.

'On the way we visited one of the 84 Village Centres now in existence – four original ones due to the enterprise of the Social Science Foundation (I think it is called), the other eighty sponsored by the Government. Each centre, through its specially trained Superintendent, aims at transforming the whole life of one particular village – health, education, agriculture, home industry, and the rest. They plan to do this for all the 40,000 villages of Egypt, but as they can only train about thirty-five social workers a year as superintendents, it was easy to calculate that this would take well over a thousand years – a discouraging fact that my enthusiastic hosts didn't seem to have thought of.

'The private centres use existing mud buildings and get the people to co-operate, for example in filling up the disease-breeding ponds from which the mud for the village's bricks has been taken : the Government insists on building new brick centres, and on paying contractors for filling up the ponds – why ?

'In the centre that I saw, the local school devotes about half its time to practical and financially productive activities – rug-making, chicken-raising, carpentry, etc. This would be impossible in England owing to child labour laws, etc., but here is welcomed as providing badly needed income for the family. Let me give one example of their appalling poverty. Bilharzia is perhaps the worst energy-sapping disease in Egypt: but the fellahin are so poor that boots and gloves, to prevent the worm larvae from penetrating their flesh, are quite out of their reach. Either the Government will have to provide them free, or the peasants' income must be raised, or the snails that carry the parasite must be exterminated: this last has been done in one area in the Fayum, but it is very expensive, both the initial clearance and the later maintenance of a snail-free condition.

'There was an excellent district nurse who had a 100 per cent record of successful deliveries, with the aid of the local midwives whom she supervises. One old crone of apparently about 90, but really I suppose not more than 65, was a great contrast to the trim, white-dressed able nurse with her broad-spaced eyes and her heavyish but attractive features (pl. 47, opposite).

'They reward the cleanest house by painting its outside and by showing it off to visitors. There is a sort of club-house where, *inter alia*, illiterate adults learn to read to avoid the embarrassment of going to school. At the school the children, garbed in blue cotton uniforms which they had made themselves, did Swedish exercises for our benefit. The authorities were beginning to think of finding local songs and dances more suitable to Egyptian children.'

More power to the Village Centres, thought I, even if they are only a drop in the ocean of Egyptian poverty and misery.

Then on to a very recent experiment – the school for training social teachers – average age 16–19. It was a little too primitive for my taste, with tents for some of the classrooms and the boys boarded in a not very satisfactory house in the village, but the curriculum was imaginative, all broadening out from local facts. Thus they go to see the local water-melon industry (in the dry part of the bed of a branch of the Nile); find out what egrets eat by seeing what creatures a captured bird vomits up; or make tables of the market prices of various commodities. And the masters seemed keen and pleasant. In the grounds the boys were making a model of the village, and obviously enjoying it.

Finally, to a Horticultural School, taking boys of 13 or 14 for, I think, three years. They learned not only gardening but building, carpentry,

6. The mummification slab for sacred bulls at Memphis with Mr Jimenez of Unesco demonstrating the scale. On the side is represented a lion-headed bed, the lions to keep away evil spirits

7. The peasant midwife and the young trained nurse at the Village Centre near Cairo

buffalo-keeping etc. (much of the work would be against our Trade Union rules!). The hundred boys slept in one huge dormitory.

Later I saw some results of the remarkable experiment of Habib Gorgi, who was chief Inspector of Art under the Egyptian Ministry of Education. He takes children from the villages who, with minimum guidance from him, are encouraged to develop their artistic talents – in sculpture, painting, weaving, and other media. Some of their productions were truly remarkable. The query remains whether these methods of individual self-development can be applied on a large scale. But certainly something new has here come out of Egypt.

Since 1948, under Nasser, striking progress has been made in several fields. But the spectre of over-population still broods over the land. Even if the High Dam is successfully built, it will only cope with the swarm of new mouths to be fed until the end of the century at the latest.

★

Hashish and other drugs are another of Egypt's problems. The Government has made considerable efforts to keep down the traffic, but selfishness and ingenuity still contrive to make a great deal of money out of this debasement of human beings. Russell Pasha is celebrated for his work as head of the Narcotics Control Service (a post from which he retired shortly after the war); he is also a keen ornithologist. In the lounge of Shepheard's Hotel, I was talking to him in this latter capacity, when a be-fezzed attendant brought me the card of a scion of a highly placed family in another Arab country whom I had met during my journeys, and who I had been given to understand was making a great deal of money out of drug-smuggling. It gave me considerable pleasure to see his hastily masked change of expression when I introduced him.

The Nile barrage makes a very pleasant outing. On the way, the sailing barges on the river and the canals are beautiful, with their huge lateen sails reaching two and a half times the height of their masts (pl. 48, opposite). A gathering of them, moored, makes a wonderful linear pattern with their great curved spars and shorter straight masts.

The junction of two great rivers into one, like Rhône and Arve by Geneva or, on a vaster scale, Missouri and Mississippi by St Louis, is an

48. *The wonderful linear pattern made by the masts and spars of the Nile sailing barges.*

absorbing sight. A much rarer geographical phenomenon is the divergence of one river into two: this is illustrated, I suppose better than anywhere else in the world, by the Nile's fork into two main streams. Here was the base of the Delta, the geographical point of origin of that huge tract of level fertile land, nearly 80 miles long and 120 miles wide, which has given its name to all other tongues of land thrust out by rivers into seas or lakes, and was in all probability the first cradle of Egyptian civilization. Close by, a peasant was ploughing with a team of an ox and a water-buffalo, yoked to a plough of primitive type that might have been in use four thousand years ago.

The barrage itself, the first piece of modern social engineering to be carried out in Egypt, was constructed rather over a hundred years ago to provide for the better irrigation of the delta. There is an interesting museum showing models of this and other irrigation projects. The lovely grounds make the place a favourite Sunday resort. To start with, it has really good lawns, almost as good as those of a London park. And it is planted with very fine trees, including some magnificent jacarandas, gorgeous with their bright blue blossom, and the trees are festooned with flowering creepers – creepers with great white datura-like flowers, creepers with short blue trumpets, bohynias, orange trumpet-vines.

One group of trees was apparently covered with huge white blossoms; but on closer view, the apparent blossoms resolved themselves into birds – white egrets, hundreds and hundreds of them resting in the branches. It was a beautiful sight, in some ways even more beautiful than the marvellous egret rookery of Avery Island in Louisiana in which I had once spent a fortnight observing and photographing, for here the birds were all egrets, instead of egrets sprinkled among a great majority of non-white herons, and their nesting colony was set conspicuously in high trees, instead of being concealed in dense shrubs growing in water. It was also an encouraging sight, for the city of white birds is the result of deliberate policy. The agricultural authorities were concerned over the diminution of this extremely useful species, and planned and protected the nesting colony at the Barrage.

*

In Cairo, it was a delight to see hoopoes everywhere in the parks. The hoopoe compels attention, with its handsome longitudinal crest, a multi-coloured fan which is alternately shut and opened at each step. It has a magic quality, and is inevitably fabulous, the kind of strange or lovely creature that is sure to gather legends round itself, like the eagle and the cobra, the peacock and the fox. The chief legend that attaches to the hoopoes is of the service they rendered, in the days when they were without crests on their heads, to the Queen of Sheba. On her visit to Solomon, they gallantly protected her complexion with the living umbrella of their wings. Solomon, duly grateful, asked what he could give them in return. The hoopoes replied 'a crown like yours'. This he was unable to grant, but he gave them the next best thing, their crown-like crest.

Other strange birds, but strange in a very different way, were the shoe-bills in the Cairo Zoo – a whole group of these rare creatures, the size of storks, striding about happily, as against the one or two that look so chilly in London. I don't think anyone really understands the adaptive value of the inflated bill, but it is among the greatest *grotesqueries* of animal life. Shoe-bills (the Arabs call them 'Father of a Shoe') come from the upper reaches of the Nile in the Sudan, and their abundance here in the Cairo Zoo could be taken as a symbol of the 'unity of the Nile Valley' on which Egyptian politicians are so busily harping.

*

Over against ancient Memphis is modern Cairo. One feature of this I was unable to visit – the modern city of the dead, counterpart of those gathered round the ancient pyramids. A friend who saw it during the war told me about it. It lies along the eastern flank of the living city, miles of streets with numbered houses, but all deserted, untenanted by the living. The houses are family death-houses; every well-to-do family possesses one. Once a year, the place is thronged, and every house becomes the scene of a family banquet, rather like All Souls' Day in many catholic countries. When a funeral brings a new occupant to one of the houses, a huge canopy is erected over the entrance, striped in fantastic and un-islamic brilliance. The north end of the necropolis is medieval and the houses get more and more modern towards the south.

My friend's description left me wondering whether this unique necropolis was not the product of the ancient Egyptians' obsessive concern with a physical after-life, projected into the Moslem present.

Let me mention just three of the monuments of Islam that struck me in Cairo. The Mosque of Ibn Tulun is one of the earliest specimens of Moslem architecture, having been built in A.D. 876. The pointed arches of its arcades antedate those of Christendom by more than two centuries, and the battlements on its massive walls seem to be the prototype of the pierced parapets of Gothic times. The heavy minaret has a curious spiral staircase. In a second mosque (whose name I have stupidly forgotten) the central court has a plan I have seen nowhere else. It is surrounded by four enormous iwans, great recesses opening on to the central space by high pointed arches, with lamps suspended by chains from their top. The effect is magnificent – soaring and solid at the same time. The Mohammed Ali mosque by the citadel dominates the city's silhouette. Its minarets are the quintessence of sharp slenderness: they stab the sky in thrilling fashion while Christian steeples point upwards in aspiration.

One curious fact, rather depressing to a European, is that whereas churches built in modern Gothic are almost always lifeless or ugly or both, modern mosques, built in the style of Santa Sophia with central low dome and four flanking minarets, are often lively and attractive buildings. Why this should be so is a problem I commend to architects.

El Azhar is not only a mosque but also a religious university devoted to traditional Arabic studies. The mosque was completed in the latter part of the tenth century, and almost at once was created a University by the Caliph, in imitation of the still older university-mosque of Kairouan in Tunisia. But whereas Kairouan is educationally primitive, El Azhar has grown into the largest of the traditional Moslem universities, with thousands of students from many countries. El Azhar is an integral part of the religious system of Islam to a greater extent than any medieval European university ever was of Christianity.

There are two large modern Universities in Egypt, at Cairo and Alexandria respectively; but the work of El Azhar is not in any way coordinated with theirs, so that two entirely different systems of higher education, with different aims and standards and curricula, exist side by side. I asked the head of El Azhar, a dignified elderly man, whether something could not be done to integrate the two systems; but he seemed to think this impossible. I came away feeling that El Azhar was a dangerous institution, combining a semi-fossilized system of ideas and methods with the explosive potential of religious belief. But nothing can well be done until the Ministry of Education becomes powerful enough to exercise real control over all forms of education. Meanwhile the modern universities are not exactly perfect, and the students are cynically used by the politicians to provide political demonstrations. Thus higher education in Egypt suffers at the hands of politics as well as of religion. The surprising fact remains that the system turns out so many good professional men.

Moslem Cairo, the largest city of the Arab world, is a new outgrowth from the site of the ancient suburb of Heliopolis, which the Greeks very confusingly called Babylon. But I have neither the knowledge nor the space to plunge into its eventful and sanguinary history.

Already in 1948 the situations seemed to have explosive possibilities: in 1952 the explosion occurred, and among other things burnt down Shepheard's Hotel and blew King Farouk out of his kingdom. The future of Egypt will lie largely in the hands of the professional men educated at the modern universities. After corruption has been purged and the grosser inequalities of wealth reduced, the competence of the engineer, the administrator, the social scientist, the doctor, the teacher will be desperately needed to make the internal adjustment of Egyptian society to modern conditions, and the sanity of the educated man to transcend nationalist fanaticism in a system of international participation.

15

PYRAMIDS

'THE MOST POMPOUS MONU-
ment of Egyptian greatness, and one of the most bulky works of manual
industry,' said Imlac, 'are the Pyramids; fabrics raised before the time of
history, and of which the earliest narratives afford us only uncertain traditions.' 'Let us visit them to-morrow,' said Nekayah. Thus Dr Johnson in
Rasselas.

Rasselas's party took tents on their camels, and, after measuring all the
dimensions of the Great Pyramid, encamped at its foot. Next day, while
Rasselas and his sister were in the interior, 'examining the chest in which the
body of the founder is supposed to have been reposited', the Lady Pekuah,
the Princess's lady-in-waiting, and her two maids were abducted by a troop
of mounted Arabs, whose chief later explained to Pekuah that all he wanted
of her was a large ransom, which was perfectly justified, since 'the sons of
Ishmael are the natural and hereditary lords of this part of the continent,
which is usurped by late invaders and low-born tyrants, from whom we are
compelled to take by the sword what is denied to justice.'

Things have changed since then, though there is still danger to the visitor's
purse, through the clamorous demands for backsheesh, with or without services rendered, by everyone from little girls to aged beggars, the extortions
of guides and donkey-men, and the hotel prices. No longer need the visitor
camp (as he still must do if he wishes to stay in Petra): the enormous El
Mina Hotel is there, just across the way, with all the resources of *le confort
international*, if he wants to stay; and anyhow he can readily motor out from

Cairo for the afternoon. But the Pyramids are still, and rightly, the first objective of nearly every visitor to Egypt.

At first almost everybody equates the Pyramids with the mighty three of Giza: only later does he realize the existence of the other sixty-odd pyramidal constructions spread out along the seventy-mile stretch of the Nile's left bank across from Memphis, memorials of the Pyramid Age.*

Familiarity (though at second-hand) had led me, not to despise the Pyramids, but to discount them. They had become international commonplaces, degraded to the level of the tourist souvenir. They had passed through so many million minds as one of the 'Wonders of the World' that their sharp edge of real wonder had been blunted. Like Niagara and Rio de Janeiro, they had been thrust down my throat so often that I was sure I was not going to be impressed by them.

But in actuality, they make an overpowering impression. It is not one of beauty, but on the other hand not one of mere bigness, though size enters into it, and there is an element of aesthetic satisfaction in the elemental simplicity of their triangular silhouette. But this combines with an element of vicarious pride in the magnitude of the human achievement involved, and with a sense of their bold novelty and their historical uniqueness, to produce an effect different from that of any other work of man.

Jomard, who was among the men of learning on Napoleon's expedition to Egypt, has well described this effect. 'The general aspect of those monuments', he writes, 'gives rise to a striking observation: seen from a distance they produce the same kind of effect as do high mountain peaks of pyramidal form, outlined against the sky. The nearer one approaches, the more this effect decreases. But when at last you are within a short distance of these regular masses, a wholly different impression is produced: you are struck by surprise, and as soon as you have reached the top of the slope, your ideas change in a flash. Finally, when you have reached the foot of the Great Pyramid, you are seized with a vivid and powerful emotion, tempered by a sort of stupefaction, almost overwhelming in its effects. . . . What you

* I have drawn heavily on J. P. Lauer's *Le Problème des Pyramides d'Egypte* (Payot, Paris, 1948) and I. E. S. Edwards's *The Pyramids of Egypt* (Penguin Books, 1947), as well as on standard and semi-popular works on ancient Egypt. Lauer, *inter alia*, has an interesting section on the building techniques employed. Edwards is particularly valuable on the historical development of the pyramid complex. Drioton and Lauer's little handbook on *Sakkarah: the Monuments of Zoser* (Institut Français d'Archéologie, Cairo), with its wealth of illustrations and reconstructions, is also most useful.

experience is in no wise the admiration provoked by a great work of art, but it is profound and impressive.'

Napoleon's mind reacted characteristically to the sight. He first demanded to know the measurement of the Great Pyramid: and then astonished his staff, on their return from climbing to the top, by pointing out that its cubic content would suffice to build a wall ten feet high and a foot thick entirely surrounding France. This is one way of bringing home its staggering bulk. Originally this solid mass of stone was over 480 feet high – 115 feet higher than the top of the cross on St Paul's; its base covered over 13 acres – an area, we are assured by the guide-books, sufficient to accommodate St Paul's, Westminster Abbey, St Peter's, and the Cathedrals of Florence and Milan all at once; and it contained over $2\frac{1}{4}$ million blocks of stone, averaging $2\frac{1}{2}$ tons in weight. It is an artificial mountain, which would reach from the seashore almost to the summit of Beachy Head.

The interior is equally impressive. The ascending gallery leading to the King's Chamber, where Cheops's sarcophagus is still to be seen, is over 150 feet long. When you are in it, the sense of the thousands of tons of super-incumbent stone deliberately piled up above your head is more oppressive than the sense of overlying rock-masses in the galleries of a natural cave. On the walls of the upward-sloping limb of the passage there are projections, against which the royal sarcophagus was rested on its final journey; and in the central chamber is the enormous object itself. It is hard enough for the visitor to crawl up the narrow ramp: what it must have been like for the workmen struggling to move the huge box of stone upwards, is difficult to conceive.

In spite of all precautions, tomb-robbers penetrated to the King's Chamber and abstracted the mummy, and doubtless the treasure round it. In 'Don Juan', Byron records his characteristic impression of the violated tomb:

> *Where are the hopes of man? Old Egypt's King*
> *Cheops erected the first pyramid*
> *And largest, thinking it was just the thing*
> *To keep his memory whole and mummy hid.*
> *But somebody or other rummaging*
> *Burglariously broke his coffin's lid.*
> *Let not a monument give you or me hopes,*
> *Since not a pinch of dust remains of Cheops.*

Here in the gallery and chamber the fine workmanship of five thousand years ago makes its full impact. There is no mortar: the blocks of granite and limestone fit to a hair's breadth: and all this was done with only copper and stone tools. The masonry of the ancient Incas (so much superior to that of their Spanish conquerors) gave me the same impression.

Most of the gallery is surmounted by a remarkable corbel vault (the true arch was still unknown), comprising seven overlapping courses, with a final roof-span of over a metre.

To climb the Great Pyramid is to receive the same impression of size in yet a third fashion. It is a real piece of rock-scrambling, in the course of which most visitors are grateful for the help of the guides. When I was on the summit, the sun was getting low in the sky. Suddenly I realized that it was casting the shadow of the pyramid far out on to the fertile valley-floor in a huge inverted V. Only once in my life had I had a comparable experience, of a man-made structure intruding into the realm of physical geography. That was when I saw the Empire State Building, a structure nearly 5000 years later in date, losing itself in a layer of cloud well above the tops of the common ruck of skyscrapers.

In passing, the pyramids of Mexico are quite different from those of Egypt. They are not tombs, but bases or platforms for the temples of the gods, while temples in Egypt are never thus raised, and the god-temples never have pyramids associated with them. The Mexican pyramids are all stepped: none has a simple triangular outline. Only a few score pyramids are known in Egypt. But some 18,000 have already been identified in Mexico: this of course includes all the local 'parish churches' of the pre-Columbian religion as well as its main 'cathedrals'. If you want to equate the Mexican pyramid with anything in the Old World, the comparison should be with the Ziggurat of Mesopotamia, though this is not to say that there is any genetic relationship.

Britain poses a minor riddle of the same sort, in the shape of Silbury Hill near the glorious megalithic centre of Avebury. It is, I believe, the only example in Britain of a true artificial hill as opposed to a mere tumulus: and my impression is that it was not built as a simple cone, but with a slight flattening of its four sides. It is tempting to believe that some band of voyagers brought the idea of a gigantic pyramid tomb to prehistoric Wiltshire, two thousand years after it first took shape in Egypt. But why is there only one such artificial hill in all Britain?

The Egyptian pyramids were built as tombs exclusively royal, and extremely outsize, but tombs none the less. This, the considered view of all competent archeologists who have worked on the subject, is indeed obvious to the ordinary visitor who has seen the interior chamber of the Great Pyramid. The pyramidal super-tomb was always associated with other buildings, notably a mortuary temple in the so-called pyramid complex. And the function of the whole pyramid complex was to ensure the survival of the king in the realm of the after-life. The pyramid itself was not just a funerary memorial, but a place where the body of the king could be safely preserved and where the rituals of survival could take effect upon it.

This, however, has not deterred a large number of people from wasting their energies on 'proving' that the pyramids were built with some quite different main end in view – as astronomical observatories, as confirmations of the literal truth of the Bible, as repositories of secret wisdom and mathematical knowledge, or even as prophetic 'records of the future'.

In the course of my career, I have been the target for a good deal of the literature of crankdom. One large section of this is devoted to the pyramids, almost invariably though somewhat arbitrarily to the Great Pyramid alone. From its measurements the pyramidologists claim to be able to deduce a great many surprising facts and prophecies. Unfortunately different sects or schools make different and often incompatible deductions, and the prophecies have almost invariably been falsified by events.

One memory is of the arrival in my laboratory at King's College of some voluminous printed documents entirely devoted to what I may call pyramidal theory. The main one was concerned to demonstrate the curious conclusion that π, the ratio of a circle's circumference to its diameter, is not incommensurable, but ends (if I recollect right) at the fourth decimal place – precisely 3·1416 instead of 3·14159265358979..... At first sight this seemed singularly uninteresting compared to the usual deductions, which either ascribe to the constructors of the pyramids a fabulous degree of esoteric knowledge, or else a miraculously conveyed preview of human history. However, on turning to the end of a second pamphlet I discovered that here was a more general conclusion after all: 'From all this it will be evident' (I quote from memory) 'that $\pi = 3\cdot1416 = H_2 + O = H_2O = $ Jesus Christ.' I wrote the author a note saying that I was much interested (which was no more than the truth) but that for the present I felt I should stick to the value of π as determined by the mathematicians; and by return of post received a reply beginning, 'Dear Sir, That's right – stick-in-the-mud British science, as usual'.

This memory was revived by reading J. P. Lauer's book. He devotes an entire section to 'The pretended secrets of the pyramids', which makes clear the fascination exercised by this kind of pseudo-scientific interpretation. After all, we may remember that Newton was deeply interested in the interpretation of the prophecies of the Book of Daniel, and actually devoted a good deal more of his time to this subject than to science and mathematics.

'Pyramidology' is, in effect, one sector of a considerable field of human activity, which however regrettable, deserves study as part of the history of human thought.

Lauer divides pyramid theories into two main groups – the mystical, including the biblical and the theosophical, and the scientific, including the astronomical and the mathematical. I recommend his book to the curious reader. He will find extraordinary examples of *petitio principii*, of falsification – or shall we say 'adjustment' – of facts to fit preconceived theories, of the invocation of 'scientific' accuracy of detailed calculation to mask a basic absence of scientific method. Above all he will realize the strength of the anti-scientific forces in the human mind – the wish-fulfilling belief in absolutes; the passion for certitude, in which the simple all-or-nothing reactions of lower nervous activities are projected into the upper reaches of the mind; the unconscious, unacknowledged belief in the magical and mystical; the mythopoeic desire for soul-satisfying explanations. If the western world had gone on using the pyramid as an architectural form, if the Great Pyramid and its rivals had been only 50 or 60 feet high instead of over 400, I suspect that there would have been no esoteric meanings found in pyramids, or revelatory prophecies emerging from their measurements.

As an example of the potency of the anti-scientific forces aroused by the contemplation of the Great Pyramid, let me take Piazzi Smyth. Piazzi Smyth, in spite of his scientific status and his official position as Scottish Astronomer Royal, in 1867 published a book entitled *Life and Work at the Great Pyramid*, largely based on his own measurements on the spot, in which he claimed, among much else, that the builders of the Great Pyramid used as unit of measurement a special and sacred 'Jewish cubit', as opposed to the profane 'cubit of Cain', that containing 25 pyramidal inches, each 1/500,000,000th part of the polar diameter of the earth, and therefore equivalent to 1·001 British inches; and attacked the Egyptologists for their obstinate insistence on acquiring erudition on the subject of 'ancient idolatry'. He also believed that the measurements of the interior galleries prefigured important dates in history. One date thus pyramidally indicated as especially important was 1813: this, he explained, was because 1813 marked the greatest recent progress in British efforts to spread the knowledge of the Bible. And some of his followers deduced the future date of the Final Tribulation and other scourges. While these have luckily not materialized at their appointed times, the pyramidal measurements failed to give the dates of the World Wars.

I have no time for other examples, however curious, of these elaborate rationalizations of irrationality. But I must recall that the measurements of the pyramids do tell us something, and something of considerable interest, about the builders. In the first place, the pyramid-builders were capable of extremely exact measurement. The individual sides of the Great Pyramid deviate from their average length of 755·79 feet by less than one part in a thousand.

Then the pyramids are oriented with extreme accuracy. The deviations of the four sides of the Great Pyramid from the true north–south and east–west directions vary from 1/11th down to less than 1/30th of a degree – an astounding measure of exactitude. Whether this orientation had some purely religious significance – the west being the entrance to the After-life, for instance – or whether, as is possible, the pyramids also served as standards of astronomical direction, we do not know.

The measurements of the Great Pyramid do yield some interesting mathematical relations. For instance, the ratio of the perimeter of the base to double the height is approximately equal to π. Further, the ratio of the shortest slope of the pyramid, up one of its mid-faces, to half the distance across its base, gives the so-called Golden Number, 1·618, which is said to provide the most aesthetically satisfying ratio between the dimensions of a construction.

However, the significance of these facts is somewhat diminished when we recall that other pyramids have different measurements. The most obvious example is the neighbouring Pyramid of Chephren, whose angle of slope is steeper than that of its immediate predecessor – 52°20′ instead of 51°50′ – a fact which from some aspects gives it the illusion of greater absolute height.

To the east of the pyramid are two great pits in the rock. These are boat-shaped, and once contained wooden ships for the use of the King in the world beyond the grave.

Down below is the Sphinx – gaunt and rather ugly now that the surrounding sand has once again been cleared away: it must have been more impressive when it emerged incompletely from the desert's accumulated encroachment. It remains a unique monument. There are plenty of other sphinxes in Egypt, but none so large and solitary. No wonder that legend gathered round it.

The riddle of the Sphinx, or at least of its function, seems now to have been solved. Sphinxes originated from lions, which were supposed to act as guardians of sacred places in general, and in particular of the gates of the underworld. This development coincided with the rise of the solar religion at Heliopolis; and eventually the lion became a sphinx, by being given the head of the sun-god in human form. In later times, avenues of sphinxes, though sometimes with a reversion to animal heads, were often built as approaches to god-temples – as at Karnak, where they make an imposing and surprising show (pl. 51, opp. p. 249).

Here at Giza, the builders of Chephren's pyramid, the successor and all-but-equal of that of Cheops, took the hunk of rock that the quarrying operations for the Great Pyramid had left, and carved it into a huge and rather disproportioned sphinx, some 240 feet long, with the face of King Chephren, originally complete with artificial beard and other insignia of royalty. To add to the complication, a statue of Chephren himself was originally placed between the great fore-paws. According to the doctrines of Heliopolis, the king on dying became identified with the sun-god: so the great sphinx represents a king, who represents a god, who represents a lion, who acts as guardian for the entire gigantic burial-ground of Giza.

The so-called 'Temple of the Sphinx' is really Chephren's Valley Building, the riverside portion of his pyramid complex. It is all very well to read in a book that a pyramid was merely part of a huge and elaborate complex of buildings, but another matter to realize at first hand how elaborate that complex actually was. It was to the Valley Building that the dead king's body was brought by water in the royal barge across the Nile. Here were performed the rites of purification, embalmment, and the so-called 'opening of the mouth'. In this last ceremony the royal statues and (at least in later times) the royal mummy itself were 'vivified', ritually endowed with various attributes of life so that they could mediate the continued existence of the dead man in the after-world.

These rites occupied many months – perhaps a year. Only after their completion was the body taken, again to the accompaniment of various rites, along the causeway to the Mortuary Temple by the side of the pyramid tomb. Chephren's causeway was over a quarter of a mile long. The Mortuary Temple was a larger building, devoted to the continuing ritual of providing sustenance for the king in his after-life. It contained a sanctuary with an altar, an outer court with statues of the king, and storehouses and magazines with reserves of food and drink. Each dead king had a body of priests devoted to his service. They seem to have lived in a 'pyramid town' attached to the Valley Building, where they enjoyed various privileges, including exemption from certain kinds of taxation.

Chephren's Valley Building is a marvel of restrained design, with its imposing square columns of red granite. Illumination was provided only by narrow slits just below the roof, so that the hall must have been a place of twilight mystery. The effect of this 'dim religious light' is enhanced by contrast with the hard blinding sunshine of the outer landscape.

Originally, no fewer than 23 statues of the King stood in the Valley Temple. The only one to survive, now in the Cairo Museum, is a remarkable work. To the modern European mind, it is surprising to think of these splendid statues standing almost invisible in the semi-darkness. But here again we are confronted with the fact that ritual representation was the primary aim. As Edwards says, the sculptures 'were not designed for display, but to provide the spirit with an imperishable substitute for the human body'; and yet the sculptors insisted on producing works of art!

*

Saqqara is not so famous as Giza, nor is its step-pyramid so overpoweringly imposing as the great pyramids of the 4th Dynasty; but the visitor finds himself in a constant state of astonishment at the unexpected facts and interesting ideas with which the monumental complex confronts him.

In the first place, it contains the oldest of the pyramids, the step-pyramid of King Zoser of the 3rd Dynasty, built some two centuries earlier than the Great Pyramid of Cheops. Before that time, even kings had been buried in mastabas – underground chambers with a low flat superstructure.

In the second place, we can here see with our own eyes that a pyramid was only a part of an enclosure containing a vast and elaborate complex of buildings. The step-pyramid's enclosure is better preserved, and reveals the basic beliefs of the Egyptians more directly, than any other.

Thirdly, it is a remarkable example of innovation, of the sudden utilization of new ideas and new techniques – in this case the new idea of a pyramid tomb and the new technique of building in stone – in violent contrast with the normal traditionalism of Egyptian life and culture.*

Thanks largely to the admirably organized excavations and restorations undertaken by the Egyptian *Service des Antiquités* under French direction, we now can see every stage in the actual change-over from old to new. For a mastaba was originally built as Zoser's future burial place, and is still there under the great mass of superincumbent masonry. What is more, five separate stages in the evolution of mastaba to step-pyramid can be discerned in the one structure.

Zoser's mastaba was a flat-topped square stone structure almost 25 feet high, deep below which was his burial-chamber, with a number of galleries radiating from it. The fact that the mastaba was revetted with dressed Tura limestone shows that it was originally planned as the final building. However, the mastaba was twice enlarged by the addition of new layers on its sides, one all round it, the second only to the east, but each faced with dressed limestone for public viewing. They were not quite so high as the original centre, so that the result was a 'step mastaba'. In the substructure, something like 30,000 stone jars and vessels were discovered, some of them of great beauty: this gives one an idea of the scale on which this abode of the after-life was constructed.

Then a step pyramid with four steps was built over the mastaba, and the building was finally re-planned and completed as a six-step pyramid, over 200 feet high – a monument far larger than anything previously erected in Egypt. Meanwhile the substructure of the mastaba was also altered, becoming less and less house-like and more and more focused on the burial-chamber. Furthermore, a quite new feature was laid out – the pyramid enclosure, surrounded by a stone wall measuring some 600 by 300 yards and containing an array of buildings. .

* Recently (see *The Times* of 27 Sept. 1949), what are described as the oldest known metal tools, including copper chisels, engraving tools and saws for cutting stone, have been found in a 1st Dynasty royal tomb of about 3000 B.C. in the Saqqara necropolis. Such tools were clearly a prerequisite for the monumental stone architecture of the 3rd Dynasty.

But I must not lose myself and my readers in a mass of detail: I must concentrate on the main features of pyramid history as it has impressed itself on my non-expert mind.

Pyramid history is part of the history of Egyptian kingly burial. To understand it, we have to keep certain key ideas in mind. The first is the divinity of the king; the second is the preoccupation with an after-life, which will be for the most part a continuation of life as lived on earth; the third is the belief that life after death can be secured by a ritual providing a physical basis for continued existence, and in no other way; the fourth is the assumption that in this ritual, symbolic representation of objects will serve as well as, or almost as well as, the actual objects themselves; and finally, a belief in the peculiar efficacy of the written word.

As we have already seen, the idea of a sacred personage embodying the fertility of the crops was extremely widespread in primitive agricultural societies. And this neolithic idea sooner or later developed into that of the sacred priest-king, with whose vigour the vigour of the community is bound up, and who must carry out a sacred ritual if the years are to be prosperous. Originally the 'king' was ritually sacrificed after a certain length of time, to ensure against any flagging of his vigour and magic force. This still happened within living memory in parts of Nigeria; but in most places, as time went on, mock kings were chosen for the sacrifice or substitute rituals employed.

Nowhere else in human history did so much of the idea persist in such a large and highly organized society as in ancient Egypt; nowhere else was the sacred priest-king magnified to such an extent as in the person of the Pharaoh. From being merely sacred, he became also divine. And being divine, it was natural that he should, if possible, share with the gods in the life of the other world. Furthermore, if the prosperity of the kingdom were bound up with his person in this mortal life, was it not natural, or at least likely, that the connection might persist after his death? There was thus a double reason for ensuring an after-life to kings; and at the outset only kings, it seems, were eligible for it. Certainly the kings' tombs were different in type and immensely larger than those of others, and the rituals of their after-life much more elaborate. In the early dynasties, only a few nobles and favourites seem to have been eligible for a future life: it was not until later in Egyptian history that the hereafter was fully democratized.

The Egyptians believed firmly, almost passionately, that the continuance of life after death depended on the continued preservation of the corpse – a

9. The construction of the Great Pyramid: each block of stone
in the artificial mountain weighs about 2½ tons

10. At Saqqara: a step pyramid and the earliest stone columns,
still with their wall-like stone supports

51. *An astonishing avenue of ram-headed sphinxes, leading to the great temple of Amon at Karnak*

52. *The two huge colossi of Memnon enthroned in solitude among the fields*

belief that could readily grow up in a desert climate like Egypt, but not in a humid climate where the body was likely to decompose quickly, nor, of course, where cremation was practised. This led to embalmment and finally to all the elaborate techniques of mummification.

This belief was supplemented by the belief that the after-life should be a replica of this life at its best; and that, in order to secure this, the dead needed the same food and equipment as here below, as well as a continuing ritual to ensure their effective transference. Hence the allotment of lands to provide for the food and the upkeep of priests to effect its transference; hence the provision of boats and jewels, robes and vessels in the tombs and sacred enclosures.

But here the symbolific power of the human mind stepped in. If the priests were negligent, the mere existence of reserve stores, or even dummy stores, in the magazines would suffice. As further insurance, a funerary stela was eventually placed in the tomb, with an inscription declaring that regular offerings had been made: the magic force of writing was supposed to suffice as a substitute for the actual offerings, even if the service of the tomb fell into neglect. If it began to seem cruel or wasteful to sacrifice live slaves to accompany the dead king, their representation in pictorial or model form, offering game or preparing food, would surely suffice. If a palace were needed for the dead king to inhabit on his returns to earth, a façade would be enough, and imitation doors carved permanently ajar would suffice to represent real portals.

Dummy food-pots and jars in place of actual provisions are already to be found in tombs of the 2nd Dynasty. Later, sculptured scenes or little models of groups of men and women harvesting or baking or weaving were used to represent the provision of food and clothing, reliefs of the dead kings and nobles fowling or feasting were carved to guarantee the continuance of such agreeable pursuits in the after-life, and statues called *answerers* were made to act for the Pharaoh in the various tasks he might be called upon to undertake in the after-world.

The portrait-statue represented the dead man in the place of burial, enabling the spirit to recognize the body when it returned from the after-world to renew its strength from the offerings, real or substitutional, that were made in the tomb.* To this end, the statue was placed in a *serdab*, a

* The theory of the soul was in reality more complex; Man had three components – a body, a *Ba*, and a *Ka*. But for such theological details I must refer my readers to the text-books.

little dark chamber with a small slit opposite the face. The statue was thus protected by being walled-in, while the slit was enough for the spirit to get in and out. The name of the deceased was usually engraved on the statue to facilitate recognition, in case the spirit had forgotten the body's features.

*

In predynastic times, a shallow grave was dug, containing the body and pots of food and drink, together with a few personal possessions, and in all probability then covered with a mound of sand to form a tumulus. With the more elaborate civilization of the dynastic era, the more elaborate construction called a mastaba appears. This originally had a superstructure of brick coated with lime stucco, containing a number of rooms and storage chambers, with a substructure below ground-level containing the burial chamber of the dead man and a few other rooms for his personal belongings.

The mastaba was a modified copy of the house of the period, and was designed as the permanent dwelling of the deceased. He could continue to occupy its symbolic rooms and be nourished on the stores, real or representational, in its magazines.

The superstructure later became a mere shell filled with rubble, while the substructure was deepened and all the stores transferred below ground, doubtless for better protection against the elements and the tomb-robbers. Stone began to be used in royal tombs, but at first only on a small scale.

When Zoser came to the throne, he must have decided to commemorate his reign and to ensure his after-life on a grander scale than any of his predecessors. Luckily he had as chief minister a man of genius – Imhotep, who achieved legendary fame as architect, astronomer, and father of medical science, and was eventually deified.

We can picture them selecting the fine site just opposite the capital, and deciding to build there a representation, not just of a palace, but of a royal fortress city. The splendid walls of limestone, with their fourteen sham double gates, were almost certainly intended as a representation of the famous 'white walls' of Memphis with which Menes had surrounded his new capital after uniting the two kingdoms of Upper and Lower Egypt.

The royal mastaba was built in the centre of the enclosure, but, though very large as mastabas go, it would have been invisible within the walls. Then suddenly the plan was changed and the first pyramid began to rise. Perhaps it was merely that Imhotep and Zoser wanted a tomb that would tower above the walls of the enclosure so as to be visible from the city of the living in the flood-plain below; or perhaps, as Edwards suggests, this motive was combined with the idea of providing a physical means by which the King's spirit could ascend to heaven. If so, this was a sign that the theology of the time was transferring the scene of the after-life from the tomb and its vicinity to the gods' celestial realm. The step-form of the pyramid may have been an expression of the idea of a gigantic stairway reaching up to heaven. Alternatively it may have been dictated by the limitations of architectural skill. After all, this was the first large stone building to be attempted in Egypt; the art of stone construction had not been explored, and the use of large blocks had not yet been thought of. Further, the easiest way to adapt traditional ideas to the new architectural form would be to build a series of mastaba superstructures of diminishing size, piled one upon another.

Whatever the symbolism and whatever the technical limitations, imposing appearance was certainly aimed at: and so, after Imhotep had discovered that a step pyramid could be built, he changed the plans and doubled its size.

Now for some of the impressions made on the man of today by a visit to Imhotep's adventurous work. First, the skill of the *Service des Antiquités*. Barely twenty-five years ago, the step pyramid rose from a waste of sand, marked by a few ridges. Excavation then revealed the remains of the great complex of buildings and unearthed lovely treasures – pots and jars and statues and ornaments now in the Cairo Museum. And finally reconstruction has restored a great deal of their original beauty to the tumbled ruins.

The entrance colonnade, which leads in from one corner, is flanked by strange-looking 'fasciculated' columns (pl. 50, opp. p. 248). They look strange because they are copies in stone of the wooden columns of an earlier age, which in their turn were copies in wood of the bundles of reed-stems, tied together at top and bottom, that formed the supports of the early mud-brick buildings.* In the same traditional spirit, the stone slabs roofing the colonnade were carved so as to look like palm-tree logs, which were the chief source of beams in predynastic buildings.

A still stranger feature is that the columns do not stand free, but are joined to the main walls of the passage on either side by side-walls of stone. Apparently Imhotep was not at all sure of the capacity of stone, the new and wonderful material, to stand alone in columnar form. We think of the free-

* See Margaret Murray's *The Splendour that was Egypt*, p. 227, for details, and for the later conflation of lotus-bud with papyrus-bundle.

standing stone column as the central feature of ancient architecture. So it eventually became: but it originated out of quite other materials, and it had to acquire its freedom from the neighbouring walls. Here in the colonnade at Saqqara we can see the first step towards its independence.

Elsewhere in Saqqara, the columns are fully engaged, backed directly on to walls. Some, however, have freed themselves from that other servitude, the direct copying of earlier materials. Thus the beautiful columns on the 'House of the North' are representations of the papyrus plant, but as emblem of Lower Egypt, not as prior building material.

This building and its companion to the south of the enclosure seem to have typified the two Kingdoms of Upper and Lower Egypt, with their emblems of lotus and papyrus respectively, united in the single realm. They are both dummies, with only a narrow passage and a minute chapel in their solid core, and presumably represented comparable buildings in the royal capital.

Then there is a court bordered by two rows of dummy chapels, containing only small niches for offerings in their solid masonry. Each had a dummy half-open door, complete with dummy pivot and socket (the hinge had not been invented), and the niches have dummy wooden barriers carved in stone on their side-walls.

This court seems to have been a representation of the court where the living Pharaoh went through the ceremony of jubilee or *heb-sed*. The original priest-kings were, we can be sure, ceremonially sacrificed after a limited reign, before their natural force began to fail, and a younger successor was crowned to give his vigour to the community. To avoid this disagreeable necessity, the heb-sed ritual was designed, to restore the king's vigour by magical means; it involved a re-enactment of the coronation, as well as the performance of various magical ceremonies by the king. The dummy paraphernalia were doubtless intended to allow the dead Pharaoh to continue the practice, thereby rejuvenating himself in the after-life, and so continuing to confer prosperity on the kingdom he had left in this world.

At the serdab, the visitor can look through two little holes and see, in the obscurity within, the replica of the statue of Zoser that dwelt here for nearly five thousand years. It is a strange experience, to be thus in the position of the dead king's questing spirit looking for its earthly landmarks.

The Mortuary Temple seems to represent some part of the palace at Memphis. It was the first true temple attached to a royal tomb: the earlier mastabas had only a small room for offerings.

There are *graffiti* in the passage of the Southern Building, which show that Saqqara was visited as a curiosity in the New Kingdom, when the buildings were falling into decay, perhaps fifteen hundred years after they were built. It is amusing to find that the tourist's habit of writing his name on walls has been going on for well over three thousand years. These inscriptions, however, are not mere scribbles: they are the work of professional scribes (naturally enough, for ordinary people could not write) in beautiful hieratic script. In one, the scribe Amenemhet (who describes himself without any false modesty as 'a clever scribe without his equal among the men of Memphis') records his professional disgust at the low quality of some other visitors' efforts: 'It is like the work of a woman who has no mind . . . I have seen a scandal: they are no scribes whom Thoth has enlightened.'

Saqqara was succeeded by a few other step pyramids. But from Cheops onwards, only true or unstepped pyramids are known. Snefru, the predecessor of Cheops, built two pyramids for himself, one of which was first constructed in steps, and later converted into a true pyramid. Edwards suggests that the form of the true pyramid was designed to symbolize sunbeams radiating down through the clouds: the king would ascend into heaven on the beams of the sacred sun. Possibly there were two rival priesthoods centring round the step and the sunbeam form of pyramid, and Snefru, after an attempt to placate both, decided that it was better to promote religious unity by favouring one only.

After Cheops, pyramids diminish in size. This was doubtless due in part to the increasing reliance on symbolism: so long as the pyramid was of the correct form, it would provide a symbolic method of celestial ascent, without the need for actual skyscraping height. But considerations of expense must also have been involved. We need not believe that Cheops was merely a brutal tyrant, diverting the common people from useful labour to work only for his selfish glorification. His hundred thousand workmen seem to have been well fed, and to have been employed on quarrying and transporting the stone mainly during the off-season, when agricultural work was at a standstill – a gigantic policy of public works. But the work was unproductive, and the four thousand skilled artificers could have been better employed. A succession of gigantic pyramids and pyramid complexes, with the lands set aside for the support of their mortuary priesthood, must have been a serious drain on the productive resources of the country.

Toynbee, in his *Study of History*, goes further. What I have called the magnification of the Priest-King in the person of the divine and all-powerful Pharaoh, he describes as the idolization of a political sovereignty incarnated in a human being, and regards this as a major cause of the failure of Ancient Egyptian civilization to grow and develop. 'The crushing incubus which this series of human idols imposed upon Egyptian life is perfectly symbolized in the Pyramids, which were erected by the forced labour of their subjects in order to render the Pyramid-builders magically immortal.'

After the chaos of the first intermediate period which followed the collapse of the Old Kingdom, pyramids were once more erected by the Pharaohs of the Middle Kingdom, some of them in the neighbourhood of Thebes in Upper Egypt. Eventually, however, it became clear from sad experience that pyramids drew attention to the royal tombs they contained, and that no device, however elaborate, would safeguard the royal tombs from robbers. So during the New Kingdom, the Pharaohs eventually decided that the actual tomb should be as secret as possible. This meant separating the tomb from its mortuary temple. The Mortuary Temples took over the functions of conspicuous monuments and memorials, while the royal graves were dug secretly in the cliffs of the famous desert valley to the west of Thebes, the Valley of the Kings. In spite of all precautions, however, the location of the new royal cemetery soon became known, and the ingenuity of the tomb-robbers was once more successful. Tutankhamen was the only one of sixty Pharaohs to be undisturbed in his tomb until modern scientific excavation gave him and his gorgeous equipment a new and more public persistence.

During later Egyptian history pyramids were used as purely architectural features in royal funerary temples and in private tombs, as well as being employed as royal tombs by the Kings of the Sudan and the Ethiopian Kingdom. But it is the oldest pyramids which are the most significant. They illustrate for us in tangible form the monstrous magnification of the Pharaoh and his functions which left such a lasting impression on Egyptian civilization: it led inevitably to the rigid centralization of power, the anti-democratic cleavage between rulers and ruled, which beset and in the long run bedevilled Egyptian history.

16

THE EGYPTIAN PAST

OUR INEXORABLE SCHEDULE LEFT us only one day for Upper Egypt – one day wedged in between two nights in the train. Between breakfast-time when we stepped out of the train and the moonlit midnight when we stepped on to it again, we saw Luxor and Karnak, the Colossus of Memnon and the Ramasseum, the Temple of Hatshepsut, the tomb of Tutankhamen and other wonders of the Valley of the Kings. This sounds wildly exhausting; but thanks to the admirable arrangements made for us by Monsieur Chevrier, of the *Service des Antiquités* at Karnak, his personal explanation of the ruins, the charming hospitality of Mme Chevrier, and the stimulus of the spectacles presented to our eyes and minds, we enjoyed every moment.

The ancient city of Thebes has vanished as completely as Memphis. And yet it was the leading city of Egypt for some fifteen centuries – indeed, so pre-eminent in that land where cities as political units played such a relatively unimportant role, that it was colloquially called *No*, the town, as we say 'town' for London. For twelve hundred years (apart from the brief period when Akhnaton left this home of Amon, the god whom he disliked) it was the royal capital and seat of government, and during this time the country rose to its greatest height of imperial power, so that unparalleled wealth poured into the place. Yet as a city it has simply disappeared.

This is partly due to its sack by Assurbanipal in the 7th century B.C., a destruction so frightful that it became a legend of horror even in that time of violence, and served as an exemplar to Nahum when he was prophesying disaster to Nineveh. However, the very thoroughness of the Assyrians' destruction saved the remains of the great temples: when the Ptolemaic kings set themselves to reconstruct some of the ancient temples of their realm, Thebes had become too unimportant a place to warrant any such effort, and the ruins were simply left as they stood.

The city's vanishing is due also to the fact that its houses and palaces, as usually in ancient Egypt, were all of brick and wood: only the abodes of the gods and of the immortal dead were built of stone, and so they alone survive.

There is today a small town at Luxor, which subsists largely on tourists: in 1911, according to the *Encyclopaedia Britannica*, 'the district was the seat of an extensive manufacture of forged antiques'. I discreetly refrained from asking my host about the present status of this promising industry.

The broad river greets the traveller emerging from the train. Across it, to the sacred west, lies the necropolis – all the monuments erected to dead Pharaohs, all the royal tombs and funerary temples. On the hither, eastern side the people lived, and the only temples were god-temples.

Luxor is the first of the god-temples to confront the traveller. It is a shock to be told that it was in one sense only a secondary sort of shrine, suburban to Thebes, whither Amon, issuing from his metropolitan temple at Karnak, was annually brought in state on his sacred boat during the inundation. After due celebrations (represented in carvings on the temple), the god returned to his more permanent and more glorious abode in Thebes.

Amon, by the way, had a curious history. Originally a minor local deity, he was chosen as chief god by the provincial governors of Thebes who put an end to the chaos succeeding the fall of the Old Kingdom by conquering Lower Egypt and driving out the Semites who had infiltrated into power there. Installed at Karnak, and endowed with new theological properties, he became the symbol of the greatness of the new empire centred on Thebes, and there, through his priesthood, wielded great political power. Akhnaton's attempt to establish the cult of Aton, though partly ideological, springing from a nobler conception of deity, was partly a revolt against the entrenched power of Amon's priesthood.

In the street outside, a snake-charmer solicited our attention. His snakes were not very impressive: I would have preferred an Indian performance. Below, the ruins spread their crowded pillars. On their fringe is a small white mosque. The authorities were planning to pull it down, as being an intrusion on the Pharaonic past. This I thought was a pity: it stands as a vivid reminder of the multiplicity of history, the protean forms in which religion may house itself in one and the same country.

A boy on camel-back passed in the street. Ancient Luxor knew almost as little of camels as it did of the future rise of Islam. For it is a curious fact that the camel seems not to have been regularly employed as a beast of burden in the Nile Valley until about 300 B.C., though camels had of course been used in desert caravans in Arabia and Mesopotamia from the time of Abraham and earlier. It is still more curious that camels were not known in North Africa proper until about the beginning of our era. We know that Marius, just before 100 B.C., used horses in his campaign against Jugurtha, which he certainly would not have done if camels had been available: and Sallust records that the first time Roman soldiers ever saw camels was in Asia Minor, when Lucullus was fighting Mithridates, between 88 and 84 B.C. Somehow camels had reached Africa by 46 B.C., for in that year Caesar captured a score from Juba at Thapsus. But they did not become abundant there until the 4th century A.D.* Before that, from the time when post-glacial desiccation took its full effect, the Sahara must have remained an impassable sea of sand, as uncrossable by organized traffic as was the Atlantic Ocean.

This extreme slowness of the camel's westward spread is to me one of the puzzles of cultural diffusion. Perhaps the ancient Egyptians had no special or urgent need of camel transport in their well-cultivated domain; and the Nile Valley then acted like a curtain, shutting out the camel from the regions to the west where it could have been so valuable, until the rise of the Roman *Imperium*, with its wide network of communications.

The glory of Luxor is the temple of Amenophis III with its severe design and its array of papyrus columns flowering in 'bud' capitals – linear descendants of the first half-hearted stone columns of Saqqara, still revealing their origin by their fasciculation and by the constricted base marking where the papyrus bundles were tied together, but now dominating the architectural scene. The outer court, added over a century later by Rameses II, is more spectacular but less restrained and less satisfying.

Some of the architrave is still in place, in the form of heavy blocks of stone reaching horizontally from capital to capital. Where roofing was required, it was effected by means of flat stone slabs. Arches, domes, and

* The story is given in some detail by E. W. Bovill in his fascinating book, *Caravans of the Old Sahara*.

even gables were unknown. This horizontality of bridging and roofing structures prevented the development of an architecture concerned with the form of enclosed space; while the Egyptian preoccupation with mere size and massiveness (which is doubtless connected with the inflation of the Pharaoh's position and power) crowded the pillars close together and inhibited the emergence of that feeling for pure proportion which enabled the Greeks to develop the vertical-horizontal construction of column and architrave to the highest pitch of beauty.

As further examples of this preoccupation with massiveness, there are the huge colossi of Rameses III astride the main gateway, obtruding the king's personal glory to the detriment of the architectural design. Close by stood two fine granite obelisks: one is still there, but the other is in the Place de la Concorde in Paris. What a diversity of fate! – one of the twins the focal point of swirling motor traffic in a modern western capital, the other mutely presiding over Egypt's dead imperial past.

Another curiosity of history is the fact that in the early centuries of our era, part of Amenophis's temple was converted into a Christian church: you can see the remains of 4th-century Christian paintings over the far more skilled Egyptian reliefs executed seventeen hundred years earlier.

Rameses' imposing pylon is adorned with scenes of the battle of Kadesh on the Orontes (p. 63), nearly a thousand miles away – a reminder of the size of the Egyptian empire.

So much for Luxor. What were the impressions made by Karnak? First, the astonishing avenues of sphinxes that converge upon it (pl. 51, opp. p. 249). They monumentalize (if I may coin a word) the combination of animal and human symbolism which the Egyptians pushed to extremes. The fluidity of that symbolism was illustrated by the great Sphinx of Giza (p. 245); it is shown here in a different way – by re-converting the sphinxes of some of the avenues into rams, which were symbols of Amon in his procreative capacity. These creatures were thus both sphinxes and rams, both guardians of the shrine and symbols of the god.

Then there is the size and scale and curious rambling quality of the great temple of Amon. The original plan of an Egyptian temple was simple enough – an outer enclosing wall; a formal entry through a pylon; an open outer court, generally flanked with a colonnade of pillars (the peristyle court); an inner court, generally roofed and supported by a forest of pillars (the hypostyle hall); and finally various small vestibules and repositories, and the inmost shrine. To pass from the pylon to the shrine was to pass from light into increasing obscurity and increasing secrecy of esoteric ritual.

However, in large and metropolitan god-temples such as this, the original unity of design was lost through the self-glorifying propensities of ambitious Pharaohs, who insisted on enlarging the temple by making additions of their own, usually in the form of new courts and new pylons.

Here at Karnak there was not room within the temple enclosure to continue additions along the main axis; so a new axis at right angles was added, giving the complex of buildings the form of a sprawling T, with its vertical and its crosspiece both some 400 yards in length (the largest English cathedral is only about 200 yards long).

A pylon constitutes the monumental approach to a temple; it has a central portal between two great towers, their sides sloping slightly inwards towards the flat top in a characteristic way, and generally bearing commemorative reliefs all over their exposed surfaces. There are no fewer than ten pylons in the great temple of Amon, each associated with a new court; thus there remains no single plan dominating the whole, as in a medieval cathedral, but merely a series of buildings proliferating one from the other, in different styles and on different scales.

Sometimes the ambitious Pharaoh destroyed some of the work of his predecessors. In the huge pylon built by Amenophis III, M. Chevrier found a number of blocks of fine white limestone, some with delicate reliefs. Further excavation revealed that these came from a small shrine built over half a millennium earlier by Sesostris I, which Amenophis had broken up and used as raw material. Eventually M. Chevrier was able to find all the blocks except two, and to reconstruct the entire building – a really miraculous achievement. Its whiteness and miniature disciplined elegance is in striking contrast with the flamboyant painted grandiosity of the later constructions.

This grandiosity reaches its climax in the famous hypostyle hall of Rameses I and Seti I. The hall itself is enormous, 338 feet across (room for five cricket pitches end to end!), and covering an area larger than that of Notre Dame in Paris. The columns are of staggering size (pl. 44, opp. p. 229): the largest are almost 70 feet high and 12 feet across, giving them a circumference equal to that of Trajan's memorial column in Rome. Like all the rest of the surface of the hall, they are covered with inscriptions and decorations and reliefs, some of them still with the traces of their original bright colouring. At the summit they expand into huge capitals symbolizing open flowers. Today, they rise free into the blue cloudless sky; but originally the hall was roofed over and the pillars stood in a twilight gloom.

The general effect is of a painted forest of crowded stone trunks. There is no sense of space or even of plan, such as one feels at once in a Gothic cathedral. Drioton writes that this springs from the mystic symbolism according to which the hypostyle hall represented the primitive dark aquatic chaos out of which the ordered world was divinely organized; thus each time that the god's sacred boat was taken out of the inner sanctuary through this gloomy forest into the light of day, the original miracle was recalled and symbolically renewed. When, as here, the passion for mere size also came into play, while the space between the hypertrophied columns was limited by the mode of construction, the effect of massive confusion becomes oppressive and slightly monstrous.

There is, of course, a plan underlying the hall's design: but it is obscured by the size and multiplicity of the pillars – 134 of them in all. The forest of smaller pillars is divided by a central nave supported by the larger ones. The only light in the place came through the stone lattice-work of small clerestory windows in the sides of the nave. The smaller pillars all have bud capitals, indicating the nightly closing up of vegetation: the central 'flower' capitals symbolize its daily opening out in response to the beams of the sun.

I am profoundly glad to have seen this piece of hypertrophied grandiosity: but also glad that this type of architecture died with the empire which gave it birth. The occasional attempts to revive it in modern Egypt are quite abortive; while the use of the Egyptian style in other countries, as in the Carreras factory in Mornington Crescent, is so gloriously inappropriate as to be funny (as I pass in the bus, I catch myself expecting to see the chorus of priests from *Aïda* emerge between the painted papyrus columns to sing to the London crowd).

One curious fact is that the whole complex was surrounded by a high wall which prevented the *profanum vulgus* outside even from seeing the wonderful buildings within. The urge to ostentatious commemoration was only allowed to manifest itself within a curtain of esoteric secrecy – another demonstration of the essentially anti-democratic quality of the system centralized in the person of the Pharaoh. The demand for a people's religion was eventually met by the development of the Osirian celebrations; but that is another story.

By way of contrast with pharaonic magnificence, it is worth recalling that the Middle Kingdom saw the beginnings of a popular literature of tales and stories. These seem to have been outlines for the guidance of the professional story-tellers who made a living by reciting tales of adventure and humour to audiences up and down the land. The most celebrated is the story of Sinuhé. This, which is perhaps founded on fact, is the first known example of the picaresque novel of travel and adventure. Mika Waltari has used it as the basis for his historical romance, *Sinuhé the Egyptian*.

There are innumerable things to see in Karnak – the obelisk set up in the middle of the temple buildings by the masculine Queen Hatshepsut; the reliefs depicting the victory of the Pharaoh over the very Jewish-looking Jews of Rehoboam's time; the pedestal on which the god's sacred boat once stood in its special chapel; the text of the treaty between Rameses II and the King of the Hittites; but I must leave their description to the guide-books.

On the artificial Sacred Lake, where nocturnal rituals were once enacted, only a few wild duck were swimming; but in the right season it is crowded with birds, the Nile Valley being one of the main avian migration routes. I remember one photograph in the *Country Life* exhibition of wild-life photography, which showed a Jack and a Common Snipe in one field of view on its banks: it was strange to think of these creatures from the bogs and tundras of northern Europe in the sultry precincts of ancient Egyptian religion.

To conclude, I revert to Karnak's enormous scale. Under Rameses III, writes Manchip White in his book on Ancient Egypt, 'the temples of Amon-Ra at Thebes possessed 90,000 slaves, half a million head of cattle, 400 orchards, 80 ships, and 50 workshops. They commanded the revenues of 65 townships.' Under the Egyptian system, the riches of an empire converged on a single chosen religious centre, a city of priests and temples, and led to its overgrowth. The hypertrophy of the columns in the great hypostyle hall of Amon was part of the hypertrophy of the sacred city of Thebes, and this was one of the results of the hypertrophy of the Pharaoh.

★

To reach the city of the dead we crossed the Nile – the identical stream that flows through Cairo, for it receives no permanent tributaries in all these hundreds of miles of its desert course. Then a car took us over the miraculous belt of flat green towards the cliff wall that marks the boundary of the desert.

In the distance, where the level land first begins to rise, the two huge colossi of Memnon sit enthroned in solitude among the fields (pl. 52, opp. p. 249).

They are almost the sole remains of the huge funerary temple of Amenophis III, before whose entrance they stood. The legend that they represented the Trojan hero Memnon grew up some fourteen hundred years later. The northern colossus had been fractured, and emitted a musical note when the sun's rays first fell upon it, supposed to be Memnon's greeting to his mother Eros, the Dawn. Unfortunately Septimius Severus restored the statue, after which the phenomenon ceased.

Alas, we had no time to turn aside to the colossi. I should have liked to have seen the effusions, many of them in verse, inscribed on their giant legs by Roman visitors in imperial times. Hadrian's court poetess was responsible for a veritable torrent of Greek verses here, written during the three-day visit of the Emperor and his consort: one of them records that Memnon greeted the imperial visitor 'as well as he could', with three different successive sounds.

Then there was the funerary temple of Rameses II, known to the Romans as the Temple of Ozymandias; and that of Rameses III, where I recall an exceptionally lively relief of the hunting of antelopes and wild bulls. And then, right up against the desert wall, the astonishing funerary temple of that astonishing woman Queen Hatshepsut. When her husband Thothmes II died, his successor, Thothmes III, the son of a concubine, was only six, and Hatshepsut was appointed regent.

As showing the complexity of royal relationships, let me recall that she was both half-sister and wife to Thothmes II and therefore both aunt and stepmother to Thothmes III, who eventually married Hatshepsut's own daughter! In passing, it is generally supposed that the pharaonic practice of marriage between brothers and sisters or half-sisters was in origin a survival from the times when descent was matrilineal. The royal succession passed through the female line: accordingly the new Pharaoh could only assume power if married to one of the bearers of that succession. The practice was reinforced by the semi-mystical idea of preserving the sacred royal breed in as pure and concentrated a form as possible. The founder of a new dynasty usually safeguarded himself and his line by marrying a princess of the old dynasty. Both Julius Caesar and Antony had to marry Cleopatra to become the acknowledged rulers of Egypt. Margaret Murray has an interesting discussion of the subject in her book *The Splendour that was Egypt*.

Not content with the regency, Hatshepsut assumed full pharaonic status, and had herself represented on her monuments with all the normal masculine attributes of the pharaoh, including the ritual false beard. Thothmes III must have resented her dominance : at any rate, after her death, he obliterated her name from many monuments and substituted his own.

Among her able advisers and ministers was a notable architect, Senemut. It is to him that we owe the mortuary temple, though its basic plan was taken from that of Menthuhetep, built in the same valley nearly five hundred years earlier.

Dehr-el-Bahri is an unforgettable place. It lies in a recess or coombe of the desert wall, with a huge almost vertical cliff as background. Yet the scale of the building is worthy of its setting. An immense processional ramp leads up to a series of terraces, and eventually into a shrine cut out of the solid rock. Two great porticoes with severe square columns flank the ramp; the terrace on to which it emerges is in the form of an open colonnaded court. Here is a building with a noble plan, unspoilt by later accretions.

Originally the terraces were planted with files of palms and sacred trees, some of them brought from distant lands, and even with beds of papyrus. In one of the porticoes are the exciting records of the most famous of Queen Hatshepsut's trading expeditions, that to the land of Punt. This is sometimes identified with Somaliland, sometimes with Southern Arabia on the opposite side of the Gulf of Aden, while Margaret Murray suggests that *punt* was merely a generic word denoting a maritime trading station. Certainly this expedition must have reached the Gulf of Aden, for one of its aims was to bring back incense for the service of Amon.

It was remarkable to recall that Hatshepsut's marvellous temple was built only a little later than Stonehenge. (Actually, Stonehenge was about contemporary with the establishment of the 18th Dynasty at the end of the second intermediate period, while Avebury, that masterpiece of our earlier megalithic style, was built when that time of trouble was being initiated by the invasion of the foreign 'Shepherd Kings'.)

It was a strange contrast to pass from Dehr-el-Bahri to the Valley of the Kings, from open glorification to imprisoned secretiveness. The Valley itself is a long desert cleft, grim and remote, lined by piles of loose scree split off from the lowering cliffs above; and the royal tombs are deliberately concealed under the barren mass of fallen stones. It is a hiding-place for royal survival instead of a stage for the public representation of royal magnificence.

Yet even within this desolate prison the glory of the Pharaohs had to be proclaimed. Before being closed, the tombs were decorated and furnished with traditional splendour, though it was hoped that no mortal eye would ever see them again. The most striking memory I retain is that of the burial chamber of Seti I. A descent of over a hundred yards traverses a series of passages and small chambers cut in the rock, and adorned with very beautiful reliefs and paintings, mostly representing the journey of the Sun through the underworld as described in one of the sacred texts. And then you come into the main funeral chamber. This was robbed of its furnishings in ancient times; the empty alabaster sarcophagus discovered here by Belzoni in 1817 is now in London, the mummy in the Museum at Cairo. But the blaze of its colour remains almost as bright as when it was laid on nearly 1300 years before Christ. The low-vaulted roof is a deep night-blue, with a chart of the heavenly bodies and other astronomical decorations; on the walls are representations of part of the Sun's journey, the Sun's sacred boat, the god's reception of the Pharaoh, and various rituals.

The tomb of Tutankhamen made a quite different impression. Roderick Cameron had the good fortune to be taken to the tomb soon after it was opened up. In his autobiographical book *My Travel's History* he records the effect of seeing 'the dimly glittering gold and the footprints in the sand made by mourners or priests dead for over two thousand years'; but for us there was only the empty rock chamber. In the Cairo Museum I had already seen the roomfuls of treasures that Howard Carter unearthed from it, and had marvelled at their superb workmanship, the beauty of some and the rather bad taste of others (as of debased *art nouveau* combined with great technical sophistication). I recall the gold mask over the head of the mummy, with its inlay of lapis lazuli and turquoise, cornelian and faience, as a moving portrait. Here, in the Valley of the Kings, the visitor has brought home to him the fact that the treasures were discovered piled higgledy-piggledy in a tomb destined for another. If the borrowed grave of a politically insignificant boy-king (he died, apparently of tuberculosis, at the age of 18) was provided with such rich equipment, what must the grave-furniture of great monarchs such as Seti I or Rameses II have been like?

★

So back across the plain and the great river, to supper and a final glimpse of Karnak, black and silver in the moonlight. Without this day at Thebes, we should never have had any real sense of the Middle Kingdom, or of the New Kingdom and its rich but often oppressive imperial grandeur. The dead past had obtruded itself into the present, and was not to be ejected.

★

I have already quoted Dr Johnson's *Rasselas* on the pyramids; it is equally apposite on Egyptian history in general (the fact that it was thrown off in a single week adds pungency to its weighty historical sentiments). When the young prince is discouraged by the lack of happiness he finds in Cairo (a lack which is equally apparent to the modern visitor), Imlac, the elderly and rather sententious sage, urges him to visit the old Egyptians' 'monuments of industry and power'. 'You forget that you are in a country, famous among the earliest monarchies for the power and wisdom of its inhabitants; a country where the sciences first dawned that illuminate the world, and beyond which the arts cannot be traced of civil society or domestic life.' To which Rasselas replies: 'My curiosity does not very strongly lead me to survey piles of stone, or mounds of earth; my business is with man. I came hither not to measure fragments of temples, or trace choked aqueducts, but to look upon the various scenes of the present world.'

In the Middle East, the various scenes of the present world are certainly of absorbing interest. Furthermore, the very magnitude of the Egyptian past is oppressive, its ancient grandeur having endured nearly three times as long as all the history of Europe from early medieval times to the present; and the quantitative burden of this oppressiveness had been immensely heightened by the two centuries of exploration and research since Johnson's time. Nevertheless, Imlac's retort was just. 'If we act only for ourselves,' he said (among a good deal else), 'to neglect the study of history is not prudent; if we are entrusted with the care of others, it is not just.'

In Egypt, history, in its strict sense of a deliberate record of events, goes further back than in any other land. Egypt is a process in time: its history is at first acquaintance like an enormous tunnel, lit more or less efficiently with lamps penetrating far into the solid blackness of the past. The length of the tunnel has been exaggerated by the legendary proclivities of the early professional historians. Chief among these was Manetho, who wrote a command history of Egypt for Ptolemy Philadelphus in the 3rd century B.C., to be placed in the great library of Alexandria (and destined to be destroyed there nearly 900 years later – though not before most of it had been copied). The date that he assigns to the beginning of the dynastic period is nearly two thousand years too early: while before that he purports to give the dynasties of gods and demi-gods or heroes for some further 30,000 years. This fabulous extension doubtless represents the long period of prehistoric settled life from the late Neolithic onwards.

Today, archeology has given us facts instead of legend. The first of the five cultures discovered in predynastic times wholly lacked metal. The second, the Badarian, was chalcolithic, with tools still of stone but a few copper objects. Woven linen was worn, and the people already grew wheat as well as barley. The third, the Amratean, made the most beautiful flint knives, but these seem largely to have been used for ritual purposes; the people had learnt how to make copper tools such as chisels. With the Gerzean, a sharp break occurs: the new culture seems to have been introduced by conquering invaders. It has been suggested with some plausibility that Manetho's break between dynasties of gods and dynasties of demi-gods represents this actual break between the Amratean and Gerzean cultures. Gold now appears, and iron too, though as a great rarity, and never used for tools. Rowing galleys are depicted, trading with foreign countries where there were pointed hills – maybe Crete, maybe Phoenicia. Quite elaborate games were played. The fifth culture is much like the fourth, but is marked by a higher standard of life – bedsteads and stools, larger storage jars for surplus food.

The main fact that emerges is that the urban revolution was most marked in Gerzean times, perhaps first stimulated by the new ideas brought by the invaders, and later by trade with foreign countries; it probably started in Lower Egypt, in the plains of the Delta, or at least was more rapidly accomplished there than in Upper Egypt in the Nile Valley proper. Social classes seem to have been differentiated within the Gerzean community, and a simple form of picture-writing is found, though it is still a long way from a true written language. Some of the ivory figurines are very beautiful.

In the latest cultural phase, the urban revolution had been fully accomplished both in Upper and in Lower Egypt, and the two regions, now in a primitive proto-literate phase, were both, it seems, organized into definite kingdoms. Civilization had thus been born in Egypt, but it had not yet been unified. The existence of these two independent kingdoms on the course of the one great river was a challenge. It was important that the regulation of irrigation should be centralized for the whole Nile basin, and steps taken to see that the water was used to the best advantage of all regions. Unification was indeed demanded by the geographical and historical situation. And towards the end of the fourth millennium the proto-historic gives place to the historic period, with the consolidation of the two kingdoms under the single rule of Menes, and the sudden appearance of a well-developed written script. The tunnel of history begins.

If I had to give a brief outline of the history of Egypt I should be tempted to begin by employing the method of space-for-time, dividing my outline into eight equal chapters, each covering one millennium, with ten pages apiece, each page representing one century. The book would begin in 6000 B.C., and the eighth chapter would not be complete until A.D. 2000.

The first two chapters would be concerned with the Neolithic – its inception, its slow progress, and its full achievement of the agricultural revolution, while most of Chapter 3 would be occupied by the more rapid urban revolution, ending with the dawn of true history. In Chapter 4 the Old Kingdom rises and falls, to be succeeded by a time of chaos. Chapter 5 contains the Middle Kingdom, and its supersession under the invading Shepherd Kings, the introduction of the horse to Egypt; the rise of the New Kingdom to imperial glory and its gradual decline; the ineffectual monotheism of Akhnaton; Moses and the Exodus; the irruption of the People of the Sea into the Eastern Mediterranean; the supersession of bronze by iron. Chapter 6 sees the decay of the empire: the conquest of Egypt first by Nubian monarchs, then by a succession of foreign invaders – Assyrians, Persians, Macedonian Greeks, and Romans. Alexandria becomes one of the great centres of the new Hellenistic culture. The seventh chapter covers the first millennium of our era. Zenobia of Palmyra invades Egypt; Christianity spreads; the desert fills with hermits and the first monasteries; Islam conquers Egypt; the library of Alexandria is destroyed; Cairo becomes the capital of the Western Caliphate. Chapter 8, to date the last: the Crusades touch Egypt. Saladin. Rise of the Mamelukes. Turkish conquest of Egypt. Napoleon in Egypt. End of Mamelukes. Mehemet Ali. Suez Canal. Franco-British control; British occupation. Full independence of Egypt. Forced abdication of the King. . . .

★

Thanks to the dry climate and the practice of furnishing tombs for the after-life, the remains of ancient civilization are better and more abundantly pre-served in Egypt than anywhere else in the world, with the possible exception of the coastal parts of Peru. The Cairo Museum is thus almost fabulously rich in ancient objects, so rich that the casual visitor is likely to become bewildered and exhausted. We representatives of Unesco had the good fortune to be escorted through its enormous collections by the Abbé Drioton, who drew our attention to the most important exhibits and explained their interest. It was a model for all museum visits. I usually suffer badly from that curious complaint, museum fatigue; but on this occasion two and a half hours left me stimulated instead of overwhelmed: and this held good for the rest of the party too.

The classical Greeks gave sculpture its full freedom: but the sculptors of the Old Kingdom of Egypt, two thousand years earlier, had already achieved great nobility in their statues. It was then that full-size representation in the round became an art in its own right, in spite of a technique based on the older two-dimensional carvings in relief. In the predynastic period, three-dimensional sculpture had attained a high development, but only on the miniature scale of small ivories. These were presumably conceived in the round: but when the sculptors ventured to tackle life-size or over-life-size statues, they reverted to a two-dimensional approach as the basis for their work.

Drioton reminded us that in all Egyptian reliefs and inscriptions, the human figure is always shown in profile, and Kings normally from the left side. In making a statue in the round, the artist first traced a left profile on the block, leaving the actual carving to skilled workmen chipping away under supervision. The result is that the left profile of a statue is usually better than the right, and both better than the full-face view. This was very noticeable in the superb black diorite statue of King Chephren from his temple by the Sphinx: the left side-view had an extraordinary delicacy and subtlety which was lacking on the right.

Most of the really first-class statues from the Old Kingdom are in Cairo, though there is the famous *scribe accroupi* in the Louvre. I remember very vividly a fine portrait statue in sycamore wood – the so-called painted scribe of Giza. 'Rather contemptuous-looking,' I wrote in my notes, 'but doubt-less servile to his superiors.' The sculptor had succeeded in making a **real** work of art out of the likeness of 'un gros bonhomme', as Drioton called him. The eyes were made of three different materials – quartz for the cornea, rock-crystal for the iris, and ebony for the pupil.

In passing, *scribe* or *secretary* was an honorific title as well as a profession. The Pharaoh had the title of Scribe of the Sun; and nobles without any knowledge of writing might call themselves scribes, just as Secretary for War or Secretary of State are titles of high office in the English-speaking world of today.

Modern European sculpture for the most part confines itself austerely to one material and abjures the use of paint, though classical Greek statues were often coloured and many of the carvings and terra-cottas of the Middle Ages and Renaissance were bright with gold and paint. But though these techniques at first sight appear barbarous to our modern western eyes, it must be admitted that in the hands of the Egyptians they can be very effective.

The painted limestone statues of Prince Rahotep and his wife Princess Nefert are good examples of this effectiveness of colour. Rahotep was son of the king, Minister both of War and of Public Works – a sad little man with a Dewey moustache, very alive after more than four thousand five hundred years.

By the time of Mycerinus, sculpture had reached a high pitch. The statue of the Pharaoh stepping forward from between two attendant goddesses combines realism with formal classical beauty in a remarkable way. By contrast, the three goddesses from the tomb of Tutankhamen, though charming, are charming in a very decadent manner.

The sculpture of the Old Kingdom could achieve an intimate and moving personal quality. I think of the statue of Seneb, cousin of the king. Seneb was a dwarf. His peers had life-size statues to represent themselves in their mastabas, but he seems to have been ashamed of his appearance, so had this miniature group executed for his tomb. His head is heavy and big, with a rather sad expression. His children, instead of being represented to one side as was customary, are put so as to fill up the space left vacant by the shortness of his legs. At his side, his wife holds his arm in both her hands in an affectionate gesture which seems to proclaim that she loved him in spite of his looks.

The early Sumerians may have reached the stage of civilization before the Egyptians; they certainly were better at mathematics; and they early developed the most elaborate techniques in their ornaments and works of art. But as artists they did not reach the level of their Egyptian contemporaries.

The arts, like so much else in Egyptian life, were centred on the Pharaoh.

Accordingly, in the so-called first intermediate period, the time of trouble that brought the Old Kingdom to an end, the arts went downhill with the kingly power. When the Middle Kingdom re-established a central monarchy the Pharaoh and his priests deliberately set themselves to revive the traditions of the Old Kingdom. They began by copying the old works of art, proceeding by means of measurement, with the inevitable result that the style seems academic and dead. Later, in the New Kingdom, after a good beginning (the portrait statue of Thothmes III is a fine piece of delicate realism), the passion for size resulted in the disagreeably enormous colossi, in which art is so often swallowed up in self-aggrandisement. Sculpture tended to become more flamboyant, the kings being shown with elaborate robes and head-dresses and insignia, and the gods and goddesses represented with profuse symbolism: everything is there, except the simplicity and dignity of earlier times. Sometimes, on the other hand, we find a romanticism tinged with melancholy.

The reign of Akhnaton is marked by a strange aberration of style. Apparently the king, in his rebellion against the old gods and their hidebound priesthood, rebelled also against the formalized flattery of traditional art. He seems to have been slightly deformed, with over-long face tapering to a small chin, over-prominent cheek-bones, nose and lips, thin legs, somewhat protruding belly and elongated skull (perhaps artificially compressed in infancy). And he must have insisted on these peculiarities being not merely represented but exaggerated in his royal representations: for some of them are veritable caricatures. Even his beautiful queen Nefertiti is sometimes represented in this same exaggerated expressionism. This must be the first case of distortion being used as a deliberate technique in the art of a civilized nation.

We gaped at the spectacle of Tutankhamen's tomb-furnishings, which occupy several rooms. I have spoken of the strange mixture of beauty and bad taste to be seen in them: here I would like to stress the astonishing refinements of technical skill which they reveal. Dr Charles Singer, who is engaged on a monumental history of technology and techniques, tells me that as specimens of pure technique and craftsmanship the products of the Egyptian New Kingdom have never been equalled, save perhaps by some of the Etruscan goldsmiths' work. On the other hand technology, in the restricted modern sense of the deliberate application of scientific knowledge to practical techniques, was little developed: what we see in Egypt is the high point of traditional skill, mobilized for the benefit of sacred royalty.

Many species of birds are represented in ancient reliefs and paintings in the Museum. The ducks are what I remember most clearly, especially the graceful pintails, which figure almost invariably in the dangling bunches of birds being brought in as mortuary offerings to the royal dead.

But the most fascinating is the painting of the rare and beautiful redbreasted Siberian goose. It was a brilliant likeness, and brought back to me vividly the group of these birds for which I was responsible when Secretary of the Zoological Society. They lived in a grassy enclosure under the shadow of some hedgerow oaks at Whipsnade – a situation as different as one could imagine from Cairo or from their Siberian home, but one in which their bizarre beauty, of russet-chestnut breast and cheek, set off against the black belly and back by strange outline designs and patches of white, was seen to best advantage against English greenery.

But what on earth was a redbreasted goose doing in ancient Egypt? Its present-day breeding distribution is confined to arctic and subarctic Siberia; in the winter it migrates south to Persia and the Aral Sea, sporadically to Iraq, and westwards to the edge of Hungary. It has been suggested that three or four thousand years ago the bird migrated further southwards than now, so that it normally reached Egypt in winter, but this is biologically unlikely. Furthermore, if such a striking creature had occurred at all regularly in ancient Egypt, we should expect that it would have figured commonly in the reliefs and paintings, instead of in this unique example.

The alternative explanation seems much more plausible – that the Pharaoh had received a present of some of these handsome birds from one of his vassals or treaty-bound potentates from the north-eastern boundaries of the Egyptian empire at its furthest extension.

I must pass over the mummified cats and falcons in their handsome mummy cases, the superb manuscripts, the paraphernalia of the toilet and personal adornment, the array of domestic utensils and furniture, the comic drawings of animals, the medical instruments, the sight of the actual features of famous kings, mummified three and four thousand years ago, and many other things that can be seen nowhere else in the world.

We emerged from the Museum with the feeling of having been immersed in a powerful civilization with a quality wholly alien to our own. Herodotus doubtless felt this same alien quality in the Egypt he visited, when he was moved to record that Egyptian customs were usually the opposite of those of the rest of the world. Certainly some of them were very peculiar.

Among the more extraordinary of minor oddities which I have come across is the fact that they made *pâté de foie gras* from the livers of hyenas. The unfortunate animals, with their limbs tied together, were forcibly fed on geese. The *pâté* may have been good, but I cannot think that hyena-stuffing was a very pleasant job. The feminine fashion, prevalent at one period, of gilding the breasts and painting the nipples blue is in its way almost equally peculiar.

Such curiosities are instances of the tendency of this rich and ingrown civilization to try out the minor techniques of living in all kinds of ways while remaining conservative in major matters. This conservatism also led to many of the peculiar results which surprised Herodotus, such as the deification of the pharaoh, the practice of consanguineous royal marriage, and the persistence of animal and half-animal divinities.

To visit the Coptic Museum was to enter another world. (I was amused, by the way, by the derivation of the word *Copt*. It was the half-derogatory Greek diminutive for the natives – *Aiguptios* – rather as Egyptians are called *Gippies* by modern British soldiers.) The techniques of art and architecture are coarser, the style disconcertingly different. The various striking works, notably the tomb-portraits, appear as precursors of a new culture rather than as survivors of an old one, and the interesting textiles bear no resemblance to ancient patterns.

In point of fact, the original art of the country had entirely died down under the Roman occupation. It was the stimulus of Christianity which led to a rebirth : but the new art was directed to different ends, and executed by different means ; it served a different class, and its forms were dictated by a new pattern of thought. André Malraux has some interesting remarks on the subject in his *Psychologie de l'Art*, though I think he minimizes the effect of the loss of technical skills, and exaggerates the degree to which the old techniques were deliberately rejected.

In any case, in passing from the Cairo Museum to the Museum of Coptic Art, we are confronted by that mysterious phenomenon, the disappearance of a civilization. Some time during the first four centuries of our era, the civilization that had been generated in the Delta over three thousand years earlier came finally to an end. For all that time, in spite of ups and downs, of changes in material conditions and in spiritual expression, there had been a definite continuity in the life of Egypt. The quality of its pattern had persisted as something organic and unitary, capable of self-reproduction and self-transformation. Now that unity had been abolished, its organic continuity was broken.

We need not bother ourselves to attempt a precise scientific definition of what is meant by 'a civilization', how far it is synonymous with a culture or how far with particular social and political institutions. At least it is clear that in Egypt there did exist an observable pattern of civilized life distinct from others, and that this pattern had a beginning and an end: it was a unit-process in time.

Looking back from the vantage-point of modern knowledge on its three thousand years of existence as one of the distinguishable units of human history, what epitaph can we write on it? It is a bewildering question. Are we to see in it what Shelley saw in the broken colossus of Ozymandias merely an example of fallen grandeur? Shall we indulge in sententious reflections on the transitory nature and decay of empires as Volney did in his *Ruines*, or as Macaulay in his prophecy about the New Zealander surveying the remains of London? Are we to draw the conclusion that all civilizations are inevitably destined to pursue the same general course and finally to fall and disappear? Should we think of ancient Egypt as the human equivalent of an ichthyosaurus or an iguanodon, as a strange and wonderful monster first thrown up and then extinguished by the forces of human evolution, without significance for the later course of history? Or are we to believe some modern anthropological enthusiasts who see in Egypt the chief source from which the elements of later civilizations radiated over the globe?

As a first step to clearing our minds, let us recall that *civilization* is used in two distinct senses. First as a general term, to denote a stage in man's social evolution, a level of human organization: and secondly as a particular term, to denote a pattern within that general type of organization, and therefore what may be called a unit of history. Particular civilizations may thus pass through and reach different levels of general civilization; and they may also show differentiation of pattern on any given level. As in biological evolution, the two distinct tendencies of advance and divergence are both at work. But whereas a biological organism can only perpetuate itself, a civilization, even if it eventually disappears as an entity, can make contributions to other civilizations and so to the advance of civilization in general.

Ancient Egypt was thus in certain ways a doomed monster, like a dinosaur. But, again like a dinosaur, it was also magnificent. The dinosaurs were the most successful experiments of life in its first conquest of the land. Egypt was the most successful and the longest-lived of man's experiments in his first conquest of civilization. Ancient Egypt solved a number of wholly new problems in ways which, though incomplete and imperfect, were remarkably efficient. In the Old Kingdom at least, it was often better adjusted to the conditions of its age than we are to those of ours. Ancient Egyptian civilization is admirable in its own right, as a new positive achievement of the human species.

On the other hand, its eventual failure and disappearance demonstrate its imperfection. As a civilization it was scarcely conscious of itself and its possible destiny: it developed nothing in the nature of critical or analytical history, only a record of events. Over-centralization, rigidity of tradition, the total absence of a democratic approach, obsession with the future life and with the pharaoh's superhuman qualities are some of the obvious factors of its imperfection: perhaps they all spring from a too rigid acceptance of pre-civilized ideas as the basis of a civilized society.

However, though Egyptian civilization disappeared as an entity, it did contribute markedly to other civilizations and to the process of civilization as a whole. Thus much of the Minoan civilization was derived from the Egyptian, though its general pattern was very distinct.

Perhaps the most obvious example of a general contribution is that of medicine, for Egyptian medical knowledge not only reached a level higher than that of medieval Europe but was at the basis of Greek medicine, and so of modern anatomy, physiology, and medical science. In astronomy and mathematics too (though not to the same extent as Mesopotamia) Egypt made its contribution. Margaret Murray reminds us that the Greek word for *chemistry* means 'the Egyptian science', being derived from *Khemi*, the ancient name for Egypt.

The high technical level of Egyptian fine metal-working certainly influenced other countries. Monumental stone architecture was an Egyptian invention, and so was history or at least continuous public record (the Egyptian past fascinated Herodotus on his visit). Even if the ideas behind the script of Egypt may have been first derived from Mesopotamia, it was that script which stimulated the birth of the alphabet in the brains of the Phoenicians. The Egyptians invented the materials of writing – paper, pen, and ink – which have been the chief tools of our literacy. And so on and so forth.

The classical age of Greece, even while despising and repudiating many elements of late Egyptian culture, looked to Egypt as a repository of ancient wisdom and immemorial culture. Egypt was to the Greeks an encouraging reminder of the respectable antiquity of human civilization and of its persistence.

*

Today the major problem of Egypt is population. Ancient Egypt may have contained five or six million people at the outside. For 1800, the figure is estimated at two and a half million: when I was born it was under eight million. Today it is twenty-one million. The great barrage at Assuan makes it possible to irrigate the land at will instead of waiting for the annual inundation of the Nile, so that two crops a year can be raised instead of one: but no longer does nature annually spread its layer of rich silt over the fields, and artificial fertilizers are required. Most of the fellahin today are either landless or possess plots too small to support a family. In any case, the population has doubled with the crops, and is pressing harder than ever on the means of subsistence. To translate Malthus's cold phraseology into concrete terms, Egypt today contains more undernourished human beings than ever before. But the desert is still there, the narrow strip of habitable soil grows steadily more and more crowded, and the contrast between the poverty and misery of the many and the wealth and luxury of the few ever greater.

Large new irrigation works are being planned. But even if they materialize, and all the seven and a half million acres of the Nile Valley are brought under perennial irrigation in the next 20 years, the increase of productive land will hardly keep up with the increase in population.

Meanwhile discontent is diverted outwards. All over the Eastern world, peoples long kept in a position of inferiority are asserting themselves in an uneasy nationalism. In Egypt, the nationalism is largely xenophobic, and the xenophobia is directed mainly against the British. It is also expansionist, and the desire for national self-assertion has joined hands with anti-British feeling in the demand for the incorporation of the Sudan.

But the nationalist movement is in the long run inevitably self-frustrating. Nationalism stimulates counter-nationalism in neighbouring countries. In the Nile Valley, Egyptian expansionist nationalism is brought up against a new-found Sudanese nationalism. To the north, Israeli nationalism has made an alarming dent on Arab nationalism in general.

Furthermore, nationalism comes up against internationalism; local politics is confronted with the hard realities of world politics. Though the Suez Canal has become Egyptian property and is efficiently handling a much larger volume of traffic, it has still to function as an organ of world communications. Peace in the Middle East is a concern of the entire Western world. The crises in ancient Egyptian history arose whenever the self-containment of the Nile Valley was broken by violent contact with other powers, whether through their expansion or that of Egypt. Today, a fresh crisis of external contact has arisen, simultaneously with the internal crisis of over-population and poverty. And in this present year of 1961, it is far from having been resolved.

It certainly will not be resolved by exclusive insistence on Egyptian nationalist claims, nor by an Islamic religious revival. In all probability it cannot be resolved save by a radical change of attitude. There must be an internal policy centred on people and a fuller realization of life, so that individual men and women feel that they are somehow significant. Failing this, the pressure of a discontented but expanding population will eventually blow up the framework of society. And there must be an external policy, based in general on cooperation with other nations through the U.N., and in particular, not on an obstinate refusal to recognize the existence of Israel and the need for Arab-Israeli coexistence.

On the material side, there is need for the inventory and proper exploitation of natural resources; and this can best be done on a regional basis. This idea of an inventory of resources is a new and characteristic product of our epoch. It could readily be extended to include both human and cultural resources, both actual and potential.

Finally, somehow or other, life must be viewed *sub specie humanitatis*, as part of a single human process. To do so is the first step towards converting history from a series of random, separate, and often mutually contradictory forays into a single and conscious joint adventure.

The present is often regarded as an age of chaos and breakdown. So it is: but it is also a crucible of change, and of change which might be constructive. For into that crucible new elements have been introduced, as well as all the materials from the disintegrating past. The most important of those new elements is the combination of science and humanism, leading to the belief that the actualization of human possibilities is our most ultimate aim, but it can only proceed in relation to hard facts, and it is dependent on our scientific knowledge.

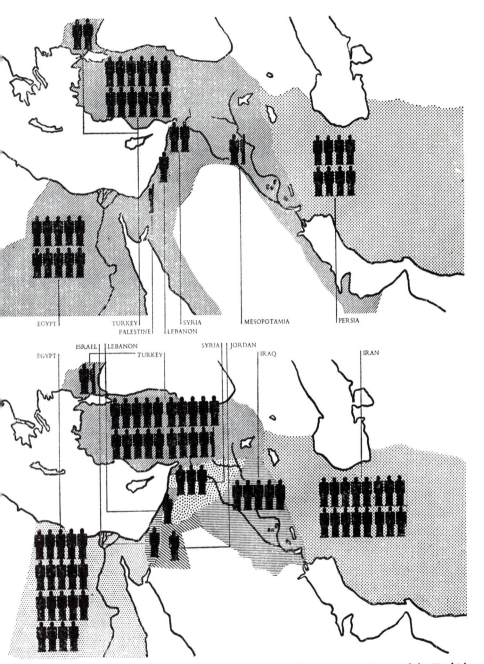

EGYPT | TURKEY | SYRIA | MESOPOTAMIA | PERSIA
PALESTINE | LEBANON

ISRAEL | LEBANON | SYRIA | JORDAN
EGYPT | TURKEY | IRAQ | IRAN

MIDDLE EAST POPULATIONS in 1900 and 1950. In 1900 most of the area formed part of the Turkish Empire, but the present-day states are indicated for comparison. (Each symbol = 1 million).

17

KNOSSOS AND THE MINOAN
CIVILIZATION

I̲T̲ ̲I̲S̲ ̲R̲E̲A̲L̲L̲Y̲ ̲A̲S̲T̲O̲N̲I̲S̲H̲I̲N̲G̲ ̲T̲O̲ remember that sixty years ago we knew next to nothing about ancient Crete. Only in 1894 did Sir Arthur Evans begin his series of excavations at Knossos. These revealed the unique Minoan civilization, which flourished for more than a millennium and a half. Minoan civilization is not quite as old as Egyptian, but dates back certainly to 3000 B.C. Throughout its existence it was the westernmost outpost of civilized life, as well as the first maritime empire. Culturally, it was a parent of Mycene, and so a grandparent of Greece.

In the Embassy at Athens, planning our visit to Crete, I remembered vividly the impression made on me as an undergraduate at Oxford by the Minoan exhibits in the Ashmolean – the unique use of the octopus as decorative motive; the snake-goddess with her modern flounced skirt but her bodice cut so as to reveal her breasts; the frescoes of bull-vaulting; the young men with broad shoulders and wasp-waists. And now we were actually going to see Knossos at first hand.

I was struck by the physical geography of Crete when I was steaming along its southern coast on the way to East Africa in 1929. Magnificent cliffs fell steeply into the sea from mountain ranges over 8000 feet high; and the ship's chart showed depths of 11,000 feet quite close offshore – a crumpling of the earth's crust involving a vertical drop of 19,000 feet in the space of a few miles. This time our plane landed at Heraklion (the latest name for Candia and Megalokastro) on the island's less steep northern face.

Heraklion is a rather depressing place, with dusty suburbs, rusty wrecks in the modern harbour, and a good deal of shoddy untidy building in the town itself. The centre has a certain bustling charm, and there are some attractive reminders of the time when it was under the dominion of Venice, notably the Morosini fountain, just about contemporary with the Great Fire of London. Not so long ago, the fountain was nearly invisible because of the rubbish and debris that had been allowed to accumulate in the little open space round it. But Sir Arthur Evans let it be known that he was sending down his photographer to take pictures of it to be published in England – and within forty-eight hours the debris had disappeared.

Now the authorities are planning to run a wide straight motor-road up to Knossos, and to lay out a new fashionable residential quarter, destroying the Venetian ramparts and filling up the moat in the process. And there is no Sir Arthur Evans to take the matter up.

Knossos lies some three miles from the coast, in a valley of the foothills. This inland situation, together with the long period of previous neolithic occupation, shows that it was originally a small local settlement which gradually and almost accidentally became the metropolis of an empire. But the other Minoan palaces so far discovered are much smaller, either perched solitary on a crag, like Phaistos, or in a quite small Minoan town, like Mallia. So Knossos was clearly the undisputed capital of a united country.

We were put up in the charmingly named Villa Ariadne. This was originally built by Arthur Evans, who beautified it by planting palms and araucarias, with a headless marble Roman bust in the place of honour. It is now occupied by Mr and Mrs de Jongh, who look after the excavations on behalf of the British School of Archeology (he is a qualified architect), and provide accommodation for British students and visitors.

The actual ownership of Knossos has been made over to the Greek Government, who allow anyone and everyone to visit the place free on Sundays. Sometimes there are thousands of people strolling about the ruins, with only two guardians to look after them. Name-carving is luckily not a common Cretan foible, but inevitably some damage is done.

Knossos is not particularly beautiful or visually impressive, like Karnak or Palmyra: its appeal is primarily to the imagination. It is approached by what is almost certainly the oldest road in Europe, its stones now grass-covered, leading up over occasional shallow steps to the so-called Dancing Floor. This (pl. 53, opp. p. 288), the only considerable open space in the palace, was apparently a formal ceremonial area where the king presided at ritual celebrations, processions, and public ceremonies and festivals. Unlike the Maidan at Isfahan, there is no formality in its design: it is just a more or less level space which happened to be there on the edge of the slope, and was later adjusted to its ceremonial functions.

The ruins revealed by Arthur Evans's excavations are almost exclusively of the Royal Palace. The surrounding town must have been quite large – some estimates put its maximum population at over 100,000; but hardly any of it has yet been excavated. Here is something to look forward to.

The palace (which housed the royal magazines and stores as well as the royal household) is a maze of tightly packed rooms and little courts and passages. Its transmutation by legend into the Labyrinths is no wonder.

The royal storehouses made a deep impression – long semi-basement cellars filled with beautiful great jars. The biggest jars are enormous, often considerably taller than a man, with abundance of handles: the handles must have been purely ornamental, since even the smaller jars were too big to have been handled. Presumably the jars served as storage-bins for the oil and wine destined for export. Many of them are decorated with patterns representing ropes – I suppose a survival of the time when their predecessors were transported in rope casings: one jar had a pattern of chains.

Arthur Evans has incurred a good deal of censure for his restoration of the chief rooms of the palace. It is true that it looks too machine-made: the concrete beams he used are ugly and have been painted in harsh colours; and, as Osbert Lancaster says in his *Classical Landscape*, the frescoes as we see them today (alas, framed in cheap and unworthy frames) are 'mainly the work of a distinguished French water-colourist',* with much speculative and probably inaccurate restoration. And it is certainly true that today it would be possible to make more satisfactory and more satisfying reconstructions.

But wooden beams would have been attacked by termites; and I am sure that it was better to reconstruct than to leave a mass of crumbling ruins,

---

* Osbert Lancaster, it should be noted, adds that, even allowing for this, the general effect produced by the paintings is 'one of immense sophistication, and a carefully cultivated taste'.

even if we may regret the errors of taste and judgment that crept in. At any rate the visitor gets a sense of the curious Minoan architecture, with its pillars tapering downwards instead of upwards, and an impression of the palace as a place that was lived in, instead of a mere ground-plan of ruins whose significance can be grasped only by an expert. Meanwhile, it would be wonderful if the reconstruction of the Little Palace could now be undertaken with the aid of modern knowledge and technique.

As it is, some of the frescoes are very lovely. I remember one frieze of partridges and hoopoes; and the strange and exciting marine creatures in the queen's apartments – fishes of various sorts, octopuses, dolphins, shells, and curious stylized sea-urchins looking like stumpy black *Opuntia* cactuses. There are also curious blue monkeys, and some lovely plants and trees; and of course the famous cup-bearer frieze with the athletic narrow-waisted young men. But sometimes the freedom of treatment becomes formlessness, or degenerates into *art nouveau* (though it is difficult to be sure how much of the effect is due to the ancient Cretan artists, how much to the modern French restorer).

The scenes with bulls are fascinating. Bull-vaulting was certainly one of the most extraordinary of human sports or rituals, worthy to rank with the still existing Mexican rite of the Voladores, in which the performers, attached to ropes, unwind themselves spirally from an enormous maypole. What a spectacle it must have been! Girls as well as boys seizing the bull's horns and swinging themselves up and over in a somersault to land on his croup. That is what the paintings and bronzes demonstrate. But we do not know if the somersault was always practised, or how the performers jumped off and escaped, or how they were trained for this fantastic activity. Nor do we know if it had become just a dangerous and exciting sport, or if it still retained the sacred ritual character that it assuredly must once have possessed.

Greek legend told of the tribute of Athenian youths and virgins sent to Crete to be sacrificed to the Minotaur. Were they in reality destined to be trained for the bull-vaulting? And was this a substitute for human sacrifice, and the Athenians a substitute for native victims? Perhaps some day, when the Minoan script has been deciphered, we shall find out more about the bull-vaulting and its significance (though most of the known tablets are short and look like being merely business records).

Unfortunately the Museum at Heraklion, which contains most of the portable objects from Knossos, was not open. The exhibits were hastily packed in the cellars when the Germans landed; and at the time of our visit it was said to be too expensive to unpack and set them up again, at any rate without special Marshall Aid. (The Germans, by the way, removed very few objects, and actually began some new excavations during the war.) But the leading surgeon of the place, Dr Yamalikis, is also a great collector, and kindly invited us to see his treasures. I recall especially various seals with ships and nets and other marine representations; a late Minoan gold bull's head, in repoussé work, with gold filigree hair; a unique representation of the Minotaur on a Middle Minoan seal, showing that the symbolic monster was native to Crete, and not merely the product of later legendary distortion in Greece; and a very extraordinary bronze, from the end of the Middle Minoan, showing the prototype of the Good Shepherd – a man in typical Minoan costume carrying a new-born lamb (with the umbilical cord represented) round his neck. It is only fair to add that some people think it a forgery; but it seems a curious subject to forge.

I remember the surprise with which as a young man I had heard of Arthur Evans's discovery of water-closets in Knossos. But there they were, right enough, in the palace – seats over a drainage-pipe. The drains were most elaborate, one system dealing with the latrines, another with the rain-water run-off. Some archeologists believe that the Minoans had even invented a system of flushing, in which water was held up to be released when wanted. Numerous baths have also come to light. They are remarkable structures of terra-cotta, in shape like an extra-wide slipper-bath, with pleasant decorations in relief. They seem to have had no plugs; but one cannot expect everything from a pre-classical civilization!

The Minoans were indeed much concerned with the practical details of domestic building. The system for utilizing the run-off of water from roofs was most elaborate: there is a story of a modern sanitary engineer who was shocked to find that the Minoans had anticipated a recently patented device by over 3000 years! The runnel down the side of the public stairway below the eastern bastion ends in a couple of obvious settling-tanks. It is built in a series of sections, each beginning with a gentle slope and ending with a steep one. This arrangement (which I have never seen elsewhere) is apparently designed to prevent splashing where the runnel turns a corner. Some of the staircases, by the way, are of 'modern' construction, with the treads overlapping to give mutual support, instead of being plastered on to a solid ramp as foundation. Light was admitted mainly through light-wells or courtyards; but there are a few casements, which the experts presume were fitted with panes of glazed parchment.

The palace gives the general impression of a building planned from within, so to speak, as a place to live in, rather than from without, as a place to look at or to be defended.

Cretan cities, indeed, were not walled. In this lack of provision for defence, they were unique in the ancient world. Apparently the Minoans' command of the seas was enough protection. But this secure and civilized existence of the Minoans, sheltered behind the wooden walls of the ships, eventually came to an end. Not long after 2000 B.C., new peoples began pouring in from the north. Eventually some of them developed nautical skill, and took to marine raiding and trading. The Achaeans were the chief of these new elements in the Mediterranean population. Their expansion displaced other populations, and caused the irruption of 'the Peoples of the Sea' along the coasts of the Levant as far as Egypt. On the mainland of Greece they had founded Mycene and other cities; and in about 1400 B.C. they invaded Crete and sacked Knossos and the other main palaces of the island. The traces of the burning of Knossos are still very apparent today. Here you can see charring, there smoke-blackened walls; sometimes oil must have leaked out and burnt on the floors, leaving dense black stains, oily to the touch when first exposed to the air. Later, the city was rebuilt, but the great days of Crete were over: it had fallen to the rank of a minor power, under alien domination. Minoan civilization probably came to its final end in the twelfth century, with the violent disturbances due to the arrival of the Dorians.

According to Sir John Forsdyke (*Times*, Mar. 4, 1952), the Minos of the Homeric poems was not a Minoan king at all, but an Achaean conqueror, who ruled in Crete about 1250 B.C. But he may have taken a traditional name for his royal title, for there are references in Greek inscriptions to an 'earlier Minos', who was King in Knossos at the height of Minoan sea-power. Forsdyke gives reasons for believing that this 'earlier Minos' is the personage portrayed on the famous Chieftain Cup in the Heraklion Museum, which he assigns to the early part of the 15th century B.C.

In any case, Minoan influence had spread to the conquerors. Mycenean civilization contained many Minoan elements, though of course it was very different in its economic and political basis; and traces of Minoan influence remained in Greek culture. These include many of the non-Aryan words which the Achaeans borrowed to denote local plants and animals. It is indeed likely that our names for various familiar flowers and trees, like olive and fig, hyacinth and violet, can be traced back, through Latin and Greek, to a Minoan origin.* In another sphere, the legend of Daedalus shows how much the techniques and inventive genius of the Minoans had impressed their successors.

★

One morning I climbed the hill beyond the valley, with the scent of the very aromatic Cretan thyme in my nostrils. From its top – a rather surprising flat plateau with small yellow buttercups carpeting an olive-grove – I could see the whole site of Knossos. The trace of the ancient main road was clearly visible. It was carried across the ravine on a massive viaduct, and was then led up to the palace on a high ramp: here it was colonnaded and probably roofed over, to serve as a processional way.

Below the Palace I could see the so-called Royal Villa – probably only a big private house. To one side was the royal mausoleum, which we had visited the day before. This was impressive in its way: a small courtyard into which the public could look down from a paved terrace-roof to see the ritual; wider courts beyond; and a rock-hewn tomb with a pillar. Unlike the Egyptians, the Minoans had no paintings or reliefs on the walls of their tombs or shrines – only plain dignified slabs of gypsum or other stone. All the tombs, by the way, were outside the town, some in the river valley, others up on the steep slopes of the hills.

Near the viaduct, I had previously been shown a little shrine, impressive in its simplicity, with its central niche and two shelves for offerings, and a small rectangular pool. Here de Jongh had been the first person to see the water well up when the supply was restored after more than three thousand years.

I could not pass an examination in Minoan archeology; but from my brief stay at Knossos, I took away a vivid picture of ancient Crete as a

---

* Recently Dr Ventris has claimed that many undeciphered tablets from Knossos are written in Greek, though the script is a syllabic not an alphabetic one. It will be extremely interesting to see if this is really so, as it would change many of our ideas on the mutual relations of late Minoan and Greek culture.

unique human creation. Before the rise of Assyria, before the great revolution of the Iron Age, Minoan Crete had built up a civilization much freer and gayer than any other in the ancient world. It was not burdened with the formality and religious pomposity of Egypt; it was not dependent on military force, nor centred round an imperial autocrat. Relying on maritime skill for security, and on commerce and the technical arts for wealth, it developed a spirit of initiative and naturalness not to be found in any other of the bronze-age civilizations. To employ a much-abused word, it was the first modern culture. Though ancient rituals were still practised, one feels that they were brought into line with a very lively existence, and that life was not lived under the weight of oppressive tradition or stifled by governmental tyranny.*

★

If the legend of Icarus is to be believed, Crete witnessed the first attempt at human flight. In modern times, it achieved the unenviable distinction of being the scene of the first large-scale airborne operation in history. That is well known: what is not so well known is that the Germans later sent some of their best men to make scientific studies on the island. One of their prominent zoologists died of heart failure while exploring the mountains in search of the rare Cretan ibex or wild goat. Dr Yamalikis had a pair of these *Aegagri*, as they are sometimes called, at his country home, and hoped to breed from them. In contrast with the Germans, the Italian troops killed and ate one small herd. There are now only a few left, but the Greek Government is trying to save the species.

The great ornithologist Stresemann was officially sent to study the Cretan avifauna. Meanwhile John Buxton, a young English poet and bird-lover, was doing the same unofficially while hiding out in the hills. Later, when he had been captured and was in a German prisoner-of-war camp, he organized a survey of the habits of the Redstart to pass the time. He managed to enter into communication with Stresemann, who was then back at the Natural History Museum in Berlin. Stresemann helped him with information about Redstarts, while Buxton was able to help Stresemann with information

* Arthur Evans's six-volume *The Palace of Minos* gives a detailed account of the excavations at Knossos. A good general book on Minoan culture is J. D. Pendlebury's *The Archaeology of Crete* (1939). See also R. W. Hutchinson on prehistoric town planning in Crete, *Town Planning Review*, 1950, **22**, 199

about Cretan birds. This is one of the few cases in which the spirit of scientific co-operation was able to circumvent or transcend the barriers of national hostility during the last war, whereas in the Napoleonic wars they were frequent.

★

The over-riding fact of Cretan geography today is deforestation, with consequent soil erosion. Save in the higher mountains, the forests have disappeared, and the hillsides are bare and often barren. De Jongh told us that the remains of quite important Minoan settlements have been found on hill sites where there is now not a vestige of soil covering the bare rock. Pendlebury in his book suggests that deforestation must already have become serious in ancient times: the eventual use of stone for door-jambs and the like seems to have been due to the increasing shortage of timber. It is the same sad story as in the Lebanon and Greece and many other countries. Until governments take action on this basic problem, most other measures are merely palliatives.

Many of the people still wear traditional costume. At one village the local landowner was just setting out on horseback to visit one of his estates – a picturesque figure in his black blouse and round cap (pl. 56, opp. p. 289). And in Heraklion it was pleasant to see some of the shopkeepers still sporting characteristically Cretan dress, with bright scarves round their middles. But the tendency to the drab uniformity of modern Western dress has set in, and I am afraid will submerge the people within the space of a generation.

This is a pity, for the traditional dress provides an outlet for self-expression, a vehicle for pride in personal appearance, which cheap modern clothes can never do. Cheapness is relevant: many of the old costumes were certainly expensive, in money or labour or both. But it should be possible to adapt them so that they are not too much of an economic strain. The trouble is that governments, obsessed with economic questions, have not seen the importance of dress for social well-being, or realized the value of cultural variety in our shrinking world. Greece is one of the countries where the trend to modern uniformity has not yet fully triumphed, and might still be reversed.

The de Jonghs had many stories about the Cretans. I particularly liked their one about Venizelos and the hens. Apparently he not only passed a law prohibiting the carrying of live hens head downwards, by their legs, but saw to it that it was enforced. When he was outed, the populace paraded all day with bunches of upside-down hens!

After the German occupation of Crete, the British encouraged the resistance of the local population in various ways. One way, since the people were very hard up for food, was by dropping food supplies from planes. And even when we in Britain were severely rationed for milk, British planes were dropping large quantities of condensed milk in Crete. When she returned to Knossos after the war, Mrs de Jongh asked a local woman about this. Had they not been very grateful for the condensed milk? Oh, yes. Didn't you find it a welcome addition to your short rations? We? Oh, no, we would never eat that stuff. Well, you found it was good for the children? No, no, we wouldn't dream of forcing it on our children. What did you do with it, then? Ah – we fed it to the little pigs, and it made them grow very big and fat, and when the English came back, we sold the pigs to them at a very good price. Yes, we were grateful for the stuff. . . .

Mrs de Jongh thought this rather a sad story : and we agreed.

★

Greece and Tunisia I also visited. Though they are not part of the Middle East, one or two points obtrude themselves into the field of this book.

Tunisia was a reminder of how a Middle Eastern culture was extended into the southern lands of the Mediterranean during the whirlwind spread of Islam ; and of how this same extension of Islam split the original unity of the Mediterranean basin into two sharply delimited halves which for over a thousand years have pursued quite different destinies.

A thousand years ago the Islamic world was culturally more advanced, and was still pressing on the Christian West. Today Islam is backward and frustrated, and the West, no longer so whole-heartedly Christian, is still in its phase of powerful expansion which started five hundred years ago.

The vigour of Islam's cultural spread along the North African littoral is vividly brought home at Kairouan. In this holy city of what is now southern Tunisia, the Moslems founded the oldest university institution in the world. The Great Mosque of Kairouan was founded in 670 immediately after the first Islamic irruption into the region: by about 800 it had begun to exercise higher educational functions, and has continued to exercise them, apart from an interruption of a few decades due to war, ever since. For centuries it boasted the main Law School of Islam, and was the parent of the three other important university-mosques of the region - El Azhar in Cairo, and the Great Mosques of Tunis and Fez.

These are today much more important as centres of higher education, while Kairouan has degenerated sadly from its high intellectual estate. Of recent years it has begun to make an effort to raise itself again. The Director of Studies proudly showed me the new classrooms, equipped with the novelty of chalk and blackboards. I had never before realized the intellectual importance of the blackboard: it must have revolutionized the entire technique of education.

It must be confessed, however, that the standards of Kairouan and even at Tunis were low, and the whole educational outlook of Islam in the region is still essentially medieval. If the Arabic countries want to take the path of progress, either they must radically reform their religious universities, or must found modern secular and scientific ones.

The previous cultural unity between the northern and southern shores of the Mediterranean was illustrated by the remains of Rome in Tunisia. In the Museum at Tunis are some of the biggest Roman mosaics in the world – monster scenes of marine life, and one of a big farm. And the Roman amphitheatre at El Djem is one of the largest in existence, and doubly impressive by the way it looms up in isolation from a featureless plain (pl. 54, opposite). Roman Carthage, though now merely a heap of ruins, for a time ran neck and neck with Alexandria for the position of second city of the Empire.

Carthage provides another connection with the Middle East, for it was the largest and indeed the only important Phoenician settlement outside the Levant. *Carthago est delenda*, Cato fulminated; and deleted it was. There is scarcely a visible trace left of the stupendous city, Rome's only rival, with nearly three-quarters of a million inhabitants. Here and there a little brickwork is revealed by the crumbling of the low cliff, and in the sea can be discerned the remains of some sort of harbour construction. The rest was razed and then thoroughly burnt.

The cultural continuity of Italy and North Africa continued into Christian times. Among the mosaics in the Museum are some Christian ones, unusual as including nude and rather voluptuous female angels. This particular African contribution to religious culture has died out: but Africa exerted a powerful influence on the development of Christian ideas and church organization, notably by being the birthplace of Augustine and the scene of

53. The 'Dancing Floor' at Knossos, scene of Minoan rituals and celebrations

54. The huge Roman amphitheatre at El Djem looms up in isolation from a featureless plain

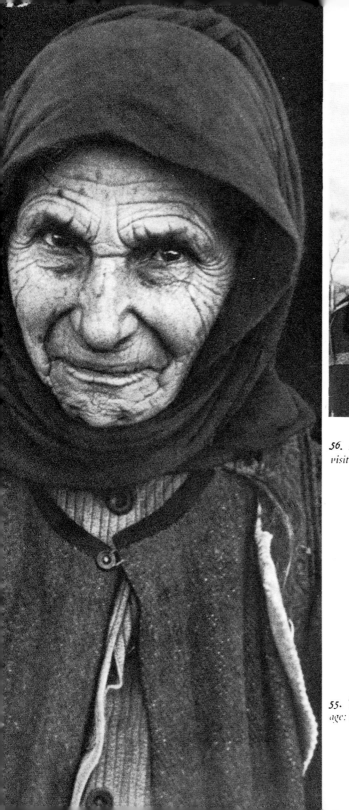

56. *A Cretan landowner setting out to visit his estates*

55. *The patient beauty of peasant old age: an octogenarian Greek grandmother*

his main activities. The strangeness of the early Christian world is illustrated by the fact that prominent men ran the risk of being kidnapped and made ecclesiastical dignitaries against their will – a sort of religious press-gang: Augustine himself only became a presbyter under compulsion. A contemporary parallel, though affecting one man only, was the nomination of Adlai Stevenson as Democratic candidate for President against his expressed inclination.

★

The impressions that Greece evoked were wholly different. The old grandmother spinning wool on a farm near Athens had all the patient beauty of peasant old age, but it was a European, not an Oriental beauty (pl. 55, opposite). The pervading culture is Christian, not Moslem. The Byzantine churches, like the great monastery at Daphni or the tiny Old Metropolitan Church in Athens, have not been converted into mosques or museums like Santa Sophia, but are still used for the same purposes as when they were built (and, one may add, with a liturgy that has scarcely changed in over a thousand years, and is now in danger of becoming a living fossil).

Delphi, that 'savage place, as holy and enchanted' as any in the world, with its monuments and inscriptions from Greek cities as far away as Marseilles, is an example of the Greeks' unique system of colonization, whereby a colony was hived off like a swarm of bees, but preserved its connection with its parent-city. It also demonstrates the emptiness of the western Mediterranean in early classical times, an emptiness which made the Greek colony system possible.

Above all, Delphi illustrates the paradox of ancient Greece – the political disunity of its separate city-states within the cultural unity of its conscious Hellenism. Mainland cities like Athens, Corinth, Thebes or Argos, colonies like Syracuse, Paestum, Marseilles or Selinus – they all produced masterpieces of Hellenic architecture, yet were all involved in inter-city rivalry and war.

The Greek *polis* or city-state was a marvellous politico-social invention which permitted an unexampled flowering of freedom, intellect and art. But it was by its nature limited in size, and could no more develop into a nation or an empire, or even into a unit of a federal state, than an insect could evolve into a mammal or a bird. A parallel has often been drawn between classical Greece and modern Europe, for Europe too is a region with a very real cultural unity, but cut up into competing and often hostile political units. But the parallel is not exact; and the difficulties in the way of some larger union are not so great in Europe as they were in Greece. We Europeans are already accustomed to representative government in place of an assembly of all citizens, and to a large and permanent bureaucracy in place of a small number of citizens temporarily charged with public office. Furthermore, the apparatus of international trade, finance and communications has been developed to a far higher pitch than in the classical world, and is at the disposal of any supernational organization that may arise. The construction of the *polis* prevented its evolution into part of a larger system: the construction of the European nation-state, though it cannot be said to favour such an evolution, at least does not preclude it. What with our warnings from past history and our empirical experiments in the present, I would expect to see this new phase of political evolution achieved within a few decades.

But my brightest impression was of the unique and decisive step taken by the Greek mind, the step to mental freedom. Before the 7th century B.C. this step had never been taken by any society, though a few individuals had struggled to make it in one or other field of existence, notably the Hebrew prophets in religion. Everywhere religion dominated, tradition was the guiding rule of life, and innovation was frowned upon; everywhere the individual was subordinated to the system.

The Greeks, in the course of three glorious centuries, freed the creative and enquiring spirit from this subservience. They turned religious ritual into great drama, mythology and moralizing into philosophy, practical calculation into pure mathematics, tendentious record into reflective history; they pursued the first, critical approach to the facts of politics, and the first rational approach to the facts of nature; they made of coinage not only a system of useful tokens but a new art-form, they freed painting, sculpture and architecture from their subservience to religion and authority, so that they could develop as arts in their own right. The Parthenon is the supreme symbol of this liberation of man's creative spirit, its pure beauty in striking contrast with the god-ridden and pharaoh-ridden Egyptian temples and pyramids.

The Middle East invented all the foundations of civilized life: Greece transposed them into the key of freedom, and in so doing threw a bridge between the ancient and the modern world.

18

AND LAST

WHEN THE MIDDLE EASTERN traveller surfaces, so to speak, from his plunges into the past, and has managed to shake himself free of the waters of history, his first general reaction is likely to be one of bewilderment and disillusion. For millennia, the region led the world in what Breasted calls the conquest of civilization, and for millennia more had a place in its forefront. Why has it now fallen so far behind?

Ur and Babylon, the Old and the New Kingdoms of Egypt; Jerusalem, Damascus, Persepolis, Alexandria, Byzantium, Cairo; the great primal inventions, of agriculture, the wheel, stone building, organized irrigation, metal-working, writing, the alphabet; the great discoveries, of primitive astronomy, of mathematics, of geography; the beginnings of philosophy, the first libraries, the dawn of monotheism, the multiple rise of sculpture and painting and architecture; the richness of Ionian, Alexandrian, Persian, Byzantine, Arabic culture; Hammurabi, Zoser, the great Pharaohs, Moses, David, Jesus, Mahomet, Zoroaster, Saladin, Avicenna, the architects of Santa Sophia, the Persian poets . . . What is there in the region's recent history to compare with this brilliance of its past?

Of course, notable men are still being produced. To take one name as exemplar of a rare personality thrusting up through layers of difficulty, there is Taha Hussein, the poor blind boy who became an inspiring writer and poet, and later Minister of Education in Egypt. And Kemal Atatürk was certainly that rare phenomenon, a really great man, whose individuality affected the course of history.

Of course, too, things are happening, often good things. There is the rebirth of Turkey and its vigorous attempt to take its place as an advanced country; but there is a long way to go, and in the process it has lost some of its new-found democratic virtues. In Egypt, there has been a marked renaissance both in material and social reform and national consciousness, with many achievements to its credit. But will it be able to catch up with Malthusian misery, and will it be able to shed its nationalist intransigence? And will the Arabs in general be able to get over the stumbling-block of Israel? There are Universities, like those of Egypt or the new National University of Syria: but the academic standards are not always high enough; and the students often lead an unsatisfactory life, and are mobilized for political purposes. There is the new efficiency of Israel: but this is having serious demographic and political consequences – the impending overcrowding of Palestine, and the creation of a huge block of dispossessed and displaced refugee Arabs.

But why multiply examples? Of course, the Middle East cannot avoid being touched and transformed by the modern spirit; injected here and there with doses of science and technology; invaded by cheap mass-produced goods; infected by nationalism, with its good ambitions and healthy pride as well as its narrowness and jealousy; confronted with Communism and its new methods of organizing power; confronted also with Western ideas about democracy and human rights. It cannot remain isolated from the world as a whole, its attempts at unification, its drastic ideological revolutions. But if it cannot live in isolation, it has managed to provide itself with a good deal of insulation against a good many modern tendencies.

Monarchy, if no longer either universal or absolute, is still powerful in some Arab countries, with the result that dynastic interests as well as political jealousies continue to bedevil Arab politics. For this among other more important reasons, Arab nationalism has not been very effective as a constructive force even within the region, and its effects have been largely negative, manifested in hostility to things non-Arab. The Arab League seems in constant danger of falling apart, and has too often served as a manifestation of Arab disunity and political inefficiency, instead of as a demonstration of what Arab unity could achieve in the way of positive benefits for Arab peoples.

The social organism of Egypt, with its staggering contrasts between riches and poverty, its pullulation of the under-nourished and under-privileged, is as different from the Welfare State organization of Scandinavia or Britain as is a crocodile from a dog. Throughout the region, there is only the dawn of a sense of social responsibility.

The region, taken as a whole, is a backward one, or as it is the fashion to say now, under-developed. Worthington sums up his survey of the nutritional position by saying that 'the whole area, with a few local exceptions, must be classed with the worst-nourished parts of the world; . . . malnutrition is widespread and starvation threatens the poorest'. Malaria, tapeworms, hookworm, bilharzia (three-quarters of the population of Egypt are affected), T.B., smallpox, typhus, typhoid, dysentery, V.D. and eye-diseases are widespread and cause grave debility, as well as much suffering. There are few regions where narcotic drugs are more widely used, in spite of all the campaigns against them; and fortunes are still being made by their illicit supply. The systems of land tenure are usually inimical to good farming and prosperous agriculture. During historic times, in spite of new irrigation schemes here and there, the desert has extended its sway over many thousands of square miles, not through any ineluctable climatic change, but through man's greed, stupidity and mistakes: the forests have largely disappeared, disastrous soil erosion has taken place, and large areas once irrigated and inhabited have reverted to desolate sterility. The status of women is on the whole low, and in some areas they suffer worse horrors at the hands of men than anywhere else in the world – for instance the revolting and barbarous practice of infibulation or so-called Pharaonic female circumcision.

If the present state of the Middle East appears discouraging, it is even more so when regarded in the perspective of the past. For three hundred years, since the time of Shah Abbas in Persia, it is fair to say that no major contribution to science or learning, to architecture or the arts (including the art of living) has been made by a region which once discovered all the bases of civilization. And when we look at the details of history, is not their only lesson a gloomy one – plus ça change, plus c'est la même chose? Are not the facts of the Middle Eastern past incompatible with an evolutionary philosophy of history?

I do not think so. I am sure that there are principles underlying the course of history, but that the present is the first age in which it is profitable to begin searching for them. Only in the last few decades have we discovered many of the elementary facts about the course of human history, regarded as a world-wide process which includes prehistory and extends back to before the origin of the present species of man. As a result, serious attempts are now being made by historians to formulate such principles and to discern the general forces at work in history: Arnold Toynbee's is perhaps the most widely known.*

The present is also the first age in which the search for principles in history can be illuminated by ideas drawn from biological evolution. Human history is, after all, a direct continuation of biological evolution, and we must expect to find useful analogies and similarities between the two processes. It is of course true that evolution in its human or psycho-social phase operates by quite other methods than those of evolution in the biological phase – by cumulative consciousness based on the transmission of relevant awareness and its products, instead of by natural selection based on the transmission of relevant mutations in the material of the hereditary constitution: but once we realize this vital difference we can discount its implications.

In days before the modern comprehensive neo-Darwinian theory of evolution, great contributions could be and were made to our knowledge of life. The comparative anatomy of organisms, leading to the detection of common plans underlying the construction of large groups; their methods of working, leading to modern physiology and ethnology; their inter-relations, leading to a scientific ecology; the cataloguing and description of the variety of life, leading to their rational and systematic classification; the study of fossils, leading to the recognition of past organic change; the study of the development of living things, leading to an analytic embryology, and of their mode of inheritance, leading to a scientific genetics – in these several ways our biological knowledge was enormously extended during the past three centuries. But a total picture, an over-all comprehension, only became possible with the realization that life was neither static nor a mere accumulation of separate units, but a single dynamic process of self-transformation.

The same sort of thing, we may be sure, will happen with history. In the past, our historical knowledge has grown enormously, through the painstaking analysis of written records, followed by that of cultural remains like pottery and architecture; the accurate dating of events; the documentation of social and institutional change; the history of art, law, religion, economics, science, and other separate aspects of human life; the comparative study of societies; the comparative study of regularities in history; the backward

* O. H. K. Spate has published an interesting critique of certain sides of Toynbee's work in the *Geographical Journal*, vol. 118 (1953), p. 406.

extension of history through the methods of archeological research, and its lateral extension through those of social anthropology; and much else. But until the central idea of mutually interacting, self-transforming cultures had emerged, it was not possible for the separate parts of history to fall into place, as part of the single pattern-process of psycho-social evolution.

In biological evolution, we have to distinguish trends of different scale and scope. Broadly speaking, there is the process of detailed adaptation, by which single species become adapted to particular local conditions; there is the process of specialization, by which groups become more efficient in some particular way of life but eventually reach a limit; there is special advance, in the improvement of one or other of the main mechanisms of existence; and there is general advance, leading to the improvement of general organization and the realization of new possibilities.

Major steps of advance are generally effected by the replacement of one dominant type by another and improved type, as when the mammals replaced the reptiles as the dominant group of land vertebrates at the end of the Mesozoic era. A certain amount of cyclical repetition occurs. Each new dominant type shows a radiation into a number of specialized trends, and successive radiations repeat the same broad features. But the repetition is never exact, and each cycle starts from the new basis of an improved pattern of construction and working. In fact, we can discern, through the welter of minor change and the succession of specialized radiations, a major trend of general progress.

General progress is manifested both in the physical and mental capacities of organisms. There is an increase in the efficiency of material organization and physiological function; there is also an improvement in the mental functions of awareness and knowing, feeling and emotion, impulse and will. And the emphasis falls increasingly on the mental aspects, until finally, in the late Cenozoic, the possibilities of physiological improvement were fast reaching their limit, and the only major advance to remain open was mental organization. It was through advance in this property of life that man became the latest dominant type in evolution.

What analogies with biological evolution can we expect to find in the cultural evolution that we call history? We should expect to find a divergent radiation of cultures, and the persistence of some simpler types of society side by side with increasing complexity of organization in other societies. But this does not mean that all are of the same evolutionary value or on the same evolutionary level. We should expect to find some cyclical recurrence in the history of successive civilizations, as has been crudely stressed by Spengler, and more scientifically by Toynbee. But this does not mean that decadence is inevitable, nor that recurrence is all: the wheel may merely turn, but the vehicle may move onwards.

We should expect to find that one-sided specialization is restrictive (as with Egypt) or self-defeating (as with Assyrian militarism); but this does not mean that greater efficiency in the various organs of society can never be reconciled with flexibility of total organization. We should expect to find types of organization admirably adapted to one set of conditions, but becoming extinct when conditions change (like the Greek city-states); but that does not mean that other types of organization may not prove capable of continuous adaptation to change. And once we survey the process as a whole, we should expect to find certain major trends standing out.

The most important trend in human history would appear to be the trend towards improvement of thought and accumulated experience, its amount and its organization, leading to better control of practical problems through skills and techniques, better expression of experience through the arts, better ways of facing and guiding destiny through improved religions and moral codes.

This is correlated with a higher level of organization of society and its institutions; and this in turn is dependent on economic and material efficiency. But in human as in biological evolution, the relative importance of the mental components increases with time, and over-emphasis on the material basis may stand in the way of the more essential kind of advance, the improved organization of thought and experience.

We also have to reckon with the fact that man's evolution is unique in one important respect: instead of splitting up into biologically discontinuous lines, he continues as a single species, and his divergences, both biological and societal, are increasingly counteracted by convergence, tending towards the creation of a common pool of thought and a common framework of action for the whole species.

We should recall the fact that in all phases of evolution advance is related to the exigencies of the immediate situation, and therefore takes place in a series of steps; but also that, whereas in biological evolution advance is the blind outcome of automatic forces, in human history it can be in part the conscious outcome of knowledge and purpose, and that 'the situation' can therefore be extended – in time, in space, and degree of generalization of thought.

Seen in this sort of perspective, the process of history, in the Middle East or anywhere else, emerges as the resultant of a number of different forces and trends. There are the trends resulting from blind physiological forces such as the urge to reproduction. There are those resulting from the urge to discover new and improved techniques; and those others resulting from the need to feel significant in the scheme of things. There are trends which are due to conscious planning; there are accidents and the unforeseen consequences of earlier action. And finally there are incalculable irruptions from outside the region.

The trends towards improved organization of thought and experience are largely restricted within the frameworks provided by organized societies; but they are in some measure capable of transcending these frameworks, and diffusing into other social units. Thus we have not only the history of distinct civilizations, but also the history of civilization in general.

Cultural evolution has produced societies as different in their plans of construction and modes of working as are the main types of animal organism – of mollusc as against vertebrate, or mammal as against fish.

Finally, we must remember that in biological evolution, progress is neither inevitable nor universal. We find stability in some lines as well as transformation in others; many specialisms are doomed to reach a limit, many groups suffer extinction; some primitive types survive unchanged side by side with higher and rapidly evolving forms; but the upper level of biological achievement is in fact more or less steadily raised.

As we might expect, the same sort of thing, *mutatis mutandis*, is found in human history. Some civilizations become fossilized, others become totally extinct; some reach a limit, others continue their transformations. But behind the divergence and the struggle, the general trends persist, and the upper level of achievement in various human functions does in fact rise.

In the light of such general analogies, the evidence of decay and decline in the Middle East is not so depressing as at first sight. It could be an incentive: what man has done once, he could do again, if he sets about it in the right way. The difficulty is to find the right way in the totally changed situation of the 20th century.

What are the chief points which demand attention in the present situation? I would say first the widespread misuse or neglect of renewable natural resources, shown in deforestation, soil erosion, neglect of irrigation systems and failure to use water-power. The neglect of water-resources is marked in Mesopotamia, but not in Egypt: and of course deforestation is not a problem where, as in Egypt, forests have never existed, though the Egyptians' lack of wood has accelerated deforestation elsewhere.

Then there is over-population: this is grave in Egypt and in Israel, but not so urgent in other parts of the region. Thirdly, there is the growing discontent of the common people with their poverty and misery. It is not just the fact of poverty and misery: it is the consciousness of that fact, coupled with the hope, engendered by modern science and diffused through modern communications, that they are remediable.

Fourthly, there is the reaction against everything that can be styled imperialist or colonial exploitation, with the resultant rise of xenophobic nationalism. One country has even refused to accept Technical Assistance because foreign personnel would be needed to plan and administer it. It is an irony of history that purely nationalist ideals should have spread from the West to take root in the Middle East just when the West has realized that they are out of date and is attempting to integrate them in larger concepts.

Then there is a religious revival, with an emphasis on orthodoxy and Islamic tradition – an escape towards the past and away from the disturbing realities of the present. There is the infiltration of western industrialism and technology and their products, which is upsetting traditional economics and traditional ways of daily life. And of course there is the effect of modern communications, from motor-buses to air-services, from newspapers to radio, which is disturbing and transforming ways of thought throughout the region.

Finally, there is modern science. The rise of natural science in the short space of three centuries constitutes one of the two or three major revolutions in human history. Through science, the organization of knowledge and technique has been cast into a new pattern and has reached a new level; any further advance must start from this as its base, and must continue to utilize science as one of its main organs.

The Middle East can be proud of the contributions it has made to progress and the organization of knowledge – the invention of writing and the alphabet; the beginnings of mathematics and astronomy; the introduction of decimal notation (even if the idea of zero was taken from India); the preservation of Greek learning and its transmission to other regions. Through accepting and utilizing those contributions, the West has been able to create modern science. It is for the Middle East now to accept and utilize modern science.

For the scientific development of the region it is necessary to think first of its natural resources – their extent, their conservation, and their improved utilization. By a curious irony, the first survey of the Middle East as a region was initiated from outside and carried through as a war measure, with the primary objective of freeing tonnage, quay space and internal communications for war materials. Enormous quantities of stores and munitions were required for the North African campaign, and also for aid to Russia via the Persian Gulf and across Persia. In order to do this, imports into the region had to be drastically curtailed; the largest and most obvious savings could be made in imported foodstuffs, by means of increasing the food-production of the area. The extent of the saving thus made possible can be realized from the fact that in three years imports were cut down to a quarter of their previous total, from 6 million to 1½ million tons per annum, and this without in any way reducing the health and efficiency of the region's seventy million inhabitants.

To carry out the general task, the British Government in 1941 set up a special agency, M.E.S.C., the Middle East Supply Centre, which was converted into a joint Anglo-American organization in the following year. In the course of its work, an Agricultural Mission was sent out in 1942, and in 1943 Dr Worthington reported on Middle East Science, and Dr Keen on the Agricultural Development of the region. The two reports provide a remarkable survey of its basic resources, and constitute a milestone in the history of the area.

When the reports appeared in 1944, it was at once clear how valuable they were, and how remarkable it was that we (for it is fair to say that the British took the initiative in the whole matter) had had vision enough in the middle of the war to arrange for and conduct a long-term survey of really fundamental problems in an entire region of the world. Now that I have been over so much of the region, a re-reading of the reports brings home their very great value, and makes me more than ever regret that they have hardly been acted on and that the admirable co-ordinating and planning mechanism provided by M.E.S.C. was not retained in the post-war period.

I have already suggested the value of a survey of cultural resources, and the possibility of utilizing them to increase the flow of visitors, with mutual benefit to them and to the region. But for any comprehensive development of any under-developed area, aid from outside is needed, aid in money, in machines, in technical know-how, in the form of foreign experts, scientists, advisers, administrators, technicians, and of training given in foreign countries to men and women from the area. Here, it seems to me, a new approach is needed, on the part of both parties to the transaction.

Current terms like Foreign Aid and Technical Assistance signify a wrong attitude. They imply that the transaction is one of charity between a rich giver and a poor receiver. Little wonder that some under-developed countries resent this approach, and even refuse the offer of assistance; and little wonder that in the richer countries many are reluctant to continue what they feel is a form of compulsory charity, and many others treat it merely as a means of salving their international conscience.

The only way in which the transaction could be made satisfactory would be by regarding it as a joint enterprise, to which both partners are contributing, and in which both are co-operating. In addition, it means replacing the uninspiring phrase *Technical Assistance* by something better expressing the idea of co-operative effort: *World Development Programme* is the sort of thing that might serve.

Any such change involves an altered outlook. As Arnold Toynbee has said in his introduction to the U.N. pamphlet on Unicef (the United Nations International Children's Emergency Fund), 'The 20th Century will be chiefly remembered not as an age of political conflicts or technical inventions, but as an age in which human society dared to think of the welfare of the whole human race as a practicable objective.'

These are weighty words, coming from a man who has made the whole sweep of history his province. I would add that such a radical change in outlook brings us up against the question of a new organization of general thought on the subject of human destiny – in other words, a new approach to the core of religious thinking.

In the long perspective of history, the present chaotic world situation can be seen as somewhat analogous to that at the end of the Roman Empire, one in which a new vivifying and unifying concept of human life and its significance is needed.

In this field of ideas, too, the Middle East has reason to be proud of the contributions it has made – in this case to the organization of religious thought. The Jews gave the world the idea of monotheism and a single true God: Christianity and Islam provided unifying religions for two enormous sectors of the world's population. But, though universalist in principle, none of these systems proved universal in practice; their 'true Gods' not only conflicted with each other, but the systems split up into competing and often hostile sub-systems.

It is for the Middle East now, profiting by these lessons from its past, to join with the rest of the free world in developing a new over-all system of ideas, a system which has religious functions in being concerned with the better comprehension and better guidance of human destiny.

The present spiritual distress is due partly to the collapse of old certainties and the incomplete digestion of new knowledge, partly to the focusing of human loyalties and aspirations round a number of conflicting creeds. Any new system, if it is to succeed, must be potentially universal in its appeal, capable of uniting the separate bits and pieces of the human species in a common attitude and way of thought.

Man today needs to evolve a new organization of thought capable of dealing with the new situation in which he finds himself, just as land vertebrates needed to evolve a new organization of bodily structure and working adapted to the new situation of terrestrial existence.

The human species is only at the beginning of this task: but it seems clear that any such system of thought will have to perform many of the functions of a religion, and that it will find itself centred round the idea of fulfilment – fulfilment of the individual personality in relation to the world of ideas and values which transcend the immediate and the specific, fulfilment of the destiny of the species as a whole through the fuller realization of more possibilities for more individuals. From another angle, the central idea emerges as that of participation in a joint enterprise.

What is more, the central ideas, of fulfilment and of joint enterprise or shared adventure, are applicable at every level of the process of human destiny, from long-term evolution to specific and immediate projects, from international organization to the development of a single human personality.

When, in 1946, I was unexpectedly invited to take over the direction of the Preparatory Commission of Unesco, I found myself faced with essentially the same problem, though in more restricted and immediate form. Obviously Unesco would have to find some guiding lines for its policy, some common ground for unity and continuity in its outlook. And this was not going to be easy, when the organization included Catholic, Communist and Moslem States, powerful industrial nations and small backward countries, countries with highly developed science and others with scarcely any scientific activity, representatives of radically different cultures. How were such disparate elements to be united in a common enterprise?

It seemed to me that it should be possible to work out an acceptable body of guiding and integrating principles for a world-wide effort in education, science and culture; and I spent most of my leave in writing a pamphlet which I hoped might serve as a basis for such a body of principles.

It was this self-appointed task which first drove me to the idea of evolutionary humanism as the inevitable key concept for any practical world philosophy adapted to the present situation. As I then wrote, 'the general philosophy of Unesco should, it seems, be a scientific world humanism, global in extent and evolutionary in background'. And I then tried to follow out some of the implications, practical as well as theoretical, of such an outlook. However, I was politically naïve in imagining that an inter-governmental body such as Unesco would adopt such a philosophy – or indeed could commit itself to any official philosophy whatsoever. Religious and ideological differences were too great, intellectual and political assumptions too different. My Executive Committee published the pamphlet under the title 'Unesco: its purpose and its philosophy'; but as a statement of their Executive Secretary's personal attitude, not of their official view.

Looking back, I am sure they were right. Discussion of general principles would have plunged the General Conference into interminable and acrimonious philosophical debate, and deflected it from its urgent practical tasks. In point of fact, it proved relatively easy to find agreement on the kinds of specific project which Unesco should undertake – removal of barriers to the spread of information, campaigns against illiteracy and ignorance, the establishment of science co-operation centres in areas where scientists were few and scattered, the encouragement of international professional bodies in all fields of Unesco's competence, the promotion of cultural and artistic interchange and of international training facilities: and out of the practical operation of such projects, the broad lines of a general Unesco policy began slowly but surely to emerge, without being deliberately formulated.

However, my further two years with Unesco as Director-General, including the experience of travel on Unesco business in various regions of the world, and perhaps especially the experience of history which was forced on me by my journeys in the Middle East, have only strengthened my conviction that some general philosophy, some such over-all system of ideas as I envisaged under the name of evolutionary humanism, will eventually be needed, though Unesco cannot be expected to provide it. It is needed as an organ of world society, of humanity as a whole. International organizations will never become fully effective as agencies of joint enterprise until a common framework of collective thought has been developed in which they can operate.

One way of stimulating the development of such a common system of thought would be for the United Nations to convene a conference, where the subject would be broadly discussed by experts, instead of by official Government representatives. An exploratory conference of this sort has already been held on the subject of world resources; and a second is shortly to be held on the urgent but controversial subject of world population. A United Nations conference on world philosophy would be the modern counterpart of one of the great Councils of the early church. It would certainly be an interesting and indeed exciting occasion, though let us hope not so exciting as the Council of Ephesus, where a disagreement over the doctrine of Christ's Person led to the Patriarch of Alexandria knocking down the Patriarch of Constantinople and trampling on him.

★

It is one of the duties and privileges of man to testify to his experience, to bear witness to the wonder and variety of the world in which he finds himself. I had the fortunate experience of being plunged into the Middle East and its history; and in this book I have tried to give my personal testimony of the impression which that experience made upon me. I am only too well aware that my acquaintance was brief and my experience superficial. But the impressions it made were profound as well as vivid; and the attempt to order them into communicable form has been a satisfying though sometimes a difficult task.

The Middle East, perhaps more than any other region, demonstrates the mingled splendour and horror of human history, with the slow and painful surge of progress behind its superficial transformations.

Humanity requires a coherent picture of itself and its world, a picture in which the conflicting variety of detail can be related to the unity of over-all pattern. And the picture must be re-drawn in every age. If this book contributes anything to such a picture, I shall be content.

INDEX

(italic figures indicate illustrations)